THE GREAT
WICKEDNESS
of CHRIST'S SAINTS, *his* ELECT, *and all* CHRISTIANS

JONATHAN BIJJA
CHARLES SPURGEON

© 2018 Jonathan Bijja Charles Spurgeon

All rights are reserved. No portion of this may be reproduced, stored in retrieval system or transmitted in any form or by any means – electronic, mechanical, photocopy, recording, scanning, or other--except for brief quotations in critical reviews or articles, without the prior written permission of the author.

The scripture quotations are taken from bibles in public domain, namely, Authorized King James Version and American Standard Version 1901.

Cover Design by Jonathan and Rajender Bisht.
Interior Design by Rajender Bisht.
Proof reading by Vicki Pipher-Moore and others

ISBN-13; 978-1-7329267-0-7 (Paperback)
ISBN-13; 978-1-7329267-1-4 (Hardcover)
ISBN-13; 978-1-7329267-2-1 (E-Book)

Printed in United States of America

HARPS AND PIPES

*Dedicated
to
the Savior
of
Lord Jesus Christ
&
his servants*

CONTENTS

INTRODUCTION 1

Section One: The great wickedness 5
1. The wickedness of saints and their present situation 7
2. The unfaithfulness of his people from the beginning 23

Section Two: Mystery of iniquity 41
3. Beast the mystery of iniquity and times 43

Section Three: The things which must soon come to pass 123
4. Turning again their captivity 125
5. Avenging of God for his servants 159
6. Gathering the remnant of his people from the ends of Earth 177

Section Four: Book of Prophecy 199
7. The Revelation of Jesus Christ 201

Section Five: Help to understand 231
8. Little help for the saints 233

About the Author 297

INTRODUCTION

The Apostle Paul wrote that the things that happened to the children of Israel in the old times are an example, and they were written down to serve as an instruction to the saints. Now, after the children of Israel came into the land, they sinned against God by breaking the covenant in that they went after the strange gods of the various peoples that were living around them. In the course of time, they became more evil than the pagans in the land, so God's wrath came upon them and scattered them abroad among the heathen nations of the earth to serve strangers and their idols of gods as a punishment. But God said his eyes are upon all their ways: they are not hid from his face, neither is their iniquity hid from his eyes. But the story of this book is about the seed of Lord Jesus, who were begotten again by his death and resurrection as written "when thou shall make his soul an offering for sin, he shall see his seed, he shall prolong his days."

It was given by God to Lord Jesus to reign for eternity from the time of his ascension to heaven. But his reign is divided into three phases, and these three phases are made for three ages. In the first phase, he needs to reign over his people in the midst of his enemies who seek to destroy his kingdom and his people, and in the second phase, he will rule the nations of the earth as written "he shall rule them with a rod of iron:" and that age will last for tens of thousands of years, and Satan will be bound throughout that age so that he no longer deceives the various sects that will be in the Christendom as he is doing now, and in that age Christendom will be filled with the knowledge of God. Now, we are living in the times of the first phase, and this first phase and present age will end with the resurrection of his servants as written "they that are Christ's (will be raised from dead) at his coming. Then cometh the end, when he shall have delivered up the kingdom to God, even the Father; when he shall have put down all rule and all authority and power. For he must reign, till he hath put all enemies under his feet." At the time of dawn the morning star will arise in hearts of his people: then saints who were sleeping in the dust will awake and the dominion will be given to them.

You have heard the words of people saying "Jesus is coming soon" for in every generation in the past centuries many expected he will come in their own generation. I say it is a good thing to look for and hasten the coming of that day. Very certainly I tell you when Lord Jesus said *"behold, I come quickly,"* he was not talking to the people of the first century or to the people of the past millenniums. John himself was carried in the Spirit into the future, and the Revelation was signified to him just before the last trumpet since it will be made known only to the servants of Lord Jesus who will be present in the last generation after the voice of an angel is heard just before the last trumpet. Very certainly John was not saying the time is at hand to the first-century people or to the people of the past two millenniums. Therefore, the words *"behold, I come quickly"*, *"He which testifieth these things saith, Surely I come quickly"*, *"for the time is at hand."* *"Seal not the sayings of the prophecy of this book: for the time is at hand"* were spoken for the sake of the generation that will be present at the time of the last trumpet. So, the Apostle John was carried into the future and received those things through an angel and prophesied those things that are in the book of Revelation in a symbolic and spiritual language before all these generations, and those things will be closed and sealed until the last generation that will be present in times of the last trumpet.

The book of Revelation contains all things that shall come to pass one after another, beginning from the first century along the way until the end of this present age, including the things that shall come to pass in the coming age and the things that will be in that age that shall come after the coming age, a period in which the New heavens and earth are created. As Lord said unto John, *"Write the things which thou hast seen, and the things which are, and the things which shall be hereafter;"* and at the time when the end will be near just before the last trumpet, Lord Jesus will make Revelation known to John through his angel. So, the book is not meant to be opened for people until the time of the last trumpet.

Daniel the Prophet wrote about the kingdoms of peoples that will exert the authority upon the people in this religion, earlier on Judaism and later on Christianity, for he spoke about the various beasts that came out of the sea to bear rule on earth. After that time, God will give the ends of the earth to Jesus Christ; he will rule over all peoples of various sects that were in this religion. Until now, the Babylonians, the Medo-Persians, the Grecians, the Romans and the Barbarians exerted their authority over the various peoples in this religion even upon the earth. Daniel was asked to seal the prophecy which was revealed to him in the last vision he got, which was noted in the last three chapters of his book, and this is the background of that vision. Daniel in those days set his heart to understand the vision he saw about the He-goat and the Ram. In those days, Daniel mourned three full weeks. He did not eat any pleasant bread, neither flesh nor wine came into his mouth and neither did he anoint himself at all until three whole weeks were fulfilled. Afterwards, a messenger was sent to him to make him understand the vision. After those things were revealed, Daniel was instructed to seal it until the time of the End even until the time of the last trumpet.

The things that were written in this book are for the servants of Lord Jesus who have the understanding among his people. No one who does wickedly against the truth of the Gospel, the Covenant, shall understand these things, but his servants who remember their God and seek him, they shall understand these things. For the fools and mockers, these things appear foolish; for the wicked, these things appear weird; for the wise, these things appear as understanding; and for those who seek our God, these things appear as joyful music. This book I ought to give freely to you, but for the sake of reaching many of you who are far, I kept this on the market for in this book were explained the true and faithful sayings of our God, which he spoke from the beginning of the world through his prophets. I thought it is a way to reach you for your God has scattered you, his people, among various denominations and sects that were in Christendom called Earth. Don't miss reading the references, meditate and dwell on the things written in this book, go back and forth and see things clearly, you may use your favorite music.

SECTION ONE:
THE GREAT WICKEDNESS

CHAPTER ONE

The wickedness of saints and their present situation

Blessed is he that reads, and they that hear the words of this prophecy, and keep the faith of these things which are written in this book: for the time is at hand.

After they came into the world, they learned and lived in the ways of people of that world, among whom they lived in the past,[1] but that Great God called them to his marvelous light,[2] the light which they never saw in the past. But pretty soon they were lost from his light, and so they went on and created light by the fire and walked in the light of fire they lit, and by walking in light they lit they have forgotten that marvelous light of their God.

When he called them out from that world in which they were alive, his word in them was like a fire that burns. But pretty soon fire departed from their mouths. And they went on relying on lies and making lies, and they have forgotten the word of his marvelous light, through which they were called into his light. They fight with one another for their lies.

God has called them to Zion, to that Heavenly Jerusalem, but they have gone into captivity among all heathen nations of Earth. He has called them to liberty, to confidence, and to have fellowship with him, for he is in Christ. But soon they were frightened and fled from Christ and lost the fellowship and confidence.

They say they know him, yet surely, they have forgotten their God who has called them into his marvelous light at the time of their new birth. If they haven't forgotten him why do they go after gods and christs of Christendom? They seek truth yet they can't find it. They wander here and there among the heathen. They go after the doctrines and theologies of Christendom. Each one of them relies on his own doctrinal horse which he rides. Who tries to remember him? Who is it that seeks his God who hid his face from his people because of their iniquities, to whom the remembrance of his God is the desire of the soul?

If I compare the Christendom to Earth and every denomination and sect to the nations of Earth, do I say that any one of these nations has the whole truth? Certainly not. Or do I say any of these nations worship the God of Jesus Christ? Certainly not. If I compare truth with the garment, then all these nations have parted it into pieces and each one took a piece of it, little or big; they patch that piece of truth to their garments of lies, to their idols of gods and christs, and these go after them because they see truth in them.

Did they know not their God? Surely they knew, for surely he called them to the fellowship of his Son through Gospel which they heard at the time of their new birth.

Surely, they know him, for he is in his son Jesus Christ. But they perverted their ways and have forgotten their God. Therefore, other lords have dominion over them.

They ride upon their doctrinal horses and theological chariots and were very proud because of their vain knowledge, yet fools they are, for they have forgotten their God. They live in cities and towns fortified with doctrines and dogmas, worshiping gods and christs made by them after the imagination of their heart. In the old time, the idol was work of their hands, made from wood; now their gods and christs are work of their hearts, made with words.

They say they live unto God, but they are alive unto the Law. They pretend to walk in liberty but walk in yoke of bondage. They keep commandments and good deeds for justification. How can they live unto God as long as they live unto Law that says you haven't loved thy God with all your heart, soul, strength, and wisdom, that you have committed adultery, theft, and that you are a covetous man? You haven't loved your neighbor as thyself, etc. For Law only condemns and never justifies: it was given for condemnation. How can both faith in his love towards them and fear of wrath towards them dwell in their mind at the same time? How can guiltiness of condemnation and joyful boldness of innocence dwell at the same time in their mind? How can they continue while Law works wrath in their conscience?

When I say Law, I mean the Ten Commandments in all its forms, both in the Old Testament and in New Testament books and in gospels, which they call the Moral Law, for these Ten Commandments themselves are a Covenant of

God for the Children of Israel of old time. These are written on tables of stone and kept in the Ark of the Covenant. These Ten Commandments are a Covenant they were obliged to keep in order to be his people; surely God himself called the Ten Commandments a Covenant of old time.

> "He declared to you his covenant, which he commanded you to perform, that is, the Ten Commandments, and he wrote them on two tablets of stone."
> ~ Deuteronomy 4:13; kjv

> "The Lord said unto Moses, Write thou these words: for after the tenor of these words I have made a covenant with thee and with Israel. And he was there with the Lord forty days and forty nights; he did neither eat bread, nor drink water. And he wrote upon the tables the words of the covenant, the Ten Commandments. And it came to pass, when Moses came down from mount Sinai with the two tables of testimony in Moses' hand."
> ~ Exodus 34:27-29; kjv

Now this ministry, which was given to Moses, was called by the Apostle as the ministration of condemnation and death. He compares Moses delivering the words of Covenant, even the Ten Commandments on stone tablets to the Children of Israel, with preaching of gospel about Jesus Christ in whom God who called them is, which was called as the ministration of life and justification, which means the Image of Christ is the New Covenant and Holy commandment in their hearts, which is by preaching of Gospel about Jesus Christ in whom God who called them is, it justifies and gives life. Surely God's Holy Covenant is Gospel that was preached about Jesus Christ in whom God who called them is. The Covenant they must keep is retaining Christ the Image of God formed in them by preaching of Gospel about Jesus Christ by Holy Spirit when that Great God called them to his fellowship in Jesus Christ; surely, they have broken this Covenant. It is through glorious Gospel about Lord Jesus the Spirit of God took them to Lord Jesus who dwelt among us, they know and see him as if they were among his disciples.

They will find themselves continuing in Sin, continually scourged in their conscience for transgression, for they keep their conscience under the Law and they will find themselves as sinners,[3] because by the works of the Law shall no flesh be justified. For where the Law is, there is transgression, guilty conscience, and fear of God's anger, and by this way they alienate themselves from the Lord Jesus Christ and God in their minds because guilty conscience brought in them by Law. They will lose strength to believe in love of God towards them, for they will lose the sight of Jesus Christ in whom God their Father is. They will become fearful to come unto the Lord's presence, again they will try to keep commandments and again they will find themselves as sinners, and this cycle always continues and Sin always abounds them by the Law and so the guilty conscience and fear. They lose the Image of Christ formed in them by preaching of the Gospel about Jesus Christ by the Holy Spirit when God called them to himself.

You hypocrites, don't you know Law won't speak to the dead and Jesus Christ has died and his people with him? How can you say they are under the Law and were obliged to keep the Moral Law? Doesn't scripture teach they were baptized by the Holy Ghost into his body who is going to die on the cross and rise? If they are dead, that means they can't hear anything or see anything. Why are you making them alive unto Law, saying they are under Law and obliged to keep it? Thus you people do wickedly against the God's Holy Covenant, which is Lord Jesus as he promised him, "I will preserve thee and give you as covenant to the people."[4] You wicked preachers, how long you destroy his people by placing old Covenant in the place of God's Holy Covenant and thus you crucify their Lord unto his people. When God made his people dead unto Law and Sin, you people make them live unto Law and Sin and dead unto God and Christ. Do you think for all this he will keep silent and leave you unpunished?

Before the days of new birth, before they ever tasted the mercy and grace of the Lord while they were under the slavery to their various passions and pleasures of the flesh, did then Law help them? Surely, they knew that they were sinners and the things they were doing were against God; otherwise, they wouldn't have come to Christ. Does Law that screamed in their conscience at them saying this is wrong, don't do this, in any way helped them against those sinful passions? No, rather it provided strength to Sin, as Apostle wrote, "when we were in the flesh, the motions of sins, which were by the Law, did work in our members to bring forth fruit unto death."[5] One might find himself still in that carnal condition, because he keeps his conscience under the obligation of Law and try to be justified before God by keeping it, not knowing God has called them unto liberty, freedom from Law and to a better Covenant. Surely yet they stood not in this Covenant, even the gospel of that marvelous light, they departed from the word which they heard in the beginning at the time of their calling and pretty soon left that Great God who is in Lord Jesus. Because they have broken the Covenant,[6] they have fallen and are spiritually dead. Therefore, they can't see Lord Jesus as they have seen in the past when God has called them, neither they can walk in God's marvelous light as in the past, for they are defiled and they can't follow Christ in white clothes.

In the past once they were under the bondage of Sin until faith is revealed through hearing of glorious Gospel, and they are made free from the dominion of Sin and Law by faith in Lord Jesus Christ and become the servants of righteousness. But that way of righteousness is not the something which is by putting conscience under Law of commandments, and by yielding themselves to subjection of demands, threatening and condemnations of Law in their conscience, and keeping commandments under the servitude fear. For by Law they have the knowledge of Sin, by it they will find themselves to be sinners and guilty of Sin, it works wrath in their conscience, it creates fear, impatience, mistrust and hatred toward Lord Jesus and God in their hearts, and Law is a power of Sin, by it Sin easily besets us, and Law says to them that are under it, "the man which doeth those things shall live by them and cursed is every one that continues not in all things."[7] But for them righteousness comes by hearing with faith about Lord

Jesus Christ in whom that Great God is; through this faith hearts are purified.

The way of this righteousness is by gazing intently on a better Covenant, even the Jesus Christ in whom that Great God who called them is, to obtain the knowledge of God and Christ, and by trying to retain the Image of Christ and not forgetting him and God, in the glorious, marvelous light, standing in awe at the Great God who is in Lord Jesus Christ. Yet this fear is far more glorious and joyful than that of servitude fear of the Law. Surely God has called them to these glorious things at that time through Holy Spirit preaching gospel about Lord Jesus Christ in whom that Great God who called them is, so that their hearts might shine in wisdom with ever abiding glory far better than the shining of the face of Moses.

For sure Children of former Israel to whom he gave Law as Covenant hasn't seen a similitude of him as Moses testified to them, "Then the LORD spoke to you out of the midst of the fire. You heard the sound of words, but saw no form; there was only a voice. And he declared to you his Covenant, which he commanded you to perform, that is, the Ten Commandments, and he wrote them on two tablets of stone."[8] But as many of whom he called through testimony about Jesus by the Holy Ghost who brought them to the fellowship of Jesus Christ in whom he is, they all have seen him, for he is in Jesus Christ, who is his express Image and brightness of his glory and God's Holy Covenant to them.

At that time, they were weak and ungodly people while being under Law and slaves to Sin in that world. But God presented himself gracious to them in Lord Jesus who died for them, and in whom they trusted for the mercy of God. For God who is in Lord Jesus called them to his marvelous light to the fellowship of Jesus Christ who was so gentle. And God gave their inward man a new birth and these newborn babies were enriched by the mercy of God and by the Gentleness of Lord Jesus. What good, what love, what obedience, and what joy he brought in them. But they forsook that God and go after gods and christs of Christendom which were made by imaginations of men. They are foolish people; they dealt treacherously with their Father, although he brought them from that world where they were perishing in darkness under the yoke of bondage of Law and Sin, he brought them unto his fellowship in Christ and gave them liberty and gave them spiritual food, but they didn't want to stay. They sought after the righteousness which is no righteousness and a salvation which is not a salvation, and a wisdom which is not a wisdom, but forgot their God and Lord Jesus who was Gentle with them, they sold themselves for their iniquities, they sold themselves for nothing. They trust in false gods and christs, they speak lies and falsehoods against their God, therefore their God has torn them, for they robbed from him his little ones and you are his little ones and he is your Father who has begotten you, and your God led you into captivity among the heathen.

They who once walked in their God's marvelous light, now they look eagerly for a brightness, but they walk in darkness, they wait for light, but there won't be light, only obscurity and confusion. They do so much labor but end up in bringing something which is a false teaching the iniquity:

a net to catch poor souls, a poison to kill. They are like a pregnant woman who writhes and cries out in their pangs to bring forth truth and deliverance but end up bringing a vanity; they long to see those days in which they were in their Father's marvelous light in fellowship of Lord Jesus, but they won't see such days anymore in their life. They cry bitterly and look for the truth and deliverance but they shall not find any. Like spiders you toil to weave false doctrines to capture people, you fight with one another for your lies, you seek eagerly to destroy simple and needy people with your teachings, you destroy spiritually poor and needy people with your lies even though what they believe is true, you praised the devils, false gods, and christs of the Christendom, but are unmindful of that Great God who had begotten you again and forgotten him who called you into his marvelous light from that world. Therefore, your God did hide his face from you all and left you to obscurity, confusion, and shame. Your minds were corrupted from the simplicity and purity that is in true Christ unto whom that Great God has called you at the time of your new birth. Footsteps of your mind were gone astray from him who is the way, you did wickedly against Holy Covenant and turned what was simplicity into the crooked path to your mind wherein there is no peace. Your iniquities have separated you and your God, and your Sins have hidden his face from you, so that he will not hear you. For you corrupted your hearts and consciences from the simplicity and purity that is in Lord Jesus, there remained not a pure heart in any of you as it was at the time when he had begotten you again and called you into his marvelous light. Therefore, there comes no longer true and pure love from your hearts toward him, and all your righteous deeds are like a filthy garment, and all of you wither like a leaf, and your iniquities, like the wind, take you away. For you abode not in him and become withered branches which the woman come and set on fire.⁹ When Saints fall to the ground from his fellowship, from his marvelous light and wither away, those who dwell in Christendom the Earth lead them to destruction with scriptures and by their flattery. They get destroyed by their lack of discernment, for they lack knowledge of their God and do wickedly against the Holy Covenant by not holding fast to the testimony of Jesus, the holy commandment delivered unto them at the time of their calling into his light. Heathen destroy them with their flattery and by false assurances and promises quoting from scriptures, and they lead them into the light of their false religion and to their idols of gods and christs, they corrupt and entangle their mind their feet with various chains of their doctrines of lies, dogmas, and falsehoods. They seek for true light the Christ to whose fellowship they were called in the beginning, but they will not find him.

Apostles John, Peter, and Paul testified about the fate of those who break the Commandment of Holy Covenant. John testified that the word they heard at the beginning through which he called them is the commandment they must keep, if it stays in them that they will abide in Christ and God, and breaking it is Sin unto death. Peter wrote those who break this holy commandment, even the testimony of Jesus, through which they were called in the beginning, that it would have been better for them that they never have known this way of righteousness, and their present state now after turning away from this commandment is worse than when they were sinners in that world. Paul also testified about those who fall away from this Holy Commandment even the Christ formed in them through preaching of Gospel by Spirit about Jesus Christ in whom that Great God who called them is, that it is impossible to renew them, for they crucified the Son of God unto themselves, saying it's impossible to restore them again to repentance, since they are crucifying once again the Son of God unto themselves and put him to open shame. For land that has drunk the rain that often falls on it and produces a crop useful to those for whose sake it is cultivated, receives a blessing from God. But if it bears thorns and thistles, it is worthless and near to being cursed, and its end is to be burned.[10]

They all now had become wicked, evil, and useless; they now only produce spiritual wickedness the iniquity, like the field that produces thorns and thistles. Their thoughts are thoughts of iniquity; they have forgotten their God. They live in fortified cities and towns among heathen, they ride upon their doctrinal horses and theological chariots, they worship gods and christs made by them after the imagination of their heart, they speak lies and falsehoods against their God, like spiders they weave false teachings to capture people, they fight with one another for their lies, and they seek eagerly to destroy simple and needy people with their teachings. They have become so many times eviler with their spiritual wickedness than when they were in that world where they were slaves to various sinful passions of mind and body before God called them to his marvelous light. They can't repent nor will they be able to repent, for they made their paths crooked. And they made Lord Jesus no longer profitable to them, for they crucified him unto themselves. I testify to everyone before the living God that this is the testimony of God against his people and who so ever teaches that Saints have not done these things, God will destroy such a man. I testify to you again before the living God that this is the testimony of God against his people. Who so ever teaches that they are not fallen and did these things let that offender be accursed. It's better for those who speak against this testimony to emasculate themselves, let all those idolaters and liars be accursed who teach to Saints of Jesus Christ that they are alive and walking in marvelous light of that Great God. They have done evil and iniquity against their God and Lord Jesus. The Sins they did before coming to Christ are nothing before the evil they did and are doing until this day after their new birth, and they become more corrupt and eviler with spiritual iniquity than when they were in that world, not knowing the Lord and Savior Jesus Christ.

They have broken the Holy Covenant, the Holy commandment, even his word, the testimony of Jesus preached to them by the Holy Spirit in the beginning, they did Sin that leads to death. They deserted that Great God who called them in the grace of Christ, they have not stayed in Christ and in his Father, for his word, the glorious testimony of Jesus preached unto them by Spirit, has not abode in them. They lost the fellowship of their God in his marvelous light, where they walked for a while in the beginning. Once by Spirit, they were like newborn babies and harmless little lambs, who walked in God's marvelous light and were pleasing and desirous to him, when he brought them from that world having begotten them again. He was so gracious unto them having saved them from the yoke of bondage and nourished them with all spiritual food through his Spirit, he taught them and led them by his Spirit, but pretty soon they went astray from him and went after false gods and christs of the various people that dwell in Christendom the Earth. They were unmindful of that Great God the one true savior and have forgotten their God who has begotten them.

Once they were like little lambs and newborn babies, gentle and harmless by Spirit of God who made them new. They have tasted of the Heavenly gift the graciousness of their Savior and Shepherd Lord Jesus, they rejoiced in his fellowship and walked with him in confidence and assurance for a while. But they had pretty soon lost his fellowship, for they did wickedly against Holy Covenant by turning away from the Christ formed in them by the preaching of Gospel by Holy Spirit about Lord Jesus in whom that Great God who called them is, and they lost the knowledge of Lord Jesus. Therefore, they corrupted themselves through another spirit to go after a strange god of Christendom, thus withdrawing themselves from God who called them to Lord Jesus their Savior. Now when they are led by another spirit, they find themselves within the growing distance between them and Jesus Christ their Savior, for they perceive the gentleness and comfort of their gracious savior is no longer there and he is getting angry against them very often. He becomes to them a cruel extractor, who gets annoyed with the slightest provocation, although they try very hard to please him with all things they can do for him, yet his displeasure is evidently seen by them. They lose all the joy of salvation which they had just a little time ago when God called them to his fellowship in his marvelous light. Now when he grows increasingly hard for them to follow and serve him, they experience frustration and a feeling of being trapped into something. They grow impatient and suspicious and all sorts of evil rises in their hearts against him. Now there remains nothing the same as a little while ago. There won't remain anything the same when God called them out of that world to the fellowship of Lord Jesus into marvelous light having begotten them. Now no longer are they as they used to be: blameless, innocent and harmless as little lambs of Lord Jesus walking in the light of his fellowship with pure conscience. They doubt their calling and conversion and think whether they are really saved at all. When they were in this misery, obscurity and confusion, being fallen from their God's fellowship, they go on turning away far in their hearts, many of them become pray for heathen of various denominations and sects that dwell in Christendom who hate true knowledge of Christ, who take them as captives by their falsehoods, lies, and evil doctrines to serve their gods and christs, thus these heathen destroy them and make them wicked as these heathen are. For their teachings are the venom of serpents, and the deadly poison of cobras.[11] Thus, you end up in committing all sorts of spiritual wickedness. You trust in confusion and worthless teachings; if any one of you departs from any kind of false doctrine, he becomes prey to another false doctrine of all those various sects and denominations the nations that dwell on Christendom called Earth, for there is no truth in any of all these denominations and sects of Protestantism,

Catholicism, Eastern Orthodoxy, Oriental Orthodoxy, Assyrian sects, Restorationism, or in any others: there is no truth anywhere in all the Christendom.

REFERENCES:

1. Ephesians 2:2-3;
2. 1 Peter 2:9;
3. Galatians 2:17;
4. Isaiah 49:8;
5. Romans 7:5;
6. 2 John 1:9; 1 John 2:24;
7. Galatians 3:12 & 10;
8. Deuteronomy 4:12-13;
9. Isaiah 27:11; John 15:6;
10. Hebrews 6:4-8;
11. Deuteronomy 32:31-33;

CHAPTER TWO

The unfaithfulness of his people from the beginning

The story of second Israel began two thousand years ago, when that Great God had sent Jesus Christ the Israel his servant to serve the Children of the former Israel, so he might bring them back unto their God by turning them away from their iniquities as spoken by the Spirit of Christ through Prophet Isaiah,

> "Listen, O isles, unto me; and hearken, ye people, from far; The LORD hath called me from the womb; from the bowels of my mother hath he made mention of my name. And he hath made my mouth like a sharp sword; in the shadow of his hand hath he hid me, and made me a polished shaft; in his quiver hath he hid me; And said unto me, **Thou art my servant, O Israel, in whom I will be glorified...** And now, saith the LORD that formed me from the womb to be his servant, to bring Jacob again to him."
>
> ~ISAIAH 49:1-3; KJV

So he went on preaching them to repent and to believe in gospel, throughout all their cities and the villages, teaching in their synagogues, and proclaiming the gospel of the kingdom, and healing every disease and every sickness, but his labor was in vain and he spent his strength for nothing, as he said through Isaiah, "I said, I have laboured in vain, I have spent my strength for nought, and in vain."

For they rejected God's word of peace, which God has preached through Jesus Christ throughout their land, whom God has set, as approved of him, before them by miracles, wonders, and mighty signs, and went on doing good through Jesus and healing all that were oppressed by the devil. For God didn't set his Son unto people as a man that causes fear or dread or terror to them; Moses caused Earth to swallow his opponents, Elijah caused fire to come down and consume soldiers, but Jesus didn't quarrel with anyone, nor did he quench them that were like a smoke to him, nor did he break them that were a piercing reed to him. For God set his son unto people as a hope of salvation, righteousness, and eternal life from a merciful God. (God was also gentle in him; he had not presented himself as a dreadful and devouring God in Christ Jesus.)

They rejected his word of reconciliation and killed Jesus Christ by hanging him on the cross, but God raised him from the dead. They also persecuted Apostles, forbidding them from preaching Gospel. Therefore, God destroyed them and gave them the spirit of slumber, eyes that they should not see with, and ears that they should not hear with; unto this day. As he said because, when I called, you did not answer; when I spoke, you did not listen (*for they did not know their visitation*). Therefore, I will destine you to the sword, and all of you shall bow down to the slaughter.[1] But God has promised that he will bring seed out of former Israel, even Jacob from the tribe of Judah and inheritor of his kingdoms,[2] which he said about the later Israel, even Jesus Christ his servant whom he has chosen.[3] The one who is going to inherit the kingdoms of the world to come, and his seed, is the Israel of the world to come, whom he has begotten again in the body of his flesh through means of his death and resurrection,[4] a people for God's own possession, for they were chosen to be his seed before the world began. They are his own nation and his own kingdom; they are his kingdom of Heaven which rules over all the kingdoms of Earth. They are of Heaven and Jerusalem above in whose light all the Nations of New Earth that will be saved will walk. All the Children of Israel will serve the *God of hosts* forever and ever, they shall reign forever and ever, and they shall be priests and ministers of God unto those nations.

Now the story of the Children of Israel of the old time is a shadow of the things to come; things happened to them as an example, but they were written down for the instruction of this Israel, on whom the end of the ages has come. For like them, they were also once slaves in that world serving their sinful passions of mind and body, but that Great God has made them free by sending Jesus Christ, and called them with a Holy calling to his fellowship in Jesus Christ, whom he has given as Covenant to you and testimony of Jesus we heard at the time of our calling, is the word of covenant. The Gospel is the word of Covenant you need to keep by faith, if it stays in you then you will also stay in God and Jesus Christ. This Israel came unto Mount Zion to his holy kingdom, and unto the city of the living God, the Heavenly Jerusalem. For God sent those who escaped from among the Children of old Israel to nations of gentiles and brought them to his Holy mountain and Jerusalem, even to his kingdom of Heaven the Holy mountain, and to Jerusalem above. Just as he spoke through his prophet saying,

> "I will send those that escape of them unto the nations, to Tarshish, Pul, and Lud, that draw the bow, to Tubal, and Javan, to the isles afar off, that have not heard my fame, neither have seen my glory; and they shall declare my glory among the Gentiles. And they shall bring all your brethren for an offering unto the LORD out of all nations upon horses, and in chariots, and in litters, and upon mules, and upon swift beasts, to my holy mountain Jerusalem, saith the LORD, as the children of Israel bring an offering in a clean vessel into the house of the LORD. And I will also take of them for priests and for Levites, saith the LORD."[5]

Therefore, Lord Jesus sent Apostles to these nations that were far. Apostle Paul confirms this to us, that those who were called by that Great God through the Gospel of Jesus Christ were called unto that spiritual city Jerusalem which is above. When he said he was sent to bring them to God,

> "I should be the minister of Jesus Christ to the Gentiles, ministering the gospel of God, that the offering up of the

Gentiles might be acceptable, being sanctified by the Holy Ghost. I have therefore whereof I may glory through Jesus Christ in those things which pertain to God."[6]

Therefore, he writes to them that were called to that Jerusalem above, that she is their mother. Not only Gentiles but even to Jews that were called, all those who were called by that Great God, with High, Heavenly, and Holy calling through Gospel unto Jerusalem above, as written in an epistle to Hebrews, "ye are come unto mount Sion, and unto the city of the living God, the Heavenly Jerusalem."[7]

But this Israel like former Israel did not stay there for much time, for as the Children of Israel of old time forsook the God who brought them from the land of Egypt and went after the other gods of then that were around them, so also they went after the other gospels and after gods and christs of the Christendom pretty soon after the time of Apostles. Therefore, he hid his face from them, and delivered them to the hand of the church of Rome the Babylonians and lead them into captivity among all the denominations and sects of Christendom and they did hard labor. He scattered them into corners of Christendom called the Earth among the denominations and sects of Christendom, which were called as nations of Earth. There they were serving night and day, gods and christs of heathen[8] which were fashioned according to the human imagination which were known to neither Apostles nor first-century Saints. Just as Earthly Jerusalem, which was foreshadow and type of Heavenly Jerusalem above, this Jerusalem above also went into captivity. For three score and a half years, even the seventy years of desolation was determined upon that Jerusalem and the whole land was desolate, so also three times and a half years, even 1,260 years of desolation was determined upon the Heavenly Jerusalem.

Lord Jesus Christ said to his disciples some of you will not see death until the kingdom of God comes in strength. Just as he said, his ministers fought with Satan that deceives whole Christendom, and with the Satan's ministers, and they had thrown Satan and his messengers down from Heaven which is Jerusalem above. God created the heavens and set lights and stars in them to give light upon the Earth, so also the kingdom of Heaven will give light unto all nations of Earth the Christendom, and it will rule over all the denominations and sects of Christendom the Earth. So all those who were called by him to fellowship of Lord Jesus were called as dwellers of Heaven and seed of Zion which is above, truly the Kingdom of Heaven came with power as God gave them victory over Satan and his ministers and enriched them in every way and in all knowledge and they lack no spiritual gifts. He gave Jerusalem above dominion over people who dwell in Christendom the Earth. But a little time after the Apostles, they started speculations about Godhead and Christology. They developed various doctrines and theologies. They fortified their dwelling places with dogmas and filled the land with treasures and with their horses and chariots of doctrines, apologies, and theologies. They relied upon them against their pursuing enemies. They moved away from the word of the testimony of Jesus which they heard from the beginning, through which they were called by God to his fellowship in Jesus Christ, even at the time of their new birth. And gone after strange gospels, they forsake Lord Jesus and God their father who has called them out of darkness from that world in which they were slaves to Sin being under Law, and they have gone after the gods and christs of Christendom; the intangible idols of nations of Earth which were made according to the imaginations of heathen of Christendom. They learned witchcrafts and sorceries from them and walked in their superstitions. They started doing wickedly against the Holy Covenant by walking against the truth of Gospel and seeking justification and salvation through good works and pious living. Yet Father was their God from that world where they were slaves to Sin being under the Law. He sent Christ who was born of woman and made under the Law and delivered them from bondage through his death and resurrection. He raised them from the dead with Christ and made them sit in Heavenly places and blessed them with all spiritual blessings. They were filled and their heart was exalted and forgot their God. They provoked him to jealousy with their abominations against his holy and jealous love. Nevertheless, God has reserved a few for himself in those days who had not defiled their garments, neither spoke lies and falsehoods nor defiled themselves with churches that were in Christendom.

They proceeded from evil to evil, and they wearied themselves to bring forth inequity, wearied themselves for making lies and falsehoods of their doctrines, theologies, apologetics, and dogmas. They have not known their God. They spoke lies and deceived one another. They haven't grown up to speak the truth, but have been immature children, tossed to and fro by the waves and carried about by every wind of doctrine. They have gone aside, and they have become filthy. They had become the workers of iniquity and they had no knowledge. They haven't prayed to their God, but they showed favor to those who did wickedly against truth of gospel and did not deliver those who were poor in spirit from the hands of the wicked people, neither did they give justice to those poor and needy whom those wicked afflicted with their rigid dogmas and burdens. They didn't know or understood they have walked in darkness and sought their God. They and their churches had made hearts of righteousness sad, which God didn't, and promised life to those who walked wickedly against truth of Gospel.

They also started praying to Saints. Yes, they burned incense to the host of Heaven against the God of hosts their God. Yes, they worshiped the host of Heaven and prayed to Saints upon their altars. They worshiped Mary their queen of Heaven and did abomination in the sight of him who is their God and Father. They filled his Heavenly inheritance with the carcasses of their abominations and detestable things. They filled Heavenly inheritance and the holy city with their idols. They settled in their wine, which are their doctrines and teachings, and didn't sought after God and have not remembered that Great God who brought them from that world wherein they were slaves to Sin, when he called them to his marvelous light at the time of their calling. They lifted their hands as sacrifice unto the host of Heaven, and as God said, they had taken the beautiful vessels of his temple, they took beautiful gold and silver vessels of his house, even his Apostles and Saints, which he gave for the service of his temple and they made unto themselves images of idols and committed whoredom with them. They set forth before these idols as fragrant incense all the spiritual things like his teaching, wisdom, and understanding he gave, his comforting word, and all the good spiritual things with which he fed them. They also sacrificed to their idols the spiritual children God gave them; they caused them to go through fire to be devoured for these idols, forcing them to become perfect in good works according to the Law in the name of imitating Saints. In all their abominations and their whoredoms they have not remembered the days of their youth, times they were in that world among whom they all once lived being polluted in the passions of flesh, carrying out the desires of the body and the mind, poor and wretched sinners, destitute of righteousness to cover their shame and nakedness. But God, who is rich in mercy, even when they were dead in their trespasses, forgave them, made them alive together with Christ and raised them up with him and seated with him in the Heavenly places in Christ Jesus. He covered their nakedness with his own skirt, with his own righteousness. Then he sanctified them and gave them wisdom, so they can have self-control over their body. He shod their minds with gospel of peace, even with sandals of fine leather to be ready unto every good work. He fed them with the bread of fine teaching, with the honey of his gracious words of knowledge which brightens eyes, with the oil of understanding which made their faces shine, so they advanced into royalty in all the Christendom the Earth, and their spiritual beauty was perfect with patience, charity, obedience, suffering and affliction with joy of Holy Ghost, generosity etc. By all good work God brought in them and they became examples to all that were in this religion, their fame went forth in all Christendom among all heathen that were in Christendom the Earth, because of the work of grace of God in them. But they trusted in their beauty and played the harlot because of their fame. They filled their ways with Idols, and they committed fornications of idolatries with an open mind with heathen nations of Christendom that were around them. Not only so, they also lusted after philosophers of this world. Because instead of trusting in their God and his love, they trusted in their beauty which was the good work of God brought in them, therefore they become weak hearted and feeble in their knees, for they trusted in the sincerity of their faith, piety, poverty, chastity, charity, obedience to all commandments, etc. For they forsook their God and withdrew from him and sought to become perfect by their virtue and good works according to the Law. This made their conscience weak, for the Law doesn't make anyone stronger or perfect but weak, for it works wrath in their conscience. Therefore, they haven't satisfied with their whoredoms and fornications with their idols, for the Law will never justify any one. Being dissatisfied, they multiplied their whoredoms and yet are not satisfied with them. Therefore, they labored tirelessly for perfection according to Law, to attain a surpassing excellence to each virtue by the imitation of Saints and strove to acquire all the qualities that were in holy men. They toiled themselves with ascetic life, living as hermits and monks, and practiced celibacy, yet in all this wickedness of them they never remembered the times they were in that world among whom they all once lived in the passions of flesh, carrying out the desires of the body and the mind, poor and wretched sinners, destitute of righteousness to cover their shame and nakedness. Therefore, they have forsaken God their Father for their idols and whoredoms. They have even used Christ's own words to crucify him unto themselves and to others, his own words in that he expounded the Law and his answer to one who sought to become perfect by good works. They oppressed those who were spiritually poor and meek in their dwelling place, for these people and their leaders vexed them wrongfully. They took them for spoil and denied their right in their Lord Jesus and God their Father and oppressed them with their rigid dogmas and burdens. They robbed his word from his people and they killed the innocent and shed their blood with their spiritual swords. They destroyed souls for dishonest gain, and they defiled his inheritance with the blood of innocents. Therefore, God's wrath came on the Jerusalem which is above, because of the evil that is done in it by his people, who defiled his inheritance with the spiritual iniquity of their idols and bloodshed.

Now when these things were happening in Christendom the Earth, every nation walking according to its own evil ways, and his Saints the Israel whom he called from darkness to his marvelous light, whom he brought from that world where they were slaves to Sin being under Law, for he called each one of them in their lifetime at the time of new birth to his fellowship in Jesus Christ, even unto Zion which is above. Instead of showing the way like lights to all those who dwell in Christendom, they transgressed against him, being taught by the heathen to follow after their ways in serving idols of their imaginations. So, God also executed his Judgments on the Christendom called the Earth. At first, he took away peace on Earth so that nations will fight with one another and kill one another with their spiritual swords, and later he laid on Christendom spiritual famine, and then he brought spiritual death on Christendom. Many people have been killed with spiritual hunger, with spiritual swords, of one another, and by false teachers of Christendom.[9]

Because of the iniquity of his people, God's anger fell on them and he forsook them and hid his face from them, and many evils fell on them and he made them become a reproach among all nations of Earth. He cast them out of his inheritance like savorless salt and they fell like stars to the ground to be trodden under foot. He scattered them to corners of the Earth among heathen nations of Earth which were denominations and sects of Christendom. There they served idols of heathen day and night, the Jerusalem above became desolate and barren, and her land destroyed and burned up, because of the indignation of her God who smote her. Therefore, God said to that Heavenly Jerusalem on whose lights nations that will be saved shall walk in New Earth, "in my wrath I smote thee,"[10] and also he said to his Saints they are responsible for God forsaking the Jerusalem above, saying, "Behold, for your iniquities, have ye sold yourselves, and for your transgressions is your mother put away."[11] He made her drink from the cup of his fury as written,

> "These two things are come unto thee; who shall be sorry for thee? desolation, and destruction, and the famine, and the sword: by whom shall I comfort thee? Thy sons have fainted, they lie at the head of all the streets, as a wild bull

in a net: they are full of the fury of the LORD, the rebuke of thy God."[12]

As scripture says, God's wrath and fury came on his people for all the spiritual wickedness they committed against their God. He made her desolate and barren and she lost her children and she went into captivity.

Apostle said their enemy would be revealed after their apostasy, so when her time drew near and transgressors had run their course, at the end of fifth century a diverse empire of various people started to stand and the Roman Empire which stopped them was already taken out of the way, people of those nations formed an alliance with Babylon of the Christendom which is church of Rome, and thus a spiritual army the ecclesiastical host of priests, pastors, bishops, theologians, monks, etc. was formed and this army reached unto host of Heaven, even Jerusalem above and threw the host of Heaven down to Earth and tread upon them, they threw down the place of God's sanctuary. They were successful in destroying the truth and prospered in their destroying the remnant of her children who keep testimony of Jesus and commandments of God, so they were spiritually killed with spiritual swords and gone into spiritual captivity among the denominations and sects of Christendom the Earth. This church at Rome ruled denominations and sects that were in Christendom, as prophet said these Babylonians are very proud, who enlarge his desire as hell, and cannot be satisfied, but gathers unto him all nations, and heaps unto him all people. Woe to them that build a city with blood and establish it by iniquity.[13] There Saints did hard labor under the papacy. Zion became barren, wilderness, desolate, forsaken by God and lost her children. All of them scattered among all other nations of Earth which were denominations and sects of Earth and Zion remained still barren and desolate without her children, and is trodden by heathen, but in all this period those who had understanding among the seed of Christ the Israel did instruct many people, yet did fell by the enemy's hand and the word of God was robbed from them and gone into captivity to the teachings of heathen, for the authority was given to the enemy to overcome them. So it happened until now, these Saints who know their God, who called them at the time of their conversion, who keep the holy faith and in whose mouth was the testimony of Jesus, they testified about him, but every one of them fell pretty soon after they started their witness to those who dwell in Christendom after their new birth. They all fell by the spiritual swords of the enemy and went into captivity to their false doctrines. For they will fall until the set period will finish, which will end in this generation. And the enemy has prospered all this period in destroying the remnant of children of Jerusalem above, who has the testimony of Jesus and commandments of God and enemy increased in glory. He shall be so until God's indignation upon his people the seed of Jesus Christ the Israel will come to an end.

Now the Children of Israel whom he has chosen, even Jesus Christ, were scattered among all heathen sects and denominations of the Christendom the Earth. Every one of them whom that Great God begotten again through the death and resurrection of Jesus Christ, and has redeemed them from the beggarly elements of this world's Law, Sin etc.

But they all sinned against him soon after their conversion, in their new estate under a new Covenant. By transgressing against the testimony of Jesus, even the Gospel, through which their God has called them to his marvelous light, every one of them pretty soon forsook his God and gone after other gospels and other christs of the sects and denominations of the Christendom the Earth and defiled themselves, and they serve the gods and christs of the heathen of the Christendom and refuse to return to their God. They have forgotten the Father's name which Lord Jesus declared to them while they were still in his light at the time of their conversion, neither is there anyone who arouses himself to take hold of his God who has called him at the time of his conversion with the holy and high calling to the fellowship of Jesus in whom he is, for their father has hidden his face from them, because of their spiritual iniquities their God has consumed them.

Now they serve spiritual heathen, the christians of these sects and denominations and they serve their gods and christs of these heathens. They were drunken with their teachings and doctrines, the wine of these heathen sects and denominations of the Christendom the Earth. Moses wrote that the wine which is the teachings and doctrines of the heathen are like the poisonous venom of serpents, their gods were vanities, not as the Holy one of Lord Jesus. These heathen took the seed of Israel into spiritual captivity to serve them and their false christs and gods, as said by prophets that they will serve idols day and night in the land of the strangers. But the ways of his people are not hidden from their God, nor their iniquity, as spoken by the prophet concerning all the children of Zion which is above, from whose mouth

God's word was departed, saying destruction and wasting are in their ways, the way of peace they know not; and there is no judgment in their goings. They have made them crooked paths: who so ever goes therein shall not know peace. They departed from their God and trust in the gods and christs of Christendom and they speak oppression and revolt, lies and falsehoods against their God. Like their forefathers they are stiff-necked and prideful people, they exalt themselves against me and tell me that I am blind and foolish and that I need to be a pupil to them and their silly preachers.

Now the Jerusalem above has been barren and wilderness for more than 1,200 years. The remnant of her children in every generation who had an understanding among her people, who had the testimony of Jesus and the commandments of God, were overcome by the enemy and fallen. She is desolate without her children and forsaken by her God. God smote her in wrath and hid his face from her, because of the iniquity committed by her children. They pierced their God who was in Lord Jesus by their unfaithfulness and foolishness, for they forsook their God for strange gods and christs and defiled themselves. Therefore, he hid his face from Zion and her children went into captivity among the heathen and she lost her children. For they departed from him for a thing of naught, for another gospel and for other gods and christs and for the righteousness of their own. They destroyed themselves by their foolishness and unfaithfulness and pierced their God who loved them with great jealous love. They destroyed unto themselves all things Father and Lord Jesus brought for them; they crucified Jesus Christ unto themselves in whom God gave them all things. Yet there were Saints who still remember their God and Lord Jesus from a long distance, from the time when they were in his fellowship in his marvelous light at the time of their new birth, which seek their God. Zion became wilderness, a solitary place, and went into captivity more than 1,200 years ago as prophesied by the prophets and she became barren land, but now her set time has come, as written, "You will arise and have compassion on Zion; For it is time to be gracious to her, For the appointed time has come."[14] For in a few years our God is going to take away from Zion's hand the cup of his wrath and his Saints shall no more drink from it, and he will put it in the hand of Babylon the church at Rome.[15]

REFERENCES:

1. Isaiah 65:12; Luke 19:44;
2. Isaiah 65:9;
3. Isaiah 53:10; Isaiah 44:1-5; 49:3; 42:1-4; 41:8-16; 43:1-10;
4. Romans 7:4; 1 Peter1:3; 1 Corinthians 12:13; Ephesians 2:16; John 12:24;
5. Isaiah 66:19-21;
6. Romans 15:16;
7. Hebrews 12:22;
8. Deuteronomy 4:28; Jeremiah 16:13;
9. Matthew 24:6-8; Revelation 6:3-8;
10. Isaiah 60:10;
11. Isaiah 50:1;
12. Isaiah 51:19-20;
13. Habakkuk 2:12;
14. Psalms 102:13;
15. Isaiah 51:23;

SECTION TWO:
MYSTERY OF INIQUITY

CHAPTER THREE

Beast the mystery of iniquity and times

Daniel saw three visions about the empires that bear rule, before God destroying Christ's enemies and making them his footstool at the time of the first resurrection. The visions were explained in a fourth vision, which was noted in chapter ten of his book, and an Angel in chapters eleven and twelve explained to him the mystery of what was going to fall upon the saints and told him to seal these things till the end. The revelation of the mystery of iniquity was progressive to him; in the first vision of the image of human, it was revealed to him that four empires will rule. The first empire was Babylon, and the third will have a huge realm and dominion over all the Earth; the fourth will be strong like Iron that breaks into pieces and subdues, and in the second vision he saw four empires represented in the form of beasts that will come out of Sea and will rule upon Earth. The third beast has huge dominion, and it has four divisions which were four heads of it, and the fourth beast was exceedingly dreadful and it devoured, broke into pieces, and stomped the residue with his feet; and from it will arise another empire; before it three provinces will be uprooted, and that kingdom will make war with the saints and overcome them for 1260 years, until the time God visits his people to deliver them. In the third vision Daniel saw two empires that were Persian and Greek, which was the third empire of the previous visions that has dominion, and from the one of its divisions of the third kingdom comes the fourth kingdom of the image, which shall continue for 2300 years. And, apart from these visions to Daniel, it has been revealed to him, as noted in the ninth chapter, the fate of Jerusalem and the coming of the Messiah who to the Jews confirms the covenant made with their fathers by God.

In the first vision he saw the dream of the king of Babylon in the night vision, which he explained to the king; it's about the human image that represents the four empires that will bear rule on Earth, which was destroyed by the stone that smote the image on its feet. Now, the timeline of those four empires starts with the Head, which is the Babylonian empire, and ends with tip of the toes and of the feet, and there was no gap of time between these succeeding empires, as there was no gap in the image and each was succeeded by another; for the image is whole and one piece. Here the emphasis in the vision was given to the latter part of the fourth empire, which comes after the third empire that has dominion and bears rule over all the Earth, the latter end of this fourth empire in its feet and toes shall be division; nations of it cleave not with one another,[1] yet this diverse empire shall have strength of Iron. But in the days of ten kingdoms, which were ten toes sprung out of feet, God shall set up a kingdom, which shall never be destroyed. The kingdom shall not be left to other people; it shall break into pieces and consume all these kingdoms, and it shall stand forever. The Iron, the clay, the brass, the silver, and the gold, all broke into pieces together, and became like the chaff of the summer threshing floors; and the wind carried them away, that no place was found for them. And the stone that smote the image became a great mountain and filled the whole Earth.²

The second vision he saw was the vision of the four beasts, which represents the four empires. In this vision emphasis was given to the fourth beast that proceeds after the third empire; it has four heads and four wings that has dominion over all the Earth. This fourth empire was dreadful and terrible, and extremely strong; it shall devour the whole Earth, and shall tread it down and break it into pieces. And from the fourth beast there comes ten kingdoms; after them comes a little kingdom that becomes larger than its fellow kingdoms, and this kingdom also subdues the three kingdoms that came before him. This horn also fights with the saints and overcomes them for a period of 1260 years, until God comes and delivers them, and the beast will be killed and its body given to fire. In this vision he saw that there comes another empire out of the fourth empire, which will overcome the saints for 1260 years. He shall speak great words against the most High, for what he does is what he speaks, and he shall wear out the saints of the most High, and think to change times and laws. They shall be given into his hand until a time and times and the dividing of time. But the judgment shall sit, and they shall take away his dominion to consume and to destroy it unto the end. And the kingdom, dominion, and the greatness of the kingdom under the whole heaven shall be given to the people of the saints of the most High, whose kingdom is an everlasting kingdom, and all dominions shall serve and obey him.

The third vision he saw was of the Ram and the He-goat. It was shown to Daniel the three kingdoms: the second, third, and fourth. It was revealed to him that the second empire was Media and Persia, which was represented as the Ram and the third empire was of Grecian. Its first empire will be broken and will be divided into four notable empires, which are represented as four horns grown out of the Goat in place of the first empire, which were four divisions of Macedonian empire, for the empire will be plucked up and go to others beside these four. A small horn grew out of one of horns of He-Goat, and it waxed into a great empire; it is the fourth Empire of the first two visions. It waxed great, to the host of heaven, and in the later time of the kingdoms of the horn, a cruel and wise kingdom shall stand; it will cast down the host the stars to the ground, and it will stomp upon them. Here is the faith and patience of these saints, who seek the fellowship of their God and want to go back to him. The enemy magnified himself even to the prince of the host and, by him, the continuity was taken away, and the place of his sanctuary was cast down. As mentioned in chapter eleven ecclesiastical armies will stand for him and they will take way the continuity by reason of transgression, and it cast down the truth to the ground, and it practiced and prospered. There will be 2300 years since the time of that a little horn, even the Republic of Rome started to appear out of one of the horns of He-Goat, to the time of Sanctuary in heaven opened again. But he will be broken without human hand, even by the stone which was cut out without the hand in the first vision.

To Daniel, it was also revealed, as noted in chapter nine, the coming of the Messiah, and confirming to the Jews the covenant by God to Fathers. It was told to him by Angel

> "Seventy weeks are determined upon thy people and upon thy holy city, to finish the transgression, and to make an end of sins, and to make reconciliation for iniquity, and to bring in everlasting righteousness, and to seal up the vision and prophecy, and to anoint the most Holy." [3]

The Messiah confirmed the covenant to Jews as spoken by Paul; "Jesus Christ was a minister of the circumcision for the truth of God, to confirm the promises made unto the fathers:"[4] For God made a covenant to Abraham saying, "In thy seed, all the kindred's of Earth shall be blessed." So he raised up his Son Jesus and sent him to bless them by turning away everyone from his iniquity. As the Apostle Peter said, So Lord Jesus confirmed the covenant by becoming the minister of Jews, as he was a Servant of God to bring Jacob back to him and gather Israel to God; he made reconciliation for iniquity and brought forth the everlasting righteousness. He also took away sacrifice for sin and oblation of the Earthly tabernacle, which was offered under the law, and the animal sacrifices that can never take away sins, as written.

> "Sacrifice and offering and burnt offerings and offering for sin thou wouldest not, neither hadst pleasure therein; which are offered by the law; Then said he, Lo, I come to

do thy will, O God. He taketh away the first, that he may establish the second. By the which will, we are sanctified through the offering of the body of Jesus Christ once for all."5

This earthly tabernacle of the first covenant signifies the way to the holiest of all was not yet manifested, but when Lord Jesus died that veil was torn from top to bottom, showing us the same thing that happened to the temple in heaven. For the way to the holy of holies of the temple that was in heaven was made, whose shadow and example was the earthly tabernacle of the first covenant which the Jews had. The Lord entered into this holy of holies of the tabernacle in heaven with his own blood having obtained everlasting forgiveness of sins and righteousness, but the earthly tabernacle that was established under the first covenant, which should be a shadow to the tabernacle in Heaven, continued in its old fashion by continuing in animal sacrifices that were taken away and in whom God has no pleasure. It is no more continued to be a shadow of the temple in Heaven. But the abominable things increased against God's grace, against the sacrifice of Christ, his blood, his priesthood, against the everlasting righteousness and salvation which he brought forth, and against the temple in Heaven. For these Jews denied all these things and have shown in this earthly tabernacle that nothing had taken place or was affected by the work of Christ and continued in their detestable things by rejecting gospel, grace of God and the sacrifice of Christ and persecuted apostles, so the Lord made it desolate and he left their house and that was determined was poured on that, as the Lord himself said as he beheld the city and wept over it.

> "If thou had known, even thou, at least in this thy day, the things which belong unto thy peace! but now they are hid from your eyes. For the days shall come upon thee, that your enemies shall cast a trench about thee, and compass thee round, and keep thee in on every side, And shall lay thee even with the ground, and thy children within thee; and they shall not leave in thee one stone upon another; because thou knew not the time of thy visitation."[6]

And as prophesied by Daniel, the prince that will come, even the Roman Empire destroyed the City and sanctuary. As spoken by Daniel, in the last vision the land of Israel will be consumed by the Roman Empire, and, as said by Daniel, the end thereof was with a flood of armies, and unto the end of the war desolations are determined. So they were carried into exile, for desolations that were decreed were poured upon the city and sanctuary which was made desolate by Lord. I also wrote about this vision, which has nothing to do with our times or the end times; neither Lord Jesus quoted this verse in Olivet discourse when he talked about the Abomination of desolation spoken by Daniel. But he quoted from Daniel Chapter eleven and twelve, when he said "there shall be great tribulation, such as was not since the beginning of the world,"[7] which he directly quoted from Daniel chapter twelve. I wrote about chapter nine because there were so many venomous serpents, wicked dogs, and workers of iniquity who twist this portion of the scripture and confuse and deceive so many people with their lies and falsehoods. For these wicked preachers of futurism and dispensationalism and their followers especially from past few centuries, use this small portion of the scripture to destroy the truth and to sell their venom of seventy lies. These liars who love lies and make lies will take their part in the lake of fire.

After almost twenty years passed since Daniel the prophet saw the third vision that he did not understand, it was revealed to him in the last vision, in which Angel came to him to make him understand that vision. In the those days, he had set his heart to understand the vision; he was mourning three full weeks and ate no pleasant bread, ate no flesh nor drunk wine, and neither did he anoint himself at all, till three whole weeks were fulfilled. In the fourth vision Angel showed him the things that shall fall upon saints, the things he saw in the third vision, which refers to many years in the future; for in the third vision he heard the length of the vision will be 2300 years, since the time that little horn starts to appear out of one of the horns of the Goat. This little horn grows great and reaches to Heaven, for ecclesiastical armies shall stand for the cruel and wise kingdom that shall arise out of the horn, and it will reach to host of Heaven and the place of their Lord's sanctuary will be cast down by it. After the expiry of that time the Sanctuary will be cleansed.

Now in the third vision he saw a Ram with two horns. The Ram was the kingdoms of Media and Persia, and the ram was pushing westward, northward, and southward; so that no beasts might stand before him. Neither was there any that could deliver out of his hand; but he did according to his will, and became great. And he saw the He-Goat, which has a notable horn between his eyes. The Goat was the kingdom of Grecia, with its first empire of Macedonia; he saw the Goat come close unto the Ram, and he was moved with choler against him and smote the Ram, and broke his two horns. There was no power in the Ram to stand before him, but he cast down the Ram to the ground, and stomped upon him; and there was none that could deliver the Ram out of his hand. Therefore, the Goat waxed very great, and when he was strong the great horn was broken; for it came up four notable ones toward the four winds of heaven.

> The Angel in chapter eleven showed him about this saying, "now will I shew thee the truth. Behold, there shall stand up yet three kings in Persia, and the fourth shall be far richer than they all: and by his strength, through his riches, he shall stir up all against the realm of Grecia. And a mighty king shall stand up, that shall rule with great dominion, and do according to his will. And when he shall stand up, his kingdom shall be broken, and shall be divided toward the four winds of heaven; and not to his posterity, nor according to his dominion which he ruled: for his kingdom shall be plucked up, even for others beside those."
>
> ~ Daniel 11: 2-4; KJV

Now the Medes and Persians were close kin; as mentioned, the Ram has two horns, and the latter one is higher than the former one. The first horn is the Median empire, and the second horn is the Persian empire, the Medes held prominent positions in the Persian empire too. Before Alexander became the king of Macedonia, the Federation of Greek states elected his father Philip as the king of Macedonia as their leader; this Macedonia was the notable horn in between the Goats eyes. Alexander led the Federation of Greek states and the Macedonian army defeated the Persians in three successive battles and conquered all its territory. The Greeks fought against the Persians with rage, as the prophecy speaks, for all the Persian emperor Xerxes did against Grecians in the past. As the vision speaks, the Goat cast the Ram down to the ground and stomped upon him, and there was no kingdom that could deliver the Ram out of his hand. And when the Macedonian horn of the Grecian Goat waxed great and when he was strong, its great horn the Macedonian empire was broken, and instead of it there came up four noticeable horns toward the four winds of heaven. As Angel in the chapter eleven said. "His kingdom shall be broken, and shall be divided toward the four winds of heaven; and not to his posterity, nor according to his dominion which he ruled:" After Alexander's death, the Macedonian empire, which was from Egypt to India, was divided into four notable kingdoms: the kingdom of Seleucus, the kingdom of Cassender, the kingdom of Lysimachus, and the Ptolemaic kingdom. For Alexander's kingdom was uprooted and was given to others besides these four Noticeable divisions.

> And Angel Said "the king of the south shall be strong, and one of his princes; and he shall be strong above him, and

have dominion; his dominion shall be a great dominion. And at the end of years they shall join themselves together."

~ Daniel 11:5; kjv

The kingdom of the south was strong, and it had two divisions. One was strong and had great dominion, which was the Ptolemaic kingdom; in the year 271 BC, Cyrenaica was created as an independent kingdom, and in year 250 BC it was annexed in the Ptolemaic kingdom.

Angel said, "the king's daughter of the south shall come to the king of the north to make an agreement: but she shall not retain the power of the arm; neither shall he stand, nor his arm: but she shall be given up, and they that brought her, and he that begat her, and he that strengthened her in these times."

~ Daniel 11:6; kjv

The war between the southern king the Ptolemaic empire and the northern king the empire of Seleucus was concluded around 253 BC with a peace agreement, when the Ptolemy gave his daughter "Berenice Syria" to Antiochus, the king of Northern Empire with the condition of repudiating his previous wife Loadice. So Antiochus II, the king of the Seleucid Empire, had transferred the succession to Berenice's children and turned over a substantial domain to his previous wife. He died in Ephesus in 246 BC, and Ptolemy II, the father of Bernice, also died in the same year. Laodice claimed her heir to the throne, but Berenice argued her son was the legitimate heir. Berenice and her child were assassinated before her brother arrived to help her.

> Angel Said " But out of a branch of her roots shall one stand up in his estate, which shall come with an army, and shall enter into the fortress of the king of the north, and shall deal against them, and shall prevail: And shall also carry captives into Egypt their gods, with their princes, and with their precious vessels of silver and of gold; and he shall continue more years than the king of the north. So the king of the south shall come into his kingdom, and shall return into his own land."
>
> ~ Daniel 11:7-9; kjv

Now when Ptolemy III, the son of Ptolemy II, heard his sister Berenice was assassinated, he had declared war against the empire of Seleucus. The army of the kingdom south the Ptolemaic empire marched into the Seleucid Empire, even up to Babylon, and they won great victories in the heartland of the Seleucid Empire With peace in 241 BC, the Ptolemaic empire was given new territories on the northern coast of Syria, including Seleucia Pieria, the present day Turkey, and the port of Antioch, for the exchange of peace. As the Angel said, the kingdom of the south the Ptolemaic empire stayed more years than the kingdom north the Seleucid Empire.

> Angel said "But his sons shall be stirred up, and shall assemble a multitude of great forces: and one shall certainly come, and overflow, and pass through: then shall he return, and be stirred up, even to his fortress. And the

king of the south shall be moved with choler and shall come forth and fight with him, even with the king of the north: and he shall set forth a great multitude, but the multitude shall be given into his hand. And when he hath taken away the multitude, his heart shall be lifted up; and he shall cast down many ten thousands: but he shall not be strengthened by it. For the king of the north shall return, and shall set forth a multitude greater than the former, and shall certainly come after certain years with a great army and with much riches."

~ Daniel 11:10-13; KJV

The sons of the kingdom of north the Seleucid Empire has assembled a multitude of forces, and the Seleucid empire has overflowed the territories belong to the kingdom of south the Ptolemaic empire. The kingdom of the north took the "Seleucia Pieria" and took Tyre of Phoenicia; they stayed quiet for a while, and after over a year the king Antiochus III of the Seleucid empire advanced into Syria, into the mainland of the kingdom of the south, the Ptolemaic empire in the year 217 BC. The king Ptolemy of the Ptolemaic empire and his ministers prepared for war and went to war with the army of the Seleucid empire, and they fought at Rafah in Syria. In the battle, thousands of the army of Seleucid were killed by the hands of the kingdom of the south, and many men were taken as prisoners. Many who fought for the kingdom of the south were native Egyptians, and this boosted their morale and became the cause of the rise of nationalism among them. The king north of the Seleucid empire did come again after a couple of decades with a great army and heavy cavalry, and it fought with the kingdom of south the Ptolemaic empire and captured Coele Syria and Judea from the kingdom of the south, bringing an end to the rule of the king of the south in Judea. But when the kingdom of the north sought to invade the kingdom of the south, it was stopped by the Republic of Rome the little horn of third vision, and after a few decades the Seleucid empire was conquered by the Parthian empire.

> Angel said "in those times there shall many stand up against the king of the south: also the robbers of thy people shall exalt themselves to establish the vision, but they shall fall. So the king of the north shall come and cast up a mount, and take the most fenced cities: and the arms of the south shall not withstand, neither his chosen people, neither shall there be any strength to withstand. But he that cometh against him shall do according to his own will, and none shall stand before him: and he shall stand in the glorious land, which by his hand shall be consumed."
>
> ~ DANIEL 11:14-16; KJV

In those times, the kingdom of the south was declining with incompetent rulers and revolts, and the strength of Rome and its increased influence in Egypt. The native Egyptians in upper Egypt were revolted, and the kingdom of Macedonia occupied its island territories. Judea, which was ruled by the king of the south, established itself independent from it, and some factions of the Jewish people exalted themselves to completely realize eschatology in the Hasmoneans, who lasted nearly a century. But they fell, and Judea came under the rule of the Roman Empire, which is the kingdom of the north now, for the time of bronze of the first vision and the third beast of the second vision and the time of four horns of the Goat came to an end, and the kingdom of the north, Rome, has occupied most of the Greek world. The kingdom of the South the Ptolemaic empire based in Egypt was weakened by internal quarrels and slowly became the de facto protectorate of Rome. And the kingdom of the north, the Roman Empire, went on to war against the Kingdom of the south, the Ptolemaic Egypt, as Octavian got the senate's vote for a proclamation of war against Cleopatra. The Armies under the Roman Empire the king of north came with warships and fought armies of the Ptolemaic kingdom on the Ionian Sea. Later, the king of the north's legions came by land through Asia, bringing the provinces under the Ptolemaic kingdom to be gathered under their control, and they eventually captured the main city of Alexandria without any resistance. For many of the armies of the Ptolemaic kingdom had either surrendered to Rome earlier on or fled, and the remaining few that were guarding the city surrendered. Thus, in 30 BC, the Ptolemaic kingdom based upon Egypt was annexed into the Roman Empire, marking the end of Hellenistic rule in the Mediterranean region and the end of the dominion of brass of image in the first vision of Daniel; now the empire is of iron, as iron is strong and breaks into pieces and subdues all things. This kingdom of the north the Roman empire did as according to its will, and nations under its dominion were unable to withstand it; this kingdom of the north stood against the land of Israel, and the land was consumed by his hand. For when the Jews revolted, the Roman Empire crushed them by sending armies. They destroyed towns and cities in Israel, and destroyed Jerusalem and temple in 70 AD. They killed many Jews, exiled or sold many into slavery.

> Angel said "He shall also set his face to enter with the strength of his whole kingdom, and upright ones with him; thus shall he do: and he shall give him the daughter of women, corrupting her: but she shall not stand on his side, neither be for him. After this shall he turn his face unto the isles, and shall take many: but a prince for his own behalf shall cause the reproach offered by him to cease; without his own reproach, he shall cause it to turn upon him. Then he shall turn his face toward the fortress of his own land: but he shall stumble and fall, and not be found."
>
> ~ DANIEL 11:17-19; KJV

In the coming years, the kingdom of the north, the Roman empire, will set itself to enter with strength of his whole kingdom, saints also in those days, and the empire had grown to its peaks in 117 AD and continued in its strength for another couple of centuries. Although saints in first century were physically persecuted, they continued to grow in true faith, as Lord said some of you standing here will not see death until the kingdom of Heaven has come in Strength. For they overcame Satan and his ministers and thrown them down from Heaven. The Roman empire did strengthen itself and continue in its vigor for coming centuries, and the king of the north the Roman empire will give daughter of women; now the daughter of women(churches) mean woman(church), just as the daughter of my people mean Jerusalem. The king of north the Roman empire became Christian empire; they organized ecumenical councils to bring a consensus among the various sects of the Christendom, and gave a lot of privileges to Christians and their leaders and bishops. They interfered in politics and governance, and they stood not for the glory of the Roman Empire; the focus shifted away from the glory of the state, and no longer was it as it was during the pagan Roman Empire, and all this has not stood in the favor of the empire or the empire was strengthened with it. After this, the king of the north Roman empire turned towards the coastland of the black sea and took people like Sarmatians as mercenaries, and later Goths who sought refuge and were promised good life but yet ill-treated. The Empire gave them a settlement land in Trace and Dacia, an autonomous foederati under their own gothic king, in 382 AD. These Goths later turned against the king of north and turned their reproach back on the Roman empire itself, and later they marched into the Roman heartland and sacked the City of Rome itself in 410 AD. Then the king of the north the Roman empire brought back his soldiers, stationed in far, remote places like Britain, were called to defend the Roman heartlands and even the Rome the fortress of his land; yet the Roman Empire stumbled, fell, and disappeared. Now I show you the mystery; this is the end of the sixth Empire, which existed in the days of Apostles Paul and John, yet two other kings will stand in his estate and the iron of the first image still continues. The first five are the Macedonian Empire, the Kingdom of Seleucus, the Kingdom of Cassander, the Kingdom of Lysimachus, and the Ptolemaic Kingdom.

> The Angel said, "Then shall stand up in his estate a raiser of taxes in the glory of the kingdom: but within few days he shall be destroyed, neither in anger nor in battle."
>
> ~ Daniel 11:20; KJV

The Angel tells Daniel that this Empire stands in the estate of the Old Roman Empire, and that it is a raiser of taxes in the glory of the Empire. Now this is true about Byzantine empire, also called the Eastern Empire, which stood in the estate of Roman empire. The taxation of the Byzantine empire was the most advanced and robust in Europe and the Mediterranean. The empire abolished the old taxation system of Rome called "collatio lustralis" in 491 AD, and reformed taxation permanently. The state treasury was filled with huge sum of funds. But this Empire still has control over the Western part of the Roman Empire, which is present day Western Europe, but eventually his power was broken in a short time due to the migration of people in Europe and by the treachery of those whom the Empire gave refuge in Roman territory.

> The Angel said, "And in his estate shall stand up a vile person, to whom they shall not give the honor of the kingdom: but he shall come in peaceably, and obtain the kingdom by flatteries. And with the arms of a flood shall they be overflown from before him, and shall be broken; yea, also the prince of the covenant. And after the league

made with him he shall work deceitfully: for he shall come up, and shall become strong with a small people. He shall enter peaceably even upon the fattest places of the province; and he shall do that which his fathers have not done, nor his fathers' fathers; he shall scatter among them the prey, and spoil, and riches: yea, and he shall forecast his devices against the strongholds, even for a time."

~ Daniel 11: 21-24; kjv

Now we enter into the most important part of the vision; from now on the vision speaks spiritually deep and very dark things, for it addresses the great craftiness of most subtle creature the Serpent, whose craftiness remained in the dark and prospered from many centuries.

The Angel speaks about the eighth kingdom, which stands in the place of Roman empire, and in whose place the Byzantine will stand for a while, and how slowly with flatteries he obtains the honor of the Kingdom. This Kingdom of Barbarian is the feet and toes of Iron and clay of the first image, and one that wears out the saints of the Most High of the second vision, and a king of fierce countenance and understanding of dark sentences of the third vision of Daniel. In those days there was a migration of Germanic peoples into the Roman territory and also within the Roman territory, and they were on constant move, having no homeland to settle; like traveling a long and winding path and never reaching the end. This eighth Kingdom is vile and despicable; in the beginning the Roman Christians and papacy gave them not the honor of the Kingdom, and these barbarians the Germanic tribes like Franks, Jutes, Lombards,

Anglo-Saxons, etc. came peaceably as mercenaries and refugees into Roman territories. For initially, barbarians came in small numbers, Franks came as refugees and mercenaries and stayed peaceably within the Empire, so also in the beginning Anglo-Saxons and Jutes entered Britain peaceably as mercenaries, so also the Lombards and other Germanic tribes came as refugees and mercenaries. They all initially came peaceably; they entered peaceably in the fattest places of the province Gaul, Britain, Pannonia, etc. The Barbarian empire was of fierce countenance and has understanding of dark sentences, meaning they were a cruel[8] and wise[9] empire; after they made a covenant with Byzantine Empire they dealt deceitfully. For when the Franks were given shelter in Toxandria, they slowly moved westward and occupied a large territory, even the whole of Gaul that belongs to the Empire. So also the Lombards moved from their allotted land and occupied Italy, and so also the Anglo-Saxons to whom Kent was given but deceitfully occupied Britain, killing native British chieftains in what is known as Treachery of Long Knives. Initially these Anglo-Saxons came as mercenaries and in small numbers; after that, many that belong to them migrated to join them. So also, when the Lombard's gathered to themselves people from other tribes to invade Italy, for all these tribes grew stronger in the years that came after they entered. And with the arms of a flood shall they be overflown from before him, and they shall be broken, for as the Angel said, his power shall be mighty, but not by his own power.[10] This Barbarian has successfully broken the Byzantine Empire, even the prince who made league with them, and occupied the whole Western Roman Empire (present-day

Europe) not by his own power, but by the power of the prince of this world. The barbarian scattered riches and spoil among these Church leaders, and they gave huge amounts of donations to monasteries, and these Franks, Lombard's and other Germanic tribes converted to Catholic Christianity, The North King the Barbarian forecasts devices against strongholds in western empire present day Europe for a time which is 360 years, and the spiritual armies the ecclesiastical hosts formed for him when Barbarians joined hands with church of Rome, these took away continuity nearly hundred years before the Barbarian with flatteries finally obtained the honor of the kingdom, it was on December 25, 800 AD; the eighth kingdom barbarian stood in the place of Roman empire, when Pope Leo III crowned Frankish Charlemagne as Emperor of the Romans.

> The Angel said "And he shall stir up his power and his courage against the king of the south with a great army, and the king of the south shall be stirred up to battle with a very great and mighty army; but he shall not stand: for they shall forecast devices against him. Yea, they that feed of the portion of his meat shall destroy him, and his army shall overflow: and many shall fall down slain. And both these kings' hearts shall be to do mischief, and they shall speak lies at one table, but it shall not prosper: for yet the end shall be at the time appointed. Then shall he return into his land with great riches; and his heart shall be against the holy covenant; and he shall do exploits, and return to his own land."
>
> ~ Daniel 11:25-28; kjv

Until now, there was no South king since the time the Ptolemaic Empire fell in, 30 BC, to the time Roman Empire, the king of the North, and the sixth king fell. Byzantine became a small piece of land in present day Turkey and Greece, having lost its southern territories to caliphate and John saw at second trumpet, as if it were a great nation burning with scriptures, was cast into the sea, third part of waters of sea become blood. And third part of people in the sea that had life has died, And third part of the missionary activity in sea got destroyed, by 640 AD, Islamic rule came into Egypt, and by 711 AD, to the Iberian Peninsula in the present day Spain and Portugal. The king of the North the Barbarian stirred up his power and courage to fight against the king of the South, the Islamic caliphate. First, in 718 AD, few Goths rebelled against Islamic rule and formed a small kingdom, Asturia, and the 732 Frankish alliance stopped the Islamic expedition into France at the Battle of Tours; not immediately, but after 400 years they regained the whole Iberian peninsula from Muslims. Although the king of the South had a great army; he has not stood and lost the Iberian peninsula, and it was conquered again by the king of the North the Barbarian. For they, the Kingdom of the North forecasts devices against him, and they who feed of the portion of meat shall destroy the Kingdom of the South, the Islamic Caliphate. For the rulers and governors of the Iberian Peninsula declared themselves as independent of the Caliphate, and by constant internal fighting among those Muslims rulers and sometimes confederating with Christian kings, the Kingdom of the North and the Kingdom of the South spoke lies and made false commitments to each other, with mischief in their hearts. The king of the North obtained great riches from gaining the Iberian Peninsula back; his heart was against the holy covenant because he already hated it, and joined with the apostates. And in the appointed time the Kingdom of the North, the Barbarian, will come toward the south.

> The Angel said, "the ships of Chittim shall come against him: therefore he shall be grieved, and return, and have indignation against the holy covenant: so shall he do; he shall even return, and have intelligence with them that forsake the holy covenant. And arms shall stand on his part, and they shall pollute the sanctuary of strength, and shall take away the daily, and they shall place the abomination that maketh desolate. And such as do wickedly against the covenant shall he corrupt by flatteries:"
> ~ Daniel 11:30-32; KJV

When these Germanic tribes first arrived into the Roman province, they were mostly pagans worshiping their polytheistic gods of mythologies like of Norse, there were efforts of conversion by Christian evangelists, but some tribes like vandals, Goths are Arians, and in the initial decades the Empire's armies of the West and of the East fought against them many times. They fought against these tribes many times, as they were considered as alien barbarians and pagans, and were not easily accepted into their society, which was Christian at that time. There were so many fights against these tribes; they fought Alemani, also called Suebi in the Battle of Staatsburg and in the Battle of the Reims; they fought with the Saxons and Franks when they tried invade northern Gaul and Britain, and they were defeated by the Romans in 370 AD, and many Saxons were killed. They defeated the Salian Franks and killed their king in the Battle of Vicus Helena in 448 AD: they fought and destroyed Arian vandals, they defeated the Ostrogothic Kingdom in the Battle of Mons Lactarius and put an end to their rule,. and in the Battle of Orleans they defeated Arian Visigoths.

Therefore the barbarians were grieved, and had indignation against the Christian faith; after that Barbarian had intelligence with them that forsook the holy covenant. So the barbarians had intelligence with the Apostates of Christian faith and converted to Roman Catholicism. The barbarians started to show regard to the papacy, and in a couple of centuries obtained the Kingdom by flatteries in 800 AD, and by the conversion of Barbarian there formed a spiritual armies of bishops, priests, preachers, ecclesiastical leaders, monks, saints, etc. for him. So this ecclesiastical host was formed for him, and these spiritual armies polluted the true followers of Christ, the saints who had testimony of Jesus and the commandments of God, and they made saints to no longer continue with Father and Son. For they are the sanctuary of God among whom he dwells, and they take away saints continuity with him, and their translators added word sacrifice in this verse with prejudice, as this Spiritual armies of ecclesiastical host did take them to spiritual captivity or plunder the truth from Saints, or spiritually kill them by the word of their teaching of scriptural interpretation, as seen by Daniel in third vision. "It cast down the truth to the ground; and it practised, and prospered."[11] These spiritual armies of bishops, priests, preachers, ecclesiastical leaders, monks, saints etc. has thrown down the truth, and also the truth of the Gospel, even the article of Justification; they polluted true saints of Christ who keep commandments of God, even to hold to the testimony of Jesus. It made them to fall to the ground, as these people spiritually killed them or took them captives. These Spiritual armies of the Beast also placed the abomination that makes desolate, not at that time, but in our times, for there was 1290 years of space in between taking away their continuity and placing the abomination that makes desolate set up. As Angel said in the twelfth chapter, "from the time that the continuity shall be taken away, and the abomination that maketh desolate set up, there shall be a thousand two hundred and ninety days." [12]Abomination means an idol or image that was worshiped, and this idol or image causes desolation, for after expiry of 1290 years this spiritual army told those that dwell in Christendom on the Earth to make such an image. This kingdom of the North the barbarian, which is also the eighth Kingdom corrupted them to do wickedly against the holy covenant by its flatteries, for these nations praised and honored all those whom they call saints; those who sought to be justified by their own good works and virtue, against the truth of the Gospel, all those wicked who teach to the saints who baptized into the body of Christ that they were still under the Law and were obliged to keep the Law. The Barbarian corrupted such people with flatteries of praise and giving them the honor of saints and great preachers of faith. Such a people from Catholics and Protestants were considered as saints in the Dark Ages and the Middle Ages, and in modern times great Christians and great preachers. There are so many wicked and workers of spiritual iniquity in past centuries and millenniums, and also now, who teach these verses of prophecy were fulfilled before Christ was born, despite of Christ's own words. "When ye therefore shall see the abomination of desolation, spoken of by Daniel the prophet," Which Lord spoke spiritually and apocalyptically about the things to come upon his saints, and the Christendom the Earth. He also said, in those days, there shall be tribulation quoting last chapter of the book of Daniel, and in those days there will be a lot deception by false teachers who were of this spiritual army of the Barbarian. Those days will shortened, for the sake of elect, for there will be two in bed, so one shall be left and the other shall be carried away into deception. For wheresoever's this abomination, the image also called as carcass is, there these christians will be gathered together.

> The Angel said, "but the people that do know their God shall be strong, and do exploits. And they that understand among the people shall instruct many: yet they shall fall by the sword, and by flame, by captivity, and by spoil, many days. Now when they shall fall, they shall be holpen with a little help: but many shall cleave to them with flatteries. And of them of understanding shall fall, to try them, and to purge, and to make them white, even to the time of the end: because it is yet for a time appointed."
> ~ DANIEL 11: 32-35; KJV

Now back in time, while the Barbarian and his spiritual armies of bishops, priests, preachers, ecclesiastical leaders, monks, saints, etc. were polluting the true followers of Christ, the saints, with their wicked teachings; but the saints who know their God who has called them to fellowship of his son, they shall be strong and fight for the cause of truth. They instruct many for some time in their lives, from the time they were being called by God, as they see the evil of those who dwell in Christendom and their wickedness, lies, and blaspheme against God. They instruct many in sack clothes bearing disgrace with which these christians reproached their God. Yet they fall in a few days after they were called by God to the fellowship of his Son through the Gospel; in between these days they instruct many, for after the days of their giving instruction is over they shall fall by the sword of the word of their teaching of scriptural interpretation, even to spiritual sword of these spiritual hosts of Barbarian. Or they will be taken to spiritual captivity to their falsehoods and lies by these hosts of Barbarian, or they will be plundered by these hosts so that they will be robbed of the truth and word they heard at the time of their calling, so that no more word of their God comes out of their mouths, not anymore. For it is no more there in their hearts. As Paul said, "word in your mouth and in your heart," that word which they heard at the time of their salvation and through which they were called won't be there in their hearts, for this spiritual host of Barbarian will steal it from them.

Now, when this was happening from a long time ago, from the eighth century, as they were falling every saint and in every generation after a few days of their instructing to people, and as they were falling and being trodden and trampled like mire in the street, as Daniel saw in third vision;

"it waxed great, to the host of heaven; and it cast down of the host and of the stars to the ground, and stamped upon them."[13] For after they fall after they instructed, they will be trampled by these spiritual hosts of Barbarian, but after many centuries a little help was given for the fallen saints; not that after the help was given they won't fall in the coming generations, but a little help was given to them, to help them from being trampled for a lifetime after they had fallen, but this little help won't keep them from falling. For they shall fall till the end of the age, as the Angel said: "And of them of understanding shall fall, to try them, and to purge, and to make them white, even to the time of the end: because it is yet for a time appointed." The Angel says they of understanding will fall, even after the little help was given and until the time of the end. Now, spiritually "understanding" is called oil which makes the face shine.[14] And the Angel says the saints will fall to be tried; their faith and their patience are put to test, as they seek their God who had once called them at the time of their conversion, to purge and to purify them.

Nearly 800 years after they took away continuity that little help has been given to saints through the rediscovery of Article of Justification, which is the truth of the Gospel. This Article of Justification was rediscovered by Martin Luther in the sixteenth century, and he found that the Church of Rome, the papacy, was Babylon, who took saints into captivity. He preached that saints could only be justified by Faith alone and, unless they die unto the Law, they can't live unto God. And good works and merits won't contribute to our Justification; He fought against the papacy, the Church of Rome, and against the spiritual host of the Barbarian that were in his day, which trampled saints. And the Article of Justification and the other truths that were related to it were restored to the Saints. For Luther Law is good if it is used for the purposes for which it was designed, and that is to check civil transgression and to magnify spiritual transgressions; for him this is the business of the Law, and here the business of the Law ends and should go no further. But many cleaved the saints with flatteries, even in Luther's day, even his close friend Philip Melanchthon taught the third use of the Law. And others like Calvin totally hijacked the things brought by Luther; this wicked man taught that saints are still under obligation to keep the moral Law, and it has not lost any of its authority over saints. He also spoke about the third use of the Law; his followers, in their confession statements of Faith, like Westminster and 1689 Baptist confession, wrote that the moral Law is ever binding on saints and they are in an obligation to keep it. These workers of iniquity and dogs wanted saints to be kept under obligation to keep their conscience under the moral Law and all their actions, words, thoughts should be judged according to its standards, so that those who were seeking to be justified by Christ also find themselves as sinners.[15] These liars teach that the Law won't condemn the saints in their conscience, and they should live unto the moral Law. These spiritual fornicators made the woman become alive unto her former husband, their old man, under the Law and to die unto Christ. These men of the past centuries and now, who were considered as virtuous Christian preachers among their denominations and sects of Christendom, shall no more be considered as noble in the coming days. As spoken by prophets, "The fool shall be no more called noble, nor the churl said to be bountiful. For the fool will speak folly, and his heart will work iniquity, to practice profaneness, and to utter error against God, to make empty the soul of the hungry, and to cause the drink of the thirsty to fail. And the instruments of the churl are evil: he deviseth wicked devices to destroy the meek with lying words, even when the needy speaketh right."[16]

> The Angel said, "And the king shall do according to his will; and he shall exalt himself, and magnify himself above every god, and shall speak marvellous things against the God of gods, and shall prosper till the indignation be accomplished: for that that is determined shall be done. Neither shall he regard the gods of his fathers, nor the desire of women, nor regard any god: for he shall magnify himself above all. But in his estate shall he honor the God of the fortress: and a god whom his fathers knew not shall he honour with gold, and silver, and with precious stones, and pleasant things. Thus shall he do in the most strong holds with a strange god, whom he shall acknowledge and increase with glory: and he shall cause them to rule over many, and shall divide the land for gain"
>
> ~ Daniel 11:36-39; kjv

This Barbarian Kingdom of the North did according to his will, for his power was mighty, but yet not by his own power. For Satan gave them his might, and the Barbarian opposed and exalted himself above all that is called god. Now, after joining hands with those who forsake the holy covenant, even the papacy, the Barbarian has rooted out paganism and other gods from Europe from among his people. He exalted himself against all that were called as gods, for these Germanic tribes regarded not the gods of their own forefathers, and neither regarded other people's gods; they destroyed the altars pagan gods of theirs, as well as others, and no god was spared by them. This Kingdom of the North the Barbarian has joined hands with the Apostates who forsake the holy covenant and has rejected the one true God the savior of mankind; by making the man a savior of himself by means of his own merits and good works and piety, he utterly rejected God, who sacrificed his Son. This Kingdom of the North the Barbarian ensured the craftiness of Satan to become prosperous in the Christendom. He spoke that God is a merciless and cruel judge, who enjoys destroying the souls of humans, and therefore everyone should try to save themselves by their merits and good works. For thus spoke the Barbarian throughout the Middle Ages and the Dark Ages. He will prosper in his craftiness and spiritual wickedness, until God's indignation upon his saints comes to an end; then they will gain victory over him, and their victory is at hand, therefore he send me to speak these mysteries to them, for who will gain victory over Beast in all the Christendom other than he that believe and understand these things.

The king of the North the Barbarian did not show any regard to the gods of their fathers like Odin, Teiwaz, Thor etc, but he quickly abandoned them. Neither did they shown regard for the pleasant rituals and festivals of their religion. He didn't shown regard for any god; he exalted himself above all that is called god, but these barbarians has honored a strange god, whom their fathers don't know, the Christ of the Apostates, the god of the Fortress the Rome. Whom he will acknowledge and increase in glory; this Christ appears like one who has not become a partaker of flesh and blood, and has not become like us in all things as a partaker of our previous estate while we were in the world before our conversion, a Christ who is a minster of Sin and death. He dealt with the Church of Rome by acknowledging this Christ of Rome, he increased in glory. In the eighth century, Charlemagne rooted paganism from Europe by force and destroyed the pillar of the Saxon god Irmin. When the Saxons of Lower Saxony of Germany revolted against the forceful conversion, he had ordered the slaughter of 4500 Saxons. They magnified on every other god and have shown no regard for the pagan gods of their forefathers.

The king of the North, the empire of Barbarians, caused those Apostates, even the bishops, Archbishops, and popes of the Church of Rome, to rule over many, for he carried them on his back. The papacy and Church of Rome had great authority in all their lands, and he gave them lands also, and this is called donation of Pepin. In 752, when Aistulf, king of the Lombards, demanded the submission of Rome and a tribute from Pope Stephen, he sought the help of the Frankish king Pepin and met him in France, where he anointed Pepin and his sons. In return, Pepin Invaded Italy and gave territories of Ravenna and other cities to the Pope, which previously belong to the Byzantine Empire, which the Lombards occupied. And in 774 AD, Charlemagne confirmed the donation, and these territories are called Papal states, which were under the Pope until 1870. So, on 25 December 800 AD, Pope Leo III had crowned him as Imperator Romanorum, which means Emperor of the Romans, thus marking the commencement of reign of Kingdom of North the Barbarian in the place of the Roman Empire, the sixth one, and the Byzantine empire, the seventh one who stood in the place of the Roman Empire, the sixth one for few days; after that his authority was broken. The imperial title of Charlemagne was "Charles, most serene Augustus crowned by God, the great, peaceful emperor ruling the Roman empire".

> The Angel said, "And at the time of the end shall the king of the south push at him: and the king of the north shall come against him like a whirlwind, with chariots, and with horsemen, and with many ships; and he shall enter into the countries, and shall overflow and pass over. He shall enter also into the glorious land, and many countries shall be overthrown: but these shall escape out of his hand, even Edom, and Moab, and the chief of the children of Ammon. He shall stretch forth his hand also upon the countries: and the land of Egypt shall not escape. But he shall have power over the treasures of gold and of silver, and over all the precious things of Egypt: and the Libyans and the Ethiopians shall be at his steps. But tidings out of the east and out of the north shall trouble him: therefore he shall go forth with great fury to destroy, and utterly to make away many. And he shall plant the tabernacles of his palace between the seas in the glorious holy mountain, yet he shall come to his end, and none shall help him."
>
> ~ DANIEL 11:40-45; KJV

The Kingdom of the South, even the Islamic nations, pushed at the Kingdom of the North, even at the Kingdoms of the barbarians. In the end in our times a few centuries ago, the Ottoman Empire of the South pushed towards the North, occupying parts of the Balkans and Eastern Europe, and occupied Hungary; it managed to come even to the gates of Vienna and tried to invade Austria. The wars were fought battles between them from the 16th century through the 18th century, but the Kingdom of the North came against him, and pushed back the Kingdom of the South. The Kingdom of the North the Barbarian, the present Western nations came against the Kingdom of the South like a whirlwind, with their military might against the South. The Western nations of the Barbarian had entered into the countries of the South, and had overflowed and passed over. He had also entered also into the glorious land, and many countries were overthrown, so in late 19th century, the British empire of the Northern Kingdom the Barbarian occupied Egypt, and he also occupied the land of Israel;, and the Italians of the Kingdom of the North occupied Libya and Ethiopia; the French empire occupied Algeria and other countries. In fact, the Kingdom of the North the Western nations occupied the whole African continent and distributed it amongst themselves. They had power over all the treasures, gold, and silver of Egypt, and even carried some precious things to their country. The children of Amman, Moab, and Edom escaped from the hand of Barbarian at that time because these Western nations of Barbarian, the King of the North had promised autonomy to them, if the Arabs revolt against the Ottoman Empire. So Jordan became as Emirate of Transjordan as part of House of Hashim.

Now in these centuries, Barbarian the Kingdom of the North increased so much in glory; he had new territories, discovered new worlds, and had settlements on the North American continent and Australia. He got the tiding from the North and East, for the alliance of the German Empire and Austria-Hungary troubled him, as the power of the central Europe German Empire competed in an arms race with the British Empire. The Kingdom of the North went forth with great fury to destroy many, so war broke out in 1914 between them, which was called the Great War or World War I and, subsequently World War II. And the Kingdom of the North conquered Palestine from the Ottoman Empire in 1917, and captured Jerusalem and set tabernacles of his palace on it. After these World Wars, the Kingdom of the North the Barbarian, even these Western nations were united, and his deadly wound of the sword, the division, amongst themselves was healed, and the Barbarian recovered from deadly destruction happened by World Wars and become healthy, wealthy, and prosperous, and increased in glory further. All the Christendom wondered after the Barbarian the Kingdom of the North, the present day Western nations of North America, Europe, and Australia. The Christians worshipped the dragon, which gave his strength and a great authority unto these western nations, and the Christians worshipped the Barbarian, saying, "Which country is like unto our Christian countries of the West? Which country is able to make war with these Western nations?" The Barbarian is showing himself as savior unto these Christians and all

Christians whose names were not written in book of life has worshiped him, saying 'Which country is like unto these Christian countries of West? Which country is able to make war with these Western nations?" Thus they worshipped Barbarian the Kingdom of the North, the eighth King.

> The Angel said, "And at that time shall Michael stand up, the great prince which standeth for the children of thy people: and there shall be a time of trouble, such as never was since there was a nation even to that same time: and at that time thy people shall be delivered, every one that shall be found written in the book. And many of them that sleep in the dust of the earth shall awake."
>
> ~ Daniel 12:1-2; kjv

After the King of the North, the eighth king, set the tabernacles of his palace on Jerusalem, and after the time of the British Empire's occupation of the land of Israel, the children of Israel declared independence in 1948, and they occupied the land and were continuing as a nation in the Middle East until now. For God has restored again the kingdom to Israel. Nevertheless, the deception of the Spiritual armies the ecclesiastical host of the Barbarian in Christendom will be so great in these days, if God won't reduce these days, no flesh will escape their deception, and everyone will be carried away in it. This king of the North, the eighth Kingdom, shows himself as the redeemer of Israel and Christians, and all those whose names were not written in the Book of Life will worship him. All the Israelis who were elected by God and whose names were written in the

Book of Life will be delivered from deception; after this time of trouble is over, many from all the tribes of Israel will receive Gospel.[17] People elected from all nations and tribes will be gathered unto Christ by his angels at the time of his coming, and at that time many of the dead will be raised. We know we have brethren from all nations and all tribes, also from these Germanic tribes of the Kingdom of the North; nevertheless, their identity is in Christ, not in the Barbarian Empire. I write this lest they argue that the Germanic tribes, the barbarians of the past, were not the Beast by pointing to some Saints who were from these Western nations.

Now you are living in the times of trouble, but people see these days as peace and safety without knowing the destruction that comes upon them, like a thief in the night, while people were sleeping. When they wake up, they will find that they were robbed, for deception comes in the darkness of ignorance.

Now our Lord quoted from the Book of Daniel when he told the disciples about the time of his coming on Mount of Olives, and he said this during the time when the abomination that makes desolate was set. There shall be great tribulation, such as was not since the beginning of the world to that time, no, nor ever shall be. And this abomination has been set in our days by the ecclesiastical host the spiritual armies of the Barbarian, for the 1290 years were expired a few decades ago, since they polluted true followers of Christ, the saints. For they are the sanctuary of God among whom he dwells, and they took away saints continuity with their God. And this spiritual army has set the abomination that makes desolate, which is a lying wonder; an Abomination, the image that gives testimony to a lie and causes people to be spiritually killed. This abomination that gives testimony to lie had stood in the Holy place of God's testimony for his Son.[18] Lord Jesus said that the generation in which abomination of desolation is set up, even this generation shall not pass away until all those things which he spoke about are fulfilled.

> Now the Apostle Paul wrote a few words about this king of the North, the eighth kingdom, the Barbarian, the present day Western nations. "Who opposes and exalts himself above all that is called God, or that is worshipped; so that he as God sits in the temple of God, showing himself that he is God. Remember ye not, that, when I was yet with you, I told you these things? And now ye know what withholds that he might be revealed in his time. For the mystery of iniquity doth already work: only he who now letteth will let until he is taken out of the way. And then shall that Wicked be revealed, whom the Lord shall consume with the spirit of his mouth, and shall destroy with the brightness of his coming: whose coming is after the working of Satan with all power and signs and lying wonders, And with all deceivableness of unrighteousness in them that perish; because they received not the love of the truth, that they might be saved. And for this cause, God shall send them strong delusion, that they should believe a lie: That they all might be damned who believed not the truth, but had pleasure in unrighteousness."
>
> 2 THESSALONIANS 2:4-12; KJV

The Apostle Paul was quoting from Daniel, chapter eleven, saying that this Barbarian (who is going to be eight one) was already working in his days, as the Romans were in a constant clash with these Germanic tribes, even before the time of Julius Caesar, as these Germanic tribes sought to enter into Gaul. But they were stopped by the Roman Empire, when the Roman Empire who restrained them will be taken out of the way, then the wicked one will be revealed, and the things prophesied about him will be revealed. And Lord Jesus will consume this Kingdom of the North with the spirit of his mouth, and will destroy him with the brightness of his coming, for light exposes everything that is hidden in darkness and also destroys the darkness. So also the brightness at the coming of the true Christ will destroy the kingdom of darkness, like a clear morning Sun that makes darkness to disappear, for this Barbarian destroyed the truth as written; he had cast the truth to the ground and prospered in destroying it. But now all Christians that were not written in the book worshiped him, saying, "Which country is like these Christian Western nations?"

Now after Barbarian came, he has shown no regard for any god, neither have these Germanic tribes shown regard to the pagan gods of their fathers, as said by Daniel, but joined hands with the Apostate Christians and shown regard to their strange god, the Christ of Rome. The Apostle Paul said that the Lord is coming after the workings of Satan with all power and signs and lying wonders. And with all deceivableness of unrighteousness in them that perish, so that all these Christians who had pleasure in unrighteousness might be punished, whom God has delivered to damnation through delusion to receive the lie. The Lord's coming will be like the flood in the days of Noah; as the flood in the days of Noah came and carried them in unawares, so shall also now in the days of Lord Jesus, so also in these years these Christians are being carried away into deception unto their damnation. As the Lord said, they shall be carried away to carcass,[19] this carcass the idol is the image of Barbarian, which this spiritual host of the Barbarian teaches Christians to make, this is the abomination that speaks, makes desolate, and stands in the place of the testimony of God, which he gave to Jesus. These Christians are being carried away unto deception by false teachers, even by the spiritual host of Barbarian to worship the miracles and signs of Satan, by believing it are work of God. As the Lord said, then shall two be in the field; the one shall be taken, and the other left. Two shall be grinding at the mill; the one shall be taken, and the other left. From the same house and same family one will be carried away into eternal destruction through deception and another shall be left.

But this ecclesiastical host of Barbarian has deluded so many people with their false teachings about the mystery of iniquity by misinterpreting 70 weeks of prophecy, which was already fulfilled by the coming of the Messiah and confirming the covenant made with their fathers. There were so many dogs and workers of iniquity in the past millenniums, and also at present times, who seek to purposefully create confusion and bring forth damnable teachings. Among such people were also John Nelson Darby and C.I. Scofield; they created so much confusion and error, so much so that translators of the bibles were also deceived by them and translated scriptures with prejudice. For they translated with prejudice where the original text in Greek simply means, "Whose coming is after ..." but they placed their own words and translated "The coming of the lawless one ...." These evil people were deceived so much that they don't even look into the context, for in the very previous verse Paul was talking about Christ's coming.

Hear all you Christians; if your gods and christs are really gods, then they would have declared at least these former things unto you. If you had served my God, He would have shown you, but surely your gods and christs are your carved imaginations about God and Christ. Have the gods and christs of any of your denominations or sects shown these things at any time in all these centuries? Then bring your evidence; yes, none has shown these things. If they can't be able to show what things were in past, how can they show the things that will be hereafter? Hear all you, his servants, whom he has begotten again and called to his fellowship at the time of your new birth; have any of the gods and christs of nations of Earth, even denominations and sects of the Christendom whom you serve, shown you these things ? Where is the God among you in all the Christendom who has declared this and proclaimed to us the former things? Present your witnesses, that you may be justified, or hear and acknowledge the truth. They are idols of your imaginations, work of your hearts, wind and confusion, and they speak deceit. They are nothing, and their work is less than nothing They can do neither good nor evil, and they shall perish from the face of the Earth, for the Christendom will be filled with the knowledge of the glory of my God, as the waters cover the sea.

Now this mystery of iniquity was revealed to John by one of the seven Angels, who had the seven vials of wrath. John was, in spirit, carried into the future and went back and forth in the future.[20] So the Angel carried him back in time after the seven vials of wrath was poured on the Christendom, which will happen shortly in our times; and the Angel showed him the mystery of iniquity, even this kingdom of the North, the eighth kingdom.

> The Angel Said, "I will shew unto thee the judgment of the great whore that sitteth upon many waters: With whom the kings of the earth have committed fornication, and the inhabitants of the earth have been made drunk with the wine of her fornication. So he carried me away in the spirit into the wilderness: and I saw a woman sit upon a scarlet colored beast, full of names of blasphemy, having seven heads and ten horns. And the woman was arrayed in purple and scarlet color, and decked with gold and precious stones and pearls, having a golden cup in her hand full of abominations and filthiness of her fornication: And upon her forehead was a name written, MYSTERY, BABYLON THE GREAT, THE MOTHER OF HARLOTS AND ABOMINATIONS OF THE EARTH."
>
> ~ Revelation 17:1-5; kjv

As the Angel showed to John, the woman, even the Church of Rome sits on many waters, which are many people and the Kingdoms of Earth, the denominations and sects of the

Christendom, committed fornication with her. Which mean that all those sects and denominations worshiped other god with her. And the inhabitants of the Earth, the Christians who dwell in the Christendom, were made to drink her teaching of her idolatry with another Christ. This Christ of Rome is the strange god of the Barbarian, the king of the North, the eighth kingdom, as said by Daniel. This Christ is the minister of Sin and death;[21] a Christ without human form; a Christ who didn't come in the flesh; a Christ who didn't become like any of the human children who were in other religions, or like us before we were called; a Christ who was not subjected unto beggarly elements of the world and died unto the Law and Sin in our old estate and rose again. But their Christ is strange God, a spirit without a human form, an angry judge who gets annoyed with the slightest provocation, a cruel extractor, etc., and the Angel carried John into the wilderness, where the remnant of Zion was,[22] who has the testimony of Jesus and kept the commandments of God, even the two olives and two lamp stands the candlesticks, they were those who has oil of understanding among his people . As Daniel wrote, even those who were of understanding that feed people in wilderness,[23] even those who knew their God, with whom the Barbarian waged war with the aid of a whore and killed them.[24] This woman Babylon sat on a scarlet colored beast filled up with works of blasphemy, and this beast is in royal appearance; for to this Barbarian Satan gave his strength and authority, and the woman was arrayed in royal robes, sitting as the queen on the nations. For the mountains the heads of the Beast, on them Church at Rome sat and exerted her authority on these nations throughout the Middle Ages until protestant horns grew out of these nations after the 17th century. This woman the Church of Rome is God's judgment upon the Christendom; upon its denominations and sects, she was a golden cup unto all the nations of the Earth the Christendom. All the denominations and sects of the Christendom had drunken her teaching and were mad. She was the mother of all the Churches that do spiritual fornications and the mother of abominations and the idolatries that were committed in Earth the Christendom.

> Thus the Angel spoke to John; "I will tell thee the mystery of the woman, and of the beast that carrieth her, which hath the seven heads and ten horns. The beast that thou sawest was, and is not; and shall ascend out of the bottomless pit, and go into perdition: and they that dwell on the earth shall wonder, whose names were not written in the book of life from the foundation of the world, when they behold the beast that was, and is not, and yet is. And here is the mind which hath wisdom. The seven heads are seven mountains, on which the woman sitteth. And there are seven kings: five are fallen, and one is, and the other is not yet come; and when he cometh, he must continue a short space. And the beast that was, and is not, even he is the eighth and is of the seven, and goeth into perdition. And the ten horns which thou sawest are ten kings, which have received no kingdom as yet; but receive power as kings one hour with the beast. These have one mind, and shall give their power and strength unto the beast."
>
> ~ Revelation 17:7-13; kjv

Now the Angel carried John to the Middle Ages, before the days of Martin Luther, for after these things he saw Martin Luther and wrote about him. "After these things I saw another angel come down from heaven, having great power; and the earth was lightened with his glory. And he cried mightily with a strong voice, saying, Babylon the great is fallen, is fallen, and is become the habitation of devils, and the hold of every foul spirit, and a cage of every unclean and hateful bird."[25] For this Martin Luther had found that the Church of Rome, the Babylon, has fallen into apostasy and became the habitation of devils and foul spirits. He cried mightily against it, and he came with great authority and spoke for the truth of the Gospel, and his glory has lightened the Christendom the Earth. Nevertheless, the mystery of iniquity was not revealed unto him.

The Angel said the Beast was not in John's time, but he was in the past to that time. For in the past, during the time of Julius Caesar and Caesar Augustus, Germania was a part of the Roman world, and it was part of the Roman Empire, which was extended unto the river Elbe. But after the Battle of Teutoburg Forest in 9 AD, the Roman Empire withdrew from Germania and its borders were confined to the river Rhine and the Danube, and these Germanic tribes of the Barbarian were confined on the other side of Rhine away from the civilized world for next few centuries. After this the Migration period started in the 4th century and lasted up to the 7th century. It was a period of extensive migrations by the Germanic tribes into and within the Western Roman Empire, or the present Europe, and these people continually moved without a permanent place to settle, like someone who has been thrown into a bottomless pit, who was ever falling in a pit without a place for foothold to stand on. These barbarians, the Germanic tribes, finally came out of the Migration period and settled in Europe, Franks and other barbarian tribes settled in France, the Lombards and other tribes in Italy, and Goths and other barbarian tribes in Spain, the Saxons, Angelis, and Jutes settled in Britain. They that dwell in Christendom, all these Christians whose names were not written in the Book of Life shall wonder after the Empire of barbarians, when they behold the Beast.

And here is the mind which hath wisdom, so therefore be wise to understand this mystery. The number seven symbolically represents the many or complete, for this Kingdom of the North, the Barbarian the eight one has many nations. This empire has many heads, which were the countries of the barbarians, and the boundaries of those countries changed at various times in the past; these heads the mountains of the barbarian Beast in the Middle Ages were countries of Barbarian, which were all the countries that existed in the Western Europe. And this woman even the Church of Rome sat on these countries of Barbarian the kingdom of North, the Eighth kingdom.

There are seven kings: five have fallen, and one is, and the other is not yet to come; and when he cometh, he must continue a short space. Here the Angel is reminding John about what Daniel the prophet wrote in chapter eleven of his book, for he is driving John's attention to the prophecy of Daniel about the eighth Kingdom, which shall proceed after the seventh kingdom, which shall continue for short period, as Daniel wrote. "Then shall stand up in his estate a raiser of taxes in the glory of the kingdom: but within few days he shall be destroyed neither in anger, nor in battle."[26] For barbarians came peaceably and occupied all of Europe, which belongs to him, the five kings were the five Kingdoms of Greece: the first one is the Macedonian Empire, and the remaining four were the Kingdom of Seleucus, the Kingdom of Cassander, the Kingdom of Lysimachus, and the Ptolemaic Kingdom. The sixth Empire, which was present during John's time, was the Roman Empire, and the seventh one, which shall continue for a short space in the place of Roman Empire, is the Byzantine Empire. The Barbarian that was and is not during John's time shall become the eighth Empire, the vile person who will not regard any God: for he shall magnify himself above all, as mentioned in the Book of Daniel. And this Barbarian is made up of the many nations, which were his seven heads; the seven mountains.

The ten horns are the ten kingdoms, which John saw in the thirteenth chapter of the Book, which did not become kingdoms yet during the Middle Ages, but after that period they had become like kingdoms with the beast; these denominations that will become denominations after those Middle Ages will be in authority as the kingdoms along with the Barbarian the Eighth kingdom, the Beast. Although these are the religious Kingdoms of the Earth, the Christendom, all these protestant denominations will have one mind in serving the Beast, and they shall give their authority and strength to these Western nations the Barbarian the Beast. These denominations praised the Beast in their Churches, and called these nations of Barbarian were godly Christian nations in the past. These people also pretend that the Barbarian the western nations were so godly in the past, but now he has become evil in these modern times with licentious and worldly living.

> "And the ten horns which thou sawest upon the beast, these shall hate the whore, and shall make her desolate and naked, and shall eat her flesh, and burn her with fire. For God hath put in their hearts to fulfill his will, and to agree, and give their kingdom unto the beast, until the words of God shall be fulfilled. And the woman which thou sawest is that great city, which reigneth over the kings of the earth."
>
> ~ REVELATION 17:16-18; KJV

These Christian denominations, the Anglicans, Calvinist/Presbyterians, Methodists, Lutherans, Baptists, Congregationalists, Anabaptists, Adventists, Pentecostals, Churches of Christ, etc, had hated the whore even the Church of Rome and had made her desolate and naked, as these protestant denominations hated the Church of Rome. Some believed it as Babylon, the whore, and some called the Pope and papacy as the Beast and with the influence of these denominations on the Western nations; even the on heads of the Beast, some of western nations had to abandon the whore completely, which they carried for several centuries throughout the Middle Ages and the whore was deserted by them and lost her influence and authority over these Western nations. These protestant denominations plucked off her royal dress of purple and scarlet, decked with gold, jewels, and pearls, which she had when she was a queen in the Middle Ages and rode upon the Beast. But after that, these denominations removed her royal authority over these nations of the Beast and made her naked. These protestant denominations did eat her flesh by sucking out the people that belong to her into their denominations, and these horns grew significantly in these Western nations by eating her flesh, and they burnt her with their teaching of the scriptures against her. For God has put in their hearts to fulfill his will against the whore, and with one mind all these ten Protestant denominations gave their denominations and their authority to the Beast, until all the God's words, even the prophecy, were fulfilled.

These ten horns of Beast, even these Protestant denominations, the ten toes of the image that Nebuchadnezzar saw; they will make war with Christ and these kingdoms of Earth, the Christendom. In the near future they will fight against Christ, on the side of Beast, but Christ will overcome them; for he is the King of all the Kingdoms of the Earth, which were the denominations and sects of the Christendom. Those that will be with him are called by God, who knew their God and were chosen to fight for him, and they are faithful to him alone and not any kingdoms of the Earth, even the denominations and sects of the Christendom. The woman Babylon, even the Church at Rome is, is the great spiritual city of the Apostate religion of another Gospel and of another Christ, it rules over denominations of the Christendom, the kingdoms of Earth.

Now that Great God who created all humans has created three spiritual dwelling places for all humans; one is the sea. It is a place where all the people belonging to other religions dwell, and the waves, even the wicked of the sea roar against the Earth, but there are whales and other living creatures that dwell in the waters of the sea.

Another place God created is the Earth/Land, the Christendom; the dry land standing out of the waters of Sea, where the people of this Christian religion dwell and where all the people belonging to denominations and sects of the Christendom dwell; all those who belong to kingdoms of Earth dwell here.

Another place God has created is Heaven, where he set lights sun, moon, and the host of Heaven; even the stars, which give light upon the Christendom the Earth. Their line has gone out through all the Earth and their words to the end of the world. They declare the glory of God, and they proclaim the work of his hands. It is the Kingdom of Heaven the Jerusalem above, the Zion his holy mountain, the Kingdom of his Son Jesus, his anointed higher than the kingdoms of Earth. They are dwellers of Heaven and children of Zion above, the lights of the world. He made these things by Lord Jesus as he said: "And I have put my words in thy mouth, and I have covered thee in the shadow of mine hand, that I may plant the heavens, and lay the foundations of the earth, and say unto Zion, Thou art my people."[27]

John saw a great wonder in Heaven, of woman who were clothed with the sun and crowned with twelve stars, and of the red dragon with seven heads and ten horns which sought to swallow up her child. All the fathers, prophets, and holy men of the old time, all God's people longed to see the coming of the Messiah, the Christ, and God gave them Son; a child was born to them. The government was on his shoulders, and he sat on the throne to rule upon all God's saints. God has set his king upon his people, his holy mountain Zion,[28] the Holy Kingdom of God. And so Christ was caught up unto God and to his throne, where he must stay until God makes his enemies his footstool and until the restoration of all things. After that he will rule all the nations of Earth, the Christendom, with a rod of iron. But until the time when God makes his enemies his footstool, he must rule his people in the midst of enemies[29] who sought to destroy his Kingdom.

The Apostles, Evangelists, and all the ministers of the Gospel proclaimed the Christ, and the Satan who accuses saints in their conscience before God using the Law and who also deceives the whole world. He and his ministers tried to establish themselves in Heaven with their perverting of the Gospel and with other gospels. But they had overcome Satan with the blood of the lamb, in whom they believed that they might be justified before God by the faith of Christ, and not by adding their good works of the Law to the work of Christ, by the word of their testimony which they give for the true Christ and proclaimed the Gospel without corrupting it, and preached it in the sight of God and Christ as sent by God. They have not loved their lives in favor of it. Satan and his ministers were unable to deceive them, and they found no place in Heaven for them to stand. So Satan and his ministers have found no place in Jerusalem above, among the Saints, to accuse them before their God using the Law to deceive them by perverting the Gospel or by other Gospels and other christs. They were cast upon the earth, and their activity was confined to the people who dwell on Earth, to nations the heathen who were in this religion and not to the saints that dwell in light, the children of Zion the Jerusalem above, who were called by God with holy, high, and heavenly calling.

So the Kingdom of God, of Christ, of Heaven the Jerusalem above, came in power in the 1st century, as the Lord said to some of his audience, "Some of you won't taste death until you see the Kingdom of Heaven come in strength."[30] And Christ ruled his people in the midst of his enemies as written "Thy people shall be willing in the day of thy power, in the beauties of holiness from the womb of the morning:"[31] because the Satan who accused them in their conscience before their God day and night was cast down. They had overcome Satan with the blood of the lamb, in which they believed that they might be justified before God by the faith of Christ, and not by adding the works of the Law and by reason of the word of their testimony to which they hold to; and they have not loved their life unto death. So when Satan saw that he was cast unto the Earth, and when he found he and his ministers were unable to overcome them by deception and lies, he was angry with the Jerusalem above, Zion the saints of most high, so he persecuted them, that they might be tried and forsake their faithfulness to the Christ. Satan persecuted and killed them, and Zion was given the wings of a great eagle to go into the wilderness by the providence of God, so she went on becoming the wilderness rapidly; in the wilderness, those who have understanding[32] and who know their God nourish her people in the parched land of the wilderness for the coming 1260 years, away from the wrath of the Serpent.

He cast out the flood of ungodly people, all the pagans in the Roman empire against them, but Earth the Christendom opened her mouth and swallowed them into it, for in the 4th century Christianity become the official religion in all the Roman empire, and all the pagans were absorbed into the Earth, the Christendom. And this effort of Satan to carry away Zion in a flood of ungodly people, which he cast after her, ended in failure when the Christendom swallowed up all the pagans of the Empire into it. Satan was wroth with the woman,[33] and he went to make war with the remaining few of her children who keep the commandments of God, by holding to the testimony of Jesus, even those who has understanding among his people, the two olive trees and two lamp stands the church of witnesses, who might feed her in wilderness.[34] The commandments were that we should continue in faith of the Gospel of Jesus Christ, the word of faith through which he called us at the time of new birth, and love one another. He went to make war with them in whom the word which they heard from the beginning, the word they heard at the time of their calling stays.

Now, after the Earth opened and swallowed up the waters the Serpent cast out of its mouth, the Roman empire, which had its borders unto the Rhine and Danube river in the East was now at that time the Christendom the Earth, and Satan went to wage a spiritual war against the remnant of the seed of Zion, who keep the commandments of God and hold to the testimony of Jesus. He stood in the sand of the sea at the borders of Roman Empire, and a Beast came out of the sea, and John describes the Beast's appearance from our time, in which the Beast reached its height of glory. For John was describing the Beast after its ten horns received the Kingdom and received authority as Kingdoms. After the internal fight amongst its nations ended, the wound of the sword and the wound by division and by fighting among themselves was healed. For after the World War II, these nations were no longer fighting among themselves, and the deadly wound incurred by wars was healed in a few decades after the World Wars came to an end. All the Christendom wondered after the Beast whose wound was healed, and Satan gave these Western nations of North America, Western and Central Europe and Australia his strength, his seat, and great authority.[35] And the Christians all over the world worshiped the Satan who gave these nations such great authority on the affairs of this world, and they saw Satan as their God, who gave to Empire of Germanic tribes the Kingdom of North, to these Western nations such a great authority. All Christians, except those whose names were written in Book of Life, worshiped the Beast, saying "which country is like these our Christian countries, which country in the world is able to fight a war with our Christian nations of the West?"[36] They worship the Beast, saying which country is able to make war with these Western nations of North America, Western and Central Europe, and Australia. If any man has an ear, let him hear.

John describes the Beast and says, "the beast which I saw was like unto a leopard, and his feet were as the feet of a bear, and his mouth as the mouth of a lion:"[37] He says the Beast was like a leopard; it is the third beast in Daniel's vision, which was the Grecian Empire, to whom the great dominion was given to rule all the Earth. To this Barbarian Empire also great dominion was given, and like the leopard has four heads; the four kingdoms toward the four directions. So also the Beast has seven heads the many countries of west, and like the leopard in the Hellenistic period, the period of transition influenced the world in arts, science, music, literature, philosophy, etc. with its civilization and exported culture; so also these Western nations influenced the nations of the world with their Western culture, technology, Science, Music, Arts, civilization and language etc., like of the leopard, the Grecian Empire. The Beast intended to change the times and laws, these past few decades is also a period of transition in the world.

The Beast feet were like that of a bear, the second beast in Daniel's vision. The bear rose on one side,[38] for the bear was Mede-Persia, and the Persians were greater than the Medians. So also among the countries of the barbarians, some will be greater than the others and will have more authority, so also the later kingdoms of west are greater than its former kingdoms. The Beast's mouth was like that of a lion, the lion in Daniel's vision was Babylonian Empire, which destroyed the Zion the people of God and threw down the earthly sanctuary of God and swallowed up the vessels of his temple. So also the Beast did, by throwing down the living sanctuary, and by swallowing the living vessels and taking them into spiritual captivity.

Now John says in the thirteenth chapter of Revelation, the Beast came out from the sea, because the Christendom swallowed up the pagan persecutors that Satan cast after the woman like a flood, and the Roman empire become the Earth the Christendom a few years after the conversion of the Emperor Constantine. Satan went to make war, and the pagan Germanic tribes came out of the sea of other religions, and they also came out from the bottomless pit too, for they came out of migration from moving from one place to another in search of permanent place to stay. And in chapter thirteen John gave us the picture of the Beast from recent times, just before the image of the Beast, the abomination that makes desolate was set up; he gives the picture of the Beast from recent times, in which it reached to the height of its glory. For in the past, during the Middle Ages, before the reformation, the woman used to ride the Beast, and the ten horns have not yet received the Kingdom and become denominations.[39] After the 16th century, these protestant denominations that came out of the Western nations became denominations, received kingdoms, and were received authority with the Beast like kingdoms, and so the horns have the crowns. And these protestant denominations, the Anglicans, Calvinist/Presbyterians, Methodists, Lutherans, Baptists, Congregationalists, Anabaptists, Adventists, Pentecostals, Churches of Christ, etc., became denominations in centuries after the reformation by Martin Luther, and have received authority similar to kingdoms with the Beast. These kingdoms of Earth gave their authority and strength to the Beast, having one purpose, for God hath put in their hearts to fulfill his will, and to agree, and to give their kingdom unto the Beast, until the words of God were fulfilled.

John saw the Beast had a wound by a sword on its head, as the sword is division and internal conflict among these nations of Germanic tribes, which almost caused destruction unto death. After the world war two ended, in few years this deadly wound was healed and these nations become one and prospered, and all the Christendom wondered after the Beast. Satan, the prince of the world, gave these nations of the Beast his strength, his throne, and a great authority, and Christians all over the world worshiped the Satan who gave his power to these Western nations. They worshiped Satan as God by calling him God, by saying God gave the great authority to these western nations amongst the nations of the world. They worshiped the Beast by saying which country is able to make war with our Christian nations of the West. It did great and blasphemous things from the 7th century; it was given for the Beast to continue for 1260 years. From the time it stood in the place of Roman Empire the sixth king, on a Christmas day in the year 800 AD; the Beast will continue for 1260 years of 360 days, after that it will go into perdition, from the time he hated the holy covenant and joined hands with the Apostates, even the Church of Rome in 7th century. He did blasphemous things against God, for the Beast opened his mouth in blasphemy against God; what the Beast does is what he speaks, and he speaks great things against the God of gods. Which means that he does great things against the God of gods, for his actions speak for him; as some say action speak louder than words, so also does the beast do blasphemy against God by doing blasphemous things against the God.

Now the name in the scripture mean the knowledge or revelation of the person, as Jesus Christ said he declared God's name to his brethren.[40] He was not saying the literal name of the letters, which can be spelled, but he was saying he revealed his Father to them; he declared him to them, and by this they know God, since his only begotten Son has declared him to them. And this crafty Beast had done blasphemous things against this name, even against the revelation and knowledge of God which the Lord gave to his saints, and against the knowledge and revelation of one who is true, the only true God. For knowing Lord Jesus is knowing God his Father. This Beast fought against the testimony of the Lord by waging a spiritual war against those who hold to the testimony of Jesus, and spiritually killing them and taking them to captivity, to lies and falsehoods, so that they might lose the testimony of Jesus in them, and might not continue with Father and Son. He cast down his sanctuary, his dwelling place, even his saints among whom God dwells through his Spirit; the Beast cast them down by polluting them, even the sanctuary of God, and he took away the fellowship of God from them, as Daniel wrote. "It waxed great, even to the host of heaven; and it cast down of the host and of the stars to the ground, and stamped upon them. Yea, he magnified himself even to the prince of the host, and by him the continuity was taken away, and the place of his sanctuary was cast down."[41] For his saints are his sanctuary, host of heaven, stars the messengers, the candlesticks or lamp stands among whom God and Christ dwells through the Spirit.

John also wrote about the other beast that came out of the Earth, the Christendom; this beast has two horns, like horns of the Lamb the Christ; the number two symbolizes the witnesses.[42] All those saints who hold to the testimony of Jesus and who have understanding and know their God, who has instructed people all these centuries as said by the Angel to Daniel, "they that understand among the people shall instruct many: yet they shall fall by the sword, and by flame, by captivity, and by spoil, many days, even to the end of time." All these were represented by two lampstands the candlesticks and two olive trees. So also these two horns of this beast represent the witnesses, and the false prophets were called as beasts of the Earth the Christendom. The second beast, the false prophet was the ecclesiastical host the spiritual armies of preachers, priests, bishops, monks, theologians, evangelists etc, and the second beast who has horns like the horns of the Lamb the Christ; this false prophet spoke like Satan, he works the works of Satan. This second beast, the false prophet, was that Spiritual armies the ecclesiastical host formed when the Barbarian, the first Beast, and the whore joined hands in the 6th century as written. "He shall even return, and have intelligence with them that forsake the holy covenant. And arms shall stand on his part, and they shall pollute the sanctuary of strength." [43]

This second beast, the false prophet, is the spiritual armies stood up for the Barbarian which cast the truth to ground and practiced the craftiness of Satan, and prospered in destroying the saints by turning them away from truth, as written. "And arms shall stand on his part, and they shall pollute the sanctuary of strength, and shall take away the continuity"[44] They took away the saints' continuity with their God, and have made them to crucify unto themselves their Lord who loved them and gave himself for their sins. This Spiritual host has taken them to spiritual captivity, has plundered the truth from the saints, or has spiritually killed them by the sword of their teaching of scriptural interpretation. This host of Barbarian, who has thrown them down and taken away the saints' continuity with their God, they are also now in this generation after 1290 years; they placed the abomination that makes desolate. The Barbarian has great authority in this world for dragon has given him his seat and authority and his strength to these nations, and Beast has authority over all the sects, denominations of the Christendom the Earth, and upon all those who dwell in the Christendom. This spiritual army the ecclesiastical host of preachers, evangelists, pastors, bishops, theologians, etc., are exercising the authority of the Barbarian, even the Western nations, in his sight upon all those who dwell in the Christendom and on all those who were in all various denominations and sects of the Christendom the Earth. These people were causing the Christendom the Earth and those who dwell in it and belong to all denominations and sects to worship the Barbarian the Beast, the present day Western nations. These Western nations who had the wound of the sword of division, these nations of the Barbarian fought amongst themselves, but now their deadly wound has healed and lived.

This spiritual army the ecclesiastical host, who reached unto the saints who dwell in heaven and polluted the tabernacle of testimony and cast it down from the past, are now doing great miracles and wonders in the sight of the Beast before the people, as said by Lord Jesus, they will show great signs and wonders. It was also said, by the Apostle Paul, that Satan works with all his might to perform signs and wonders. Now the miracles and signs testify, witness and show the glory, as written: "This beginning of miracles did Jesus in Cana of Galilee, and manifested forth his glory, and his disciples believed on him"[45] *and* "Jesus of Nazareth, a man approved of God among you by miracles and wonders and signs, which God did by him in the midst of you,"[46] *and* "This sickness is not unto death, but for the glory of God, that the Son of God might be glorified thereby,"[47] *and* "God also bearing them witness, both with signs and wonders, and with divers miracles, and gifts of the Holy Ghost, according to his own will?"[48] *and* "Jesus saith unto her, Said I not unto thee, that, if thou wouldest believe, thou shouldest see the glory of God?"[49] So the miracle shows the glory and testifies, as Lord Jesus said, "I have greater witness than that of John: for the works which the Father hath given me to finish, the same works that I do, bear witness of me, that the Father hath sent me"[50] As Lord Jesus said, the miracles and wonders he did bear witness to him, for God, his Father, bears testimony to his son Jesus by these miracles and signs that he sent him, and he was approved of him. They show the glory of God in the face of Jesus Christ, his son, who is the express image of his person and the brightness of his glory. That he who believes in him believes not on him, but in his Father who sent him. And he that sees him sees his Father who sent him.

This ecclesiastical host the spiritual armies of bishops, preachers, evangelists, pastors, theologians, etc, the host that was formed for the Barbarian; this second beast, the false prophet, maintains that this Barbarian was godly in the past, that these nations of Barbarian are Christian nations, and God has given them that great authority in the world. And so the Christendom the Earth and those that dwell in it, these Christians that belong to various sects and denominations, worship the Barbarian, saying "who is like our Christian nations, which nation in the world, is able to make war with our Christian nations of the west?" They also worship Satan, who gave to the Barbarian his seat and great authority, saying God gave them these things; this spiritual host, the second beast, the false prophet, is in all denominations and sects of the Christendom the Earth and makes people from all denominations and sects to worship the Beast. No denomination or sect is unaffected by the work of the second beast, and also one third of Christians who belong to various denominations and sects believe in the miracles of Satan that were happening in the Christendom. Now, John wrote that the second beast that came out from the Christendom performed great miracles, even causing fire to come down from Heaven unto Earth before the people, so also now these false preachers of the Christendom are doing by the power of Satan. These deceivers call these are works of the Holy Ghost, and that God is renewing the Church; thus they blaspheme the Holy Ghost by calling Satan the Holy Ghost. This false prophet, the second beast that came out of the Christendom the Earth, this spiritual host of the Barbarian, said to those that dwell in the Christendom, even to all these Christians, to make an image unto the Beast. The image of the Barbarian who was wounded by the sword and lived, the image of these Western nations in these times who had a wound by their internal conflict, few decades after World Wars their wound was healed and they lived. All these Christians worship Satan by saying God has given that great authority, as they see these nations as Christian nations. Now the Beast, whose deadly wound was healed and prospered, this is the appearance and form of these Western nations who had wound, but it was healed, lived and became prosperous nations among the nations of this present world. All this is the actual person and reality of the Beast, whose image this false prophet, these spiritual armies of the Beast teaches to the Christians who dwell in the Christendom to make, these spiritual armies teach Christians to make this image of the Beast, whose wound was healed, it lived and prospered, and to whom Satan gave great authority. The Satan to whom these Christians worship, saying God gave these western nations glory and authority among the nations of the world.

Now these spiritual armies the ecclesiastical host the false prophet says to make an image to the Beast, the image is of getting healed and live and become prosperous, so that all those Christians who hear the false prophet make image out of their own lives, they make an image so that their own personal difficulties, sicknesses, poverty, etc will be healed, and they will live and prosper in this world like the Beast. And to this image these Christians make, these preachers give life by the power of Satan, by healing their sicknesses, difficulties in life, poverty, etc. So these dwellers of Christendom make the image of the Beast to be healed of their worldly problems, financial difficulties, illnesses, etc. just like the Beast whose wound was healed, lived, and prospered in this world. When they make this mental image by hearing the spiritual Host of these preachers, evangelists, pastors, etc, this spiritual host will heal and resolve their problems, thus giving life by the power of Satan to the image they made. Thus they deceive those who dwell in the Christendom by their miracles; the miracles and signs are meant to witness, like miracles and signs by the Holy Ghost gave testimony, and these miracles of Satan also give testimony.

For when this spiritual host, the false prophet, healed and resolved the problems of these dwellers of the Christendom the Earth, it gave life to the image by his miracles done by the power of Satan. These miracles and signs, the things happened to those Christians, will testify and destroy the Christians who have not yet believed in those miracles as works of God; for they are lying wonders,[51] and they testify falsely that God is on their behalf and is working for them, they lie that Satan's work is God's work and show Satan as God, and the teachings of Satan as God's. For the image of the Beast whose deadly wound was healed, lived and prospered, made by the Christians hearing false preachers now given life by these preachers, will speak, for these great miracles and wonders of Satan will speak and testify falsely that they are done by God, causing other Christians who have not yet believed in those miracles to believe in those miracles by saying it is done by God or Christ. Thus this image of Beast speaks and makes others to be spiritually killed and desolated by making them do blasphemy against the Holy Ghost and calling Satan a Holy Ghost. For thus they call the Holy Ghost by whom Lord Jesus, Apostles, and first century saints did miracles, Satan. For they say that the Holy Ghost, the Spirit of God, is this spirit, even the Satan who is performing his miracles now. All those who believe in these miracles and signs of Satan, and worship the image of the beast, will do the unforgivable Sin of blaspheming the Holy Ghost and shall perish forever. For this second beast, the ecclesiastical host the spiritual armies of the Beast, placed this abomination, the image of the Beast, in the holy place of God's glory, his testimony for his Son, and in the place of work of God and his Holy Spirit. All these Christians who have not believed nor loved the truth, the express image of the person of God, but have loved this world and unrighteousness, they will be deluded to believe these miracles of Satan. God's fierce anger, without any mercy, will be on them forever. They will be tormented in the presence of the Holy Angels, the messengers of God, and in the presence of Lord Jesus with that which is spiritually called as fire and brimstone. Their filthy cries of torment will rise forever and ever, they will not be forgiven. And they will be tormented day and night.

Now this image of the Beast is called, by Daniel, an abomination and by Lord Jesus an abomination and carcass.[52] The scripture refers to the idols and images that were worshiped as abominations and carcasses.[53] The Prophet Daniel wrote about this image, saying, "they shall place the abomination that maketh desolate." And this abomination stands in the place of God's glory, and in the place of the testimony of God which he gave unto his Son Jesus by mighty signs and miracles. It should not stand in such a holy place, yet it stands on such a holy place, as written: "ye shall see the abomination of desolation, spoken of by Daniel the prophet, standing where it ought not."

Now the spiritually heart is called a "forehead," and the stubbornness of the heart is called the hard forehead, as written, "all the house of Israel are impudent and hardhearted. Behold, I have made thy face strong against their faces, and thy forehead strong against their foreheads. As an adamant harder than flint have I made thy forehead: fear them not, neither be dismayed at their looks, though they be a rebellious house."[54] So also the spiritually "heart" is also called the "hand" by scriptures, and the courage of the heart is called the strength of hand, and the right hand is the strong hand, as written. "Jonathan Saul's son arose, and went to David into the wood, and strengthened his hand in God."[55] *And* "Because with lies ye have made the heart of the righteous sad, whom I have not made sad; and strengthened the hands of the wicked, that he should not return from his wicked way, by promising him life," *and* "they strengthen also the hands of evildoers, that none doth return from his wickedness."[56] Now the Barbarian, the first Beast, had a wound, and it was healed, lived, and prospered among all the nations of the world. And the Christians who dwell in the Christendom the Earth, worship Satan, saying that God had given that great authority to these Western nations of Barbarian the Beast in the world. This their belief is the mark of the Beast, that God is on their behalf and He is on the rise, so they also say "In God we trust." These nations of

Barbarian believe that God has given that great authority in this world.

Now the second beast that came out of the Earth the Christendom, these spiritual armies the ecclesiastical host of preachers, evangelists, pastors, theologians, etc, caused all those who dwell in the Christendom to receive the mark of the Beast. They were causing all kinds of Christians, both small and great, to receive this mark of the Beast,[57] that God is on their behalf and he is on the rise. For all these Christians in the Christendom believed and trusted strongly that God is on their behalf and He is on the rise; that same God who has given such authority to the Barbarian, to these Western nations, is on the rise. Those who dwell in the Christendom have the strong belief in their heart that God is on their behalf and is working things for them in their lives. This mark of the beast, that God is on their behalf and He is on the rise, so they say "In God we trust," as these nations of Barbarian believe that God has given that great authority to them in this world. This very mark of the Beast is on the hearts of all these Christians who dwell in the Christendom. Now the spiritually name of the person is knowledge about that person; therefore Lord Jesus also said, I declared your name to them, for he gave the knowledge of his Father and revealed Him to his brethren. So also the name of the Beast is the knowledge that these Christians have about the Beast, about these Western nations. For they perceive that the God of these Western nations is on the rise and that He is on their behalf, and that He has given this great authority to Western nations among the nations of the world. All these Christians have this name of the Beast on their forehead and hand, for they believe and trust strongly in their heart that God is on the rise, is on their behalf, and is working for them in their lives.

Thus this second beast, the spiritual host of the Barbarian, is causing all those who dwell in the Christendom to receive this mark or name of the Beast on their heart that is their forehead, and their hand. So that no one without this mark or name on their heart would be able to buy in the Christendom, and without having this mark or name no man could receive the things that were taught and preached in the Christendom. For it is believed in the Christendom the Earth, that the God of these Western nations is on the rise, and he gave them this great authority as it is now, and these Christian preachers will teach to their hearers that God is on rise and is on their behalf and works for these Christians. Neither no man can sell in the Christendom if he teaches or preaches to these people without having the mark or name of the Beast. For these Christians are everywhere, who had this faith and trust on their forehead or hand, this mark or name imprinted on their heart, for they believed that God is on their behalf and that He is on rise and wants to work for them in their lives, and they will not receive his teaching. If anyone comes to them without having a word related to their faith and trust, they won't receive from him; if he doesn't have this mark or name or number they won't buy from him, and they won't believe someone who says that God's anger is on the Christendom, and that he has given them to destruction. No man can buy, which is receiving the teaching, the spiritual food, and neither no man can sell, which is teaching others, the things he has, in the Christendom, among any of its denomination and sect, without having this mark or name or number of the name, for they are in the strong delusion that God is on their behalf and is working for them, or will work for them to solve their problems in their lives.

All these Christians will be damned and will drink the wine of the wrath of God without any mercy, for they have gone after Satan, who gave great authority to the Beast, and worshiped Satan in the place of God, and put their faith and trust in him. They are robbed; they are snared, and they don't know they were robbed, for they are sleeping now in the day of their calamity; destruction came upon them by unawares. John wrote that the number of the name of the beast is also a number of Man, whose number is 666, in all the scriptures this number is mentioned only in one place, in Ezra 2:13, where it is written, "The children of Adonikam, six hundred sixty and six." The meaning of the name of "Adonikam" is "a lord rising or risen." The name of the Beast, which is the knowledge or revelation these Christians have about the Beast, about these Western nations, for they perceive that the God of these western nations is on the rise and that he is on their behalf; He has given this great authority to Western nations among the nations of world. This number on their right hand or forehead the heart is their strong belief that God is on the behalf of the Christians and is on the rise and is working or will work for them, and they worship the Dragon who gave the Beast his seat and great authority in the world, calling him God. And they also worshiped the Beast, saying, "Which country is like Beast, which country is able to make war with these Western nations of the Barbarian?"

Lord Jesus also spoke of the things that will happen at the time of the end of this age, when his disciples asked him about this matter on Mount Olives. He gave them a brief overview of the things to happen in these two thousand years,[58] and stopped at the event of the abomination of desolation[59] and explained the things that happened at the time in that generation. For Lord Jesus spoke of all those things in an apocalyptic manner and with scriptural terminology. He opened his mouth and explained all the things that will take place in these two thousand years in a very brief manner, and he spoke about the things that will take place in Christendom, which is spiritually called the Earth. He said there will be many false Christs on Earth, and there will be famines and pestilences in the Christendom. There will be wars and earthquakes on Earth, and nation will rise against nation, upon the Christendom; these are also mentioned in the second, third, and fourth seal in the Book of Revelation. And Lord Jesus said , end is not yet and that these events are the beginning of sorrows. He said that from that time, these nations of the Earth, who were the denominations of the Christendom, shall deliver the saints to be spiritually afflicted and to be killed. These things were mentioned in the fifth seal of the Book of Revelation of Jesus Christ, which God gave unto him. The saints will be hated for their testimony of Jesus and for truth, by all these denominations and sects that are in the Christendom the Earth. Many will be offended, and shall betray one another and hate one another. Many false teachers will arise and deceive many, and because of the spiritual iniquity of false teachings, lies, and deceptions abound in the Christendom, the love of many will wax cold.

Those who endure till the end will be saved from the spiritual iniquity that is in the Christendom, as also written; "of them of understanding shall fall, to try them, and to purge, and to make them white."[60] Here is Patience and faith of saints, for enemy has made a spiritual war with the saints who have the testimony of Jesus, and overcame them and killed them spiritually and took them to captivity. As written in the Book of Revelation of Jesus Christ, his witnesses will be killed for a span of 1260 years. As written, the enemy will cast the truth to the ground, but they will rise again at the end of a 1260 year period. The Gospel of this Kingdom will be preached in the world unto a witness against all these denominations and sects that were in the Christendom. And then shall the end come.

After these things, the Lord Jesus spoke about the last generation, in which the abomination of desolation will be set up. And he said this the generation shall not pass away until they see the sign of the son of man appear in Heaven. I wrote in this book about the abomination of desolation, spoken by Daniel the prophet, that you might see it and understand this abomination; even the image of the Beast that speaks and causes people to be spiritually killed. The glory and miracle of Satan, even the image of the Beast that causes destruction, stood in the place of God's glory, and in the place of the miracles he performed and gave testimony to his Son Jesus, which was mentioned in the books of the glorious Gospel of Lord Jesus. Verily, an Abomination is standing in the place of God's glory and his works, which you saw when we heard the glorious Gospel and were called through it to his fellowship at the time of your new birth and conversion.

Lord Jesus spoke all these things in an apocalyptic manner, and signified with scriptural terminology; for surely he knows the scriptures will fall into the hands of his enemies, who will destroy his saints. Now Judah is ruled from Jerusalem, and Judah are the people of God who hear the word from his messengers and the preachers of his word, and the messengers who bring his message were called Zion and Jerusalem, as written. "O Zion, that bringest good tidings, get thee up into the high mountain; O Jerusalem, that bringest good tidings, lift up thy voice with strength; lift it up, be not afraid; say unto the cities of Judah, Behold your God!"[61] Likewise, giving suck and having with child is also spiritual terminology here in this context; it's about the saints who were giving suck to their spiritually young ones, and those who were in the process of begetting spiritual children, as written. "My little children, of whom I travail in birth again until Christ be formed in you"[62] *and* "though ye have ten thousand instructors in Christ, yet have ye not many fathers: for in Christ Jesus I have begotten you through the gospel,"[63] *and* "we were gentle in your midst, as a nursing mother would cherish her own children." [64]

Likewise, winter and the Sabbath is also spoken about apocalyptically, allegorically here. They can't see clearly, or do anything, while they are entangled under the Law. It will condemn their conscience, in everything they do, for the Law will never justify anyone in his conscience before God. They will always have guilty conscience before God, so they will have feeble knees. Verily, Lord Jesus knows he is going to redeem them from the bondage of the Law, yet he said to pray it might not be on Sabbath day; not that he is saying the people in the last generation need to keep Sabbath. For all of those who were baptized into his death and resurrection are made free of the dominion of the Law by his body. Therefore Paul also writes, "Let no man therefore judge you in meat, or in drink, or in respect of an holy day, or of the new moon, or of the sabbath days:"[65] But many of them entangle themselves into the bondage of the Law; they keep their conscience under the commandments of the Law, and judge their thoughts and actions according to the Law. They find themselves guilty and their hearts condemn them before God. While they are becoming fearful and fleeing from Christ, how can they understand these things when the Law works wrath in them and love waxes cold, and when they seek to be justified before God by works of the Law and do wickedly against the truth of the Gospel. Likewise, in the time of winter, it is difficult to travel; so also it is difficult for a spiritual journey if the love and zeal in their hearts waxes cold and if their hearts are occupied with the cares or sorrows of this life and this world, or by the love of the money or things of this world. So they should always guard their hearts, that they might control it's affections in the early stages, before it becomes too late. They should pray that their hearts might not run after these things, but fill with love and zeal towards their God and Jesus Christ their Lord, that they might seek the Father, their only God, and Jesus Christ their Lord, in whom he is, with all their hearts souls, wisdom, and strength.

Now is a great tribulation, for Satan, with the help of the Barbarian, waged war with the saints who have the testimony of Jesus, the true Gospel in their mouths and hearts. They spiritually killed them, for they have fallen by the sword and spiritual captivity, so that nowhere in the world might true Christ be preached, for his witnesses were spiritually killed by the enemy. Not only so, but this spiritual host of the Beast has set the abomination that makes desolate; now Satan does great miracles and signs in all the Christendom through this spiritual host. This ecclesiastical host the spiritual armies of preachers, pastors, evangelists, bishops, theologians, etc., are making all the people receive the mark of the Beast, that no one might not preach or receive the things preached in the Christendom without having the mark of the Beast. Never was such a thing in the world from the beginning of creation, when all the witnesses of God had fallen and were killed by the enemy, and God's indignation is still continuing on his saints, for he hid his face from them. Satan and his ministers doing miracles deceiving the whole Earth, and there is a false heaven from many centuries past, for with craftiness Satan created a false religion, deceiving all the denominations and sects of the Christendom. These people say they are walking in God's light and his fellowship, and deceive and are deceived. But the serpent knows he has a few years left in the Christendom, and his ruling is coming to an end upon Earth. He is aggressively seeking to destroy the Earth, which is the Christendom, for from past few decades Satan and his associates the Beast and False prophet are seeking to destroy Christendom, by depopulating it through low birth rate using tools like feminism, promiscuity, abortions, birth control pill, etc, by the abomination that makes desolate, and now by mass immigration of non-Christians.

So all of you who read this book and understand the things that were written in it, all of you flee from among them; every one of you flee from his Church, everyone flee from among all these Christians that dwell in the Christendom. Every one of you who understands and sees the abomination of desolation spoken by Daniel the prophet let every one of you flee from among those that dwell in the Christendom. You might be a leader, or a pastor, or someone in the mission field, or a layman; let none of you enter into his Church for anything, and let none of you return back to his Church for anything. If any one of you goes back to his Church for anything, desires to keep himself in their company, or are not willing to leave his Church, or wants to return back to it, for friends or for anything; he shall lose himself. For remember Lot's wife; whosoever wants to keep his life shall lose it. If you want to keep your life intact as it is and are not willing to lose everything you have, you shall lose your life. And whosoever loses his life now shall preserve it. Don't let anyone deceive you by saying, it is Jesus or God that is doing healing or miracles and not those Charlatans (the preachers), for very certainly whosoever calls the works of Satan as the work of God and believes it done by God will bare his punishment for worshiping the image of Beast. For the destruction has come upon the Christendom the Earth, like in the days of Noah and like in the days of Lot. So let every one of you flee from among them. Don't listen to anyone; if he says here is Christ preached truly, or there Gospel will be preached without corrupting it, don't believe that liar either. Don't go there to listen to them. Therefore if they say this small congregation is good here the true word is preached, or that Church is good there preaching is good and is according to scriptures, or there in that place, you will find true and uncorrupted gospel will be preached, don't believe those liars or go to those places. Moreover be careful with those who speak so much about the false teachings and false gospels in the world and say to you here or there true Gospel or Christ is preached, or pose as if they are preaching it, don't believe them, don't go after them or to the places they suggest or any other place. You know it verily certainly that he told you not to believe such people or go after them, for when true Gospel is preached, when true Christ will be preached in the world again, it shall be all over the world, not in any isolated pockets. When the true Christ will be preached, and he will be preached everywhere and in the entire world, like a lightning that comes in the East and shines unto the West. But before that, all this spiritual host of this religion will be destroyed. They will all fall to the ground; their false religion is rolled like scroll and all the light of this religion that is upon all the Christendom, upon all the sects and denominations, shall be darkened.

I tell to all of you who seek God and Lord Jesus; all of you who still remember God and Lord Jesus from that old time when you were converted to Christ, all of you who long to see those days back in your life, when God called you into his fellowship in the marvelous light at that time when you first believed; all of you who long to see those days come back, when you heard the Gospel of Lord Jesus Christ and believed in him for first time, and want to look into those things again like in the beginning; here is a word for all of you.

> "He said unto the disciples, The days will come when ye shall desire to see one of the days of the Son of man, and ye shall not see it. And they shall say to you, See here; or, see there: go not after them, nor follow them. For as the lightning, that lighteneth out of the one part under heaven, shineth unto the other part under heaven; so shall also the Son of man be in his day."
> ~ LUKE 17:22-24; KJV

So you are like your spiritual ancestors from the past 1300 years, who were spiritually killed in the few days after they were enlightened, and haven't seen those days of the glorious Gospel again, like at the beginning of the conversion, for you, by the Spirit, have seen the days of the son of man, through the Gospel. As if you were also among the Disciples and have seen those things. Nevertheless, you may see him again before this generation passes away, and when these spiritual hosts of this religion will be thrown down to ground and all the Heavens above the Christendom will be darkened and rolled like scroll. After this his sign will appear again, and in that day he will be like the lightning that lightens out of the one end under Heaven, and shines unto the other end under Heaven. Now you, who are in this generation, are living in the days of the son of man, which will be like the days of Noah and like the days of Lot.

For in this generation will this present age will come to end. So, therefore, come out from them and do not enter their Churches again, of any denominations and sects. Flee from among them like Lot, without looking back. Remember Lot's wife; if you seek to save your life, you lose it. If you lose it, you shall keep it. And they shall say to you, see here, or, see there. Go not after them, and do not follow them. Don't believe them, for where so ever the carcass is, eagles will be gathered together. Now the carcass is nothing but an abomination, idol, and image that is worshiped, as written; "they have defiled my land, they have filled mine inheritance with the carcasses of their detestable and abominable things."[66] For all these Christians gather themselves wherever the carcass is, and all those Christians of all the denominations and sects join themselves to worship the carcass.

So come out from among those that dwell in the Christendom; come out from all these denominations and sects. Come out and seek your only God, even the Father, and Jesus Christ, your Lord. Destruction is upon the Christendom, for he told us, "in that night there shall be two men in one bed; the one shall be taken, and the other shall be left. Two woman shall be grinding together; the one shall be taken, and the other left. Two men shall be in the field; the one shall be taken, and the other left. And they answered and said unto him, Where, Lord? And he said unto them, Wheresoever the body is, thither will the eagles be gathered together."[67] All of these will be taken into deception, and they all shall gather themselves to the image of the beast and receive the mark of the Beast. No flesh will be saved if God won't reduce these days; but for the sake of his elect, he will reduce these days. Therefore, come out from them and seek that Great God, who spoke unto us through the mouth of his prophets from the beginning, who roars with a mighty and transcended voice from behind from those ancient times unto us who are in this generation. So return unto your God, against whom you have sinned; he has torn you, and he will heal you; he has smitten you, and he will bind you up. Press hard on to know that Great God. As surely as the sun rises, He will appear, and he shall come unto you like rain, as former and latter rain. So seek God and Lord Jesus Christ.

REFERENCES:

1. Daniel 2:43;
2. Daniel 2:35 & 44; Isaiah 26:15; 2:2; 54:3; Revelation 21:10;
3. Daniel 9:24;
4. Romans 15:8;
5. Hebrews 10:8-9;
6. Luke 19:42-44;
7. Daniel 12:1;
8. Deuteronomy 28:50;
9. Proverbs 1:6;
10. Daniel 8:24;
11. Daniel 8:12;
12. Daniel 12:11;
13. Daniel 8:10;
14. Matthew 25:4; Psalms 104:15; Ecclesiastes 8:1;
15. Galatians 2:17;
16. Isaiah 32:5-7;
17. Revelation 7:4;
18. John 5:36-37;
19. Matthew 24:28; Luke 17:37;
20. Revelation 1:10; 4:2; 17:3; 21:10;
21. Galatians 2:17; 3:19; 2 Corinthians 3:7-9;
22. Revelation 12:6 & 14; Matthew 24: 8-9; Micah 4:10;
23. Daniel 11: 33-36;

24. Revelation 11:7; 13:7; Isaiah 51:18-20; Daniel 8:24;
25. Revelation 18:1-2;
26. Daniel 11:20;
27. Isaiah 51:16;
28. Psalms 2:6;
29. 1 Corinthians 15:25; Psalms 110:1;
30. Mark 9:1;
31. Psalms 110:3;
32. Daniel 11:33-35;
33. Revelation 12:17;
34. Zechariah 4:12; Daniel 11:33-35;
35. Revelation 13:2;
36. Revelation 13:4;
37. Revelation 13:2;
38. Daniel 7:5; Daniel 8:3;
39. Revelation 17:12;
40. John 17:6; Psalms 22:22;
41. Daniel 8:10-11;
42. Deuteronomy 19:15; 1 Timothy 5:19; Luke 10:1;
43. Daniel 11:30;
44. Daniel 11:31;
45. John 2:11;
46. Acts 2:22;
47. John 11:4;
48. Hebrews 2:4;
49. John 11:40;
50. John 5:36;
51. 2 Thessalonians 2:9;
52. Matthew 24:28; Luke 17:37;
53. 53.2 Kings 23:13; Leviticus 26:30; Ezekiel 43:9;
54. Ezekiel 3:7-9;
55. 1 Samuel 23:16;
56. Jeremiah 23:14:
57. Revelation 13:16;
58. Matthew 24:4-14;
59. Matthew 24:15-31;
60. Daniel 11:35;
61. Isaiah 40:9;
62. Galatians 4:19;
63. 1 Corinthians 4:15;
64. 1 Thessalonians 2:17;
65. Colossians 2:16;
66. Jeremiah 16:18;
67. Luke 17:34-37;

SECTION THREE:
THE THINGS WHICH MUST SOON COME TO PASS

CHAPTER FOUR

Turning again their captivity

From the beginning of the world, God spoke through the mouth of his servants the prophets that his people shall sin against him, his wrath shall fall on them, he will hide his face from them and he will deliver them to the hands of their enemies and they shall fall and go into captivity.

That Great God, who knows his works from the beginning of the world, spoke the end from the beginning. Even our God commanded Moses to write a song that shall be a witness for him against the Children of Israel.

Moses wrote song in this manner:

"Give ear, O ye heavens, and I will speak; and hear O earth, the words of my mouth. My doctrine shall drop as the rain, my speech shall distil as the dew, as the small rain upon the tender herb, and as the showers upon the grass: Because I will publish the name of the Lord: ascribe ye greatness unto our God. He is the Rock, his work is perfect: for all his ways are judgment: a God of truth and without iniquity, just and right is he.

They have corrupted themselves, their spot is not the spot of his children: they are a perverse and crooked generation. Do ye thus requite the LORD, O foolish people and unwise? is not he thy father that hath bought thee? hath he not made thee, and established thee? Remember the days of old, consider the years of many generations: ask thy father, and he will shew thee; thy elders, and they will tell thee. When the most High divided to the nations their inheritance, when he separated the sons of Adam, he set the bounds of the people according to the number of the children of Israel.

For the LORD's portion is his people; Jacob is the lot of his inheritance.

He found him in a desert land, and in the waste howling wilderness; he led him about, he instructed him, he kept him as the apple of his eye.

As an eagle stirreth up her nest, fluttereth over her young, spreadeth abroad her wings, taketh them, beareth them on her wings: So the LORD alone did lead him, and there was no strange god with him. He made him ride on the high places of the earth, that he might eat the increase of the fields; and he made him to suck honey out of the rock, and oil out of the flinty rock;

Butter of kine, and milk of sheep, with fat of lambs, and rams of the breed of Bashan, and goats, with the fat of kidneys of wheat; and thou didst drink the pure blood of the grape. But Jeshurun waxed fat, and kicked: thou art waxen fat, thou art grown thick, thou art covered with fatness; then he forsook God which made him, and lightly esteemed the Rock of his salvation.

They provoked him to jealousy with strange gods, with abominations provoked they him to anger. They sacrificed unto devils, not to God; to gods whom they knew not, to new gods that came newly up, whom your fathers feared not. Of the Rock that begat thee thou art unmindful, and hast forgotten God that formed thee.

And when the LORD saw it, he abhorred them, because of the provoking of his sons, and of his daughters. And he said, I will hide my face from them, I will see what their end shall be: for they are a very froward generation, children in whom is no faith. They have moved me to jealousy with that which is not God; they have provoked me to anger with their vanities: and I will move them to jealousy with those which are not a people; I will provoke them to anger with a foolish nation. For a fire is kindled in mine anger, and shall burn unto the lowest hell, and shall consume the earth with her increase, and set on fire the foundations of the mountains. I will heap mischiefs upon them; I will spend mine arrows upon them. They shall be burnt with hunger, and devoured with flame, and with bitter destruction: I will also send the teeth of beasts upon them, with the poison of serpents of the dust. The sword without, and terror within, shall destroy both the young man and the virgin, the suckling also with the man of gray hairs. I said, I will cut them to pieces, I would make the remembrance of them to cease from among men: Were it not that I feared the wrath of the enemy, lest their adversaries should behave themselves strangely, and lest they should say, Our hand is high, and the LORD hath not done all this.

For they are a nation void of counsel, neither is there any understanding in them. O that they were wise, that they understood this, that they would consider their latter end! How should one chase a thousand, and two put ten thousand to flight, except their Rock had sold them, and the LORD had shut them up? For their rock is not as our Rock, even our enemies themselves being judges. For their vine is of the vine of Sodom, and of the fields of Gomorrah: their grapes are grapes of gall, their clusters are bitter:

Their wine is the poison of dragons, and the cruel venom of asps.

Is not this laid up in store with me, and sealed up among my treasures?

To me belongeth vengeance, and recompense; their foot shall slide in due time: for the day of their calamity is at hand, and the things that shall come upon them make haste.

For the Lord shall judge his people, and repent himself for his servants, when he seeth that their power is gone, and there is none shut up, or left.

And he shall say, Where are their gods, their rock in whom they trusted,

Which did eat the fat of their sacrifices, and drank the wine of their drink offerings? let them rise up and help you, and be your protection.

See now that I, even I, am he, and there is no god with me: I kill, and I make alive; I wound, and I heal: neither is there any that can deliver out of my hand. For I lift up my hand to heaven, and say, I live forever.

If I whet my glittering sword, and mine hand take hold on judgment; I will render vengeance to mine enemies, and will reward them that hate me.

I will make mine arrows drunk with blood, and my sword shall devour flesh; and that with the blood of the slain and of the captives, from the beginning of revenges upon the enemy.

Rejoice, O ye nations, with his people: for he will avenge the blood of his servants, and will render vengeance to his adversaries, and will be merciful unto his land, and to his people."

~ Deuteronomy 32; kjv

Moses begins his song with calling the heavens and earth to hear his words, for prophet Moses spoke regarding those who dwell in the heavens, which were saints; the seed of Jesus Christ the Israel whom God has chosen; and about the denominations and sects who dwell in Christendom the Earth. The words of his prophecy that God told him to write are like rain, showers, small rain and dew that fall upon the herbs and grass, for he publishes the name of our God and his greatness, he spoke about works of our God and his judgments, and when our God's judgments are on Earth, people of world will learn righteousness.[1] But the wicked shall not learn righteousness nor perceive our God's majesty. He is the Rock of defense, from him and in him is our Salvation. His ways are judgment; he is God of truth without any iniquity, just and most upright is he.

In the beginning, Jesus Christ suffered for his people that were scattered all over the world and rose again from the dead. They are the seed of Jesus Christ the Israel whom God has chosen. After he died and rose again, our God sent apostles to the nations, where they were among heathen of the world that had never heard about our God. They went and preached Jesus Christ so that the sufferings of Christ for his people won't become ineffective to them. That great God who transcends the time and space beget them again unto a new life through the resurrection of Christ.[2] They were saved from the domain of darkness through the fleshly body of Jesus Christ, the way[3] God made for them through the death and resurrection of his Son.[4] They were liberated from domain, power, and principality with Christ,[5] so that they might serve God their Father in newness of life without any hindrance,⁶. They were all translated to the kingdom of his Son in light⁷. So apostles brought them all from the domain of darkness,⁸ from the land of slavery to sin being under the domain of law,⁹ they brought them to their God in Heaven to Jerusalem above,¹⁰ to his holy kingdom Zion. As spoken by God through the prophet, "they shall bring all your brethren for an offering unto the LORD out of all nations upon horses, and in chariots, and in litters, and upon mules, and upon swift beasts, to my holy mountain Jerusalem, saith the LORD, as the children of Israel bring an offering in a clean vessel into the house of the LORD."¹¹ Therefore Lord Jesus sent the apostle Paul to those nations that far.¹² Apostle Paul came to know the previous verse and confirms this that these verses spoken by the prophet Isaiah were fulfilled by his ministry, for he wrote, "I should be the minister of Jesus Christ to the Gentiles, ministering the gospel of God, that the offering up of the Gentiles might be acceptable, being sanctified by the Holy Ghost."¹³ That great God who saved their spiritual forefathers in the first century also saved these like them in every generation from the dominion of darkness by calling them through Gospel of Jesus Christ. He brought them to Jerusalem above to his fellowship in his marvelous light.

But unlike first-century saints, they haven't retained their inheritance in his marvelous light for a long time.¹⁴ For like them, you were enlightened and kept on high like the host of heaven to give light upon those that dwell in Christendom the Earth, but because of your transgressions the enemy cast you down to the ground.¹⁵ For you have corrupted yourselves by going astray from your God, to another gods and christs that were in Christendom, to other gospels.¹⁶ You did wickedly against the covenant and have fallen from the grace; you are foolish and unwise people. Is he not your Father who brought you through his Son Jesus? Now the things that happened to the children of Israel of old time are examples;[17] they are written for your admonition. As he led them from bondage to the inheritance through his prophet, so also God led you from the bondage in that world while you were among the children of this world, to eternal inheritance in light through Jesus Christ, about whom Moses wrote, God will raise a prophet like me. Like children of Israel of old times, you acted foolishly and wickedly against your God. For he showed in old times, in days of foreshadows, that there will be a nation, a kingdom that will be called his own inheritance, a kingdom of people who shall be as a priests of him unto all the nations of the Earth.[18]

Now the Jesus Christ is the Israel whom God has chosen; you are his seed whom God beget again through death and resurrection of Christ[19]. And the Christendom at present is the Earth and all denominations and sects are nations of the Earth, his saints the seed of Jesus Christ the Israel whom he has chosen shall rule this Earth, as written, "they sung a new song, saying, Thou art worthy to take the book, and to open the seals thereof: for thou was slain, and hast redeemed us to God by thy blood out of every kindred, and tongue, and people, and nation; And hast made us unto our God kings and priests: and we shall reign on the earth," *and* "Instead of thy fathers shall be thy children, whom thou mayest make princes in all the earth. I will make thy name to be remembered in all generations: therefore shall the people praise thee forever and ever"[20] *and* "the Lord God giveth them light: and they shall reign forever and ever."²¹ You are his inheritance, purchased by the blood of his Son from all nations and tribes of this literal Earth. He alone led you through his Spirit, who was scattered among all the nations, tribes, tongues of this literal earth. He called you to his fellowship in his Son in whom he is. He spoke to you through his Son Jesus, whom he has chosen that you all might know and believe him, that you might know Father is that great God who spoke all these things from the beginning. He declared and has saved, and he showed when there was no strange god among you.

Therefore Lord Jesus and you are his witnesses as written, "Ye are my witnesses, saith the LORD, and my servant whom I have chosen: that ye may know and believe me, and understand that I am he: before me there was no God formed, neither shall there be after me. I, even I, am the LORD; and beside me, there is no savior." ²² He made you ride on high places of the Earth. His divine power has given you all things toward life and godliness He gave you all the spiritual food you need through Christ. You sucked the honey of his gracious words of knowledge of wisdom, the oil of understanding from Christ, who is your teacher appointed by God. You were fed with milk, fat and hard meat of wisdom; he gave you to drink the wine of pure teaching. But you waxed fat and lightly esteemed the God of your Salvation. You have pierced your God who is in Lord Jesus by your unfaithfulness and foolishness in leaving your God for false christs and false gospels of vanities against his holy and jealous love. You and your fathers provoked him to jealousy with your abominations by going after strange gods of the Christendom. You have gone after the strange gospels, christs and gods of the Christendom, which you didn't know before he called you or at the time of conversion, after the strange christs and gods whom apostles and first-century saints followed not. You were unmindful of your God who begot you again and forgot that great God who has called you into his marvelous light from darkness.

When your God saw it he abhorred you, because of the provoking of his sons and of his daughters. And he said, "I will hide my face from them, I will see what their end shall be: for they are a very froward generation, children in whom is no faith." So also he did hide his face from you as written, "Because they trespassed against me, I hid his face from them and gave them to the hand of their enemies."[23] As you have provoked him to anger by your vanities and gods that were not God, so he also provoked you the with spiritual heathen of the Christendom the Earth, who were called by his name and were not his people, who were known in the world at present as saints, christians, ministers of God, true preachers of the word, more godly, virtuous and better Christians than you. They took away your name and your position; they tread the holy city, the heavenly Jerusalem;[24] they, as stars, show light unto denominations and sects of the Christendom. You are fallen to the ground and disliked by denominations and sects of the Christendom the Earth; you were among the heathen of the Christendom like accursed bearing the indignation of your God.

Many mischiefs have fallen on you from the sixth century onwards. You were burnt with hunger for the lack of the spiritual food, devoured with flame, for spiritually flame and sword are one. Your fathers and you were spiritually killed by the spiritual swords of enemies, which is their teaching and interpretation of scriptures as written "they shall fall by the sword, and by flame."[25] He also brought bitter destruction on you, all of you overcome by your enemies and spiritually killed and gone into captivity among denominations and sects. He also sent on them the teeth of beasts of the Earth the Christendom that were false prophets who devoured your fathers and you, the poison of the teachings of these serpents on them. Within was the terror produced in the conscience by the law, and outside was the spiritual sword of enemies to destroy the young man, old man, undefiled, an infant. This was the fierceness of anger of jealousy of our God come on you, for your iniquity was grievous, for you provoked him to jealousy like with unfaithfulness of woman. Therefore he tore you into pieces and wounded you with grievous wounds of an enemy. They fell by sword and into the spiritual captivity among the heathen nations of the Christendom the Earth as written, "The house of Israel went to captivity among heathen, Because they trespassed against me, I hid his face from them and gave them to the hand of their enemies and they all fell by sword." [26]

Your spiritual enemies are of a foolish nation; there is no counsel or understanding in them. They devour you with their spiritual swords and took you captive to their lies and falsehoods and exalt themselves against us, but they don't understand their latter end when God's anger will turn away from his people. How can one put thousand to flee and two a ten thousand, except God their savior has sold them, their God has shut them. For their God has hid his face from them. For gods and christs of your enemies are not as our God: Their teaching is of the Sodom, of the fields of Gomorrah, their grapes are grapes of gall, their clusters are bitter. Their teaching is the poison of dragons and the cruel venom of asps. Our God says he stored in his memory all evil our enemies have done to us and our fathers; he reserved his anger for the day of his wrathful vengeance upon them.[27] He says vengeance belongs to him as he is our God and our Father. He will recompense and avenge the blood of his servants,[28] for the day of their calamity at hand, the things that will come upon our enemies shall make haste.[29]

God will judge his people; he will plead the cause of his people. The enemies will overcome his servants until God comes and delivers judgment on behalf of his Saints, as is written, "I beheld, and the same horn made war with the saints and prevailed against them; Until the Ancient of days came, and judgment was given to the saints of the most High."[30] For he will repent of himself for his servants when their power is gone and no one left, for you all are fallen and blind. What can you do? You not even know that you are blind and dead. He will say, "Where are their gods", the idols in whom they trusted, even all those false gods and christs of the denominations and sects the heathen nations of Christendom the Earth, whom you served and to whom you offered your spiritual sacrifices of your praises in your teachings? Father is this great God who spoke all these things through the mouth of his prophets from the beginning. He alone does all things declaring the end from the beginning and from ancient times things that are not yet done. He says, "My counsel shall stand, and I will do all my pleasure."

But God was angry with you because of the iniquity of your fathers and you, and he chastised you by bringing great calamities on you. Although it is tough for you to bear his chastisement, for you are like children sighing and feeling the bitterness of chastisement as your years are going away like smoke and your hearts are burned like furnace. It's like an end of the world to us, but God knows he kills and make alive, he wounds and he heals. Therefore seek our Father that Great God and return to him, for he has torn you, he will also bind you; he has slain you, he will also make you alive. Therefore don't do wrongly against his chastisement by turning blind eye toward it or being indifferent toward it, saying all things are vanity or I don't care the things of this life, etc. what if the reproaches and sorrows in life is a chastisement of our God, so that we might be grieved in our heart seeing Father struck us and we might seek him and return to him. For God destroys the plans for life and desires of heart, and will make your years pass away like smoke, when he chastises a man he takes away what is precious to him and makes it like eaten up by a moth. He will shut you in a pit and in darkness and you will become like a dead long ago and gone far into captivity and your years pass away like a smoke. For he said I will tare them to pieces and go away, I will carry them and there will be none to deliver them, I will go away and return to my place, until they admit their guilt and seek my face, in their distress they will seek me early. Yet you made not your prayer before your God that you might turn from your iniquities and understand his truth. Neither you nor your spiritual forefathers have grieved in heart that

God lead them into captivity to serve the Church of Rome. For you are all blind toward his chastisement.

And he will say to you, the children of Jerusalem the Heaven, he will live forever, for he is the redeemer of her who has lost her seed, for Satan was angry with the kingdom of Heaven and waged war against them through the beast. But now your God is coming to save you and he will render vengeance to his enemies and will reward them that hate him. Your hearts shall live and flourish like young grass of the morning.

Let the nations rejoice with his saints, for he will avenge the blood of his servants, render vengeance to his adversaries, and be merciful unto his land and to his people. God will destroy them that were seeking to destroy the Christendom the Earth, even the Satan, Beast, False Prophet, etc; he will also punish the Whore. In that day, God will be the King of all Christendom the earth[31] and God said he will make his judgment for a light unto people.[32] For the kingdom is God's, and he is the governor among the nations. He makes wars to cease unto the end of the earth; he breaks the bow, and cuts the spear in sunder; he burns the chariot in the fire. So let the nations be glad: He will execute righteousness and judgment for all who were oppressed. He will deliver spiritually poor and needy, and he will save all meek of the Christendom.[33] Seek God, all you meek of the earth, which have wrought his judgment; seek righteousness, seek meekness. It may be you shall be hidden in the day of the God's anger.[34] He shall judge the people righteously, and govern the nations upon earth. He will merciful to his land and his people as written that Jerusalem above, which is their mother:

> "Thou shalt no more be termed Forsaken; neither shall thy land any more be termed Desolate: but thou shalt be called Hephzibah, and thy land Beulah: for the LORD delighteth in thee, and thy land shall be married. For as a young man marrieth a virgin, so shall thy sons marry thee: and as the bridegroom rejoiceth over the bride, so shall thy God rejoice over thee."[35]

He will make a covenant of peace, an everlasting covenant with his people, with the seed of his beloved Jesus Christ the Israel whom he has chosen. And he will merciful unto the Jerusalem above as written, "In a little wrath I hid my face from thee for a moment; but with everlasting kindness will I have mercy on thee, saith the LORD thy Redeemer. my kindness shall not depart from thee, neither shall the covenant of my peace be removed."[36]

Isaiah wrote that God's wrath came on Jerusalem above, which is the mother of all his saints, collectively all his servants and his people are Zion. He called them to the fellowship of his Son, saying unto them, "You are my people." Isaiah wrote the Jerusalem above will become desolate and barren without her Children; because of the sin of his people, God's wrath shall come upon her. For thus said their Father, "Behold, for your iniquities have ye sold yourselves, and for your transgressions is your mother put away."[37] Isaiah wrote that God's wrath will come on the Jerusalem above and her sons. She shall become barren, desolate; the desolation, and the destruction, the famine, and the sword shall come on her, and all her Sons shall fall to the ground and lie in the streets filled with fury of her God. They that afflict her shall tread on her like the street, likewise Daniel said enemies will cast them down and tread on them. It is also mentioned in the book of Revelation of Jesus Christ that Zion will become wilderness and the holy city shall be trodden for 1,260 years. The remnant of her children who has the testimony of Jesus, who were two candlesticks the lampstands, and olive trees, shall be defeated, spiritually killed and lie dead in the street for a period of three and half days, which is three and half years, the 1,260 years. But God said to Zion that after that period, he will take cup of his wrath from her hand. He will put into the hand them that afflicted her, even the Babylon the Whore, as spoken by him, "Thus saith thy Lord the LORD, and thy God that pleadeth the cause of his people, Behold, I have taken out of thine hand the cup of trembling, even the dregs of the cup of my fury; thou shalt no more drink it again: But I will put it into the hand of them that afflict thee; which have said to thy soul, Bow down, that we may go over: and thou hast laid thy body as the ground, and as the street, to them that went over."[38]

Isaiah wrote Jerusalem above shall become desolate and will become a wilderness, and God will not show mercy or favor to his servants in all this period of 1,260 years, because of their spiritual wickedness and foolishness. And the enemy shall prosper all this period until the indignation comes to an end as written, "he will prosper until the indignation is finished," Isaiah wrote, "the defenced city shall be desolate, and the habitation forsaken, and left like a wilderness."

God hasn't shown you favor throughout this period, for you are spiritually wicked, evil and prideful, and there is no understanding in you. You departed away from your God, speaking oppression and revolt, conceiving and uttering from the heart words of falsehood and lying against God. You speak lies and falsehoods against your God. Like spiders, you weave false doctrines to capture people, you fight with one another for your lies, and you seek eagerly to destroy simple and needy people with your teachings. You destroy spiritually poor and needy people with your lies even though what these needy believe is true. Therefore our God did hide his face from all of you and left you to obscurity, confusion, and shame. Your minds were corrupted from the simplicity and purity that is in true Christ unto whom Father has called you at the time of your conversion. Footsteps of your mind were gone astray from him who is our way; you did wickedly against the Holy Covenant and turned what was simplicity into the crooked path to your mind wherein there no peace. You are fallen after you were enlightened and become like the field that produced thorns and thistles after drinking rainwater[39]. Just as Isaiah wrote about your Spiritual iniquity,

> "your hands are defiled with blood, and your fingers with iniquity; your lips have spoken lies, your tongue hath muttered perverseness. None calleth for justice, nor any pleadeth for truth: they trust in vanity, and speak lies; they conceive mischief and bring forth iniquity. They hatch cockatrice' eggs and weave the spider's web: he that eateth of their eggs dieth, and that which is crushed breaketh out into a viper. Their webs shall not become garments,

neither shall they cover themselves with their works: their works are works of iniquity, and the act of violence is in their hands. Their feet run to evil, and they make haste to shed innocent blood: their thoughts are thoughts of iniquity; wasting and destruction are in their paths. The way of peace they know not; and there is no judgment in their goings: they have made them crooked paths: whosoever goeth therein shall not know peace."[40]

You are a people of no understanding: Therefore, he that made you hasn't shown mercy on you, and he that formed you showed no favor to you. And there is none that calls upon his name, which Lord Jesus revealed unto you at the time of our calling. No one arouses himself to take hold of him, for Father has hidden his face from us, and has consumed us, because of our iniquities. Because of your spiritual wickedness, your God did hide his face from your mother Jerusalem above, as he said to her, "In my wrath I smote thee, I forsaken thee; in a little wrath, I hid my face from thee."[41] She become wilderness, barren, desolate without her children, as her children were spiritually killed and went into captivity, as also written in the book of prophecy that she will go into the wilderness, into her place, for 1,260 years. As written, "Zion said, The LORD hath forsaken me, and my Lord hath forgotten me. I have lost my children, and am desolate, a captive, and removing to and fro."[42] Likewise all the prophets spoke that his people the Seed of Christ, the Israel whom he has chosen, will transgress against their God and will go into the Captivity.

Apostle Paul also wrote first there will be falling away, after that the enemy that will destroy you shall be revealed. Just as Daniel the prophet said, when the transgressors have come to the full, a king of fierce countenance, and understanding dark sentences, shall stand up. He shall destroy the mighty and the holy people, even the remnant of her children who keep the testimony of Jesus and commandments of God. And he shall prosper until the indignation of God on his people comes to an end. When the barbarian and whore, even the apostates who forsake the Holy Covenant joined hands back in the seventh century and a spiritual army an ecclesiastical host was formed for the Beast. That host polluted the sanctuary and cast the tabernacle down, even the saints, and took away their continuity with their God and at the beginning of the eighth century, nearly a century after these things, the Barbarian got the honor of Kingdom and become the eight king on the December 25th 800 AD. His dominion will continue for 1,260 years from that period; after that period, which will expire in few years, he will go into perdition.

Now you are living at the end of the sixth trumpet. In few more years, the days of the sixth trumpet will come to an end, the sixth trumpet which was noted in the Book of the Revelation of Jesus Christ. Now at this time, God is going to turn away the captivity of his people, as also mentioned in the books of prophets. As spoken of by the prophet concerning the Jerusalem above, "Awake, awake, stand up, O Jerusalem, which hast drunk at the hand of the LORD the cup of his fury; thou hast drunken the dregs of the cup of trembling, and wrung them out."[43] So also written in the

Book of Revelation of Jesus Christ that after three and half days, which is symbolically three and half years, which is 1,260 days, and so after 1260 years period of witness and being spiritually killed by the enemy, now the meaning of candlesticks the lampstands is churches, these two witnesses who were candlesticks the lampstands and olive trees that the oil of understanding will rise and stand on their feet. So these things happened as said by Daniel; these witnesses who have oil of understanding will instruct, but they shall fall a long time until the time of the end: "they that understand among the people shall instruct many: yet they shall fall by the sword, and by flame, by captivity, and by spoil, many days. Now when they shall fall, they shall be helped with a little help: but many shall cleave to them with flatteries. And of them of understanding shall fall, to try them, and to purge, and to make them white, even to the time of the end."[44] All of you who had a testimony of Jesus and given witness to those that dwell in the Christendom after you have been enlightened, when God has called you into his fellowship through Gospel. All of you of the understanding, you have known the holiness of your God, who called you into his marvelous light. You have seen and understood the ways of these christians and their preachers are very evil and won't depict God's character. You have seen how they speak foolishly, pridefully, and wickedly against your God. You have seen how these christians and their preachers reproach your God. You hated them with a perfect hatred and testified against them. But pretty soon all of you had fallen and the enemy spiritually killed you after those days after your conversion; yet now you shall rise again to life and go back

Zion above, where unto you have been called at that time of your conversion, for Father is going to take his great strength to himelf to rule.

The enemy shall overcome his saints until the indignation of their God comes to an end, and they have been given into the hand of the enemy for a period of 1,260 years. But now in these times and in this generation, God had mercy on his people, as written by Moses the Prophet: "He repent himself for his servants, when he seeth that their power is gone, and there is none shut up or left." For now, the set time to show mercy on Zion, his people, has come as written: "Thou shalt arise, and have mercy upon Zion: for the time to favor her, yea, the set time, is come."[45] Now that time has come, and he sent me to show you, his servants, the things that shall soon come to pass. For these mysteries were sealed until this last generation as also spoken by the Angel to Daniel, "O Daniel, shut up the words, and seal the book, even to the time of the end."

But I say unto the unbelieving, liars, prideful and the scornful wicked, I know your lofty looks against me and how you people exalt yourselves against me and refuse to listen to me and want me to be your pupil and to your silly preachers of your denominations and sects. Therefore you say I need to learn from your learned men, from men of past centuries and they that are now spiritually tall and great men in your sight. Now listen to me, you who are haughty and wise in your own conceits, I didn't come to speak these things on my own, but they whom you say our God and our Lord, even my Father and Lord Jesus, has sent me to speak these things to the servants of Lord Jesus. Therefore he who refuses to obey my voice and speak against the things written in this book will receive his punishment from God.

Now that great God shall plead the cause of his people, he will contend for their cause, although you have forsaken your God and destroyed yourselves with the vanities, gone after strange gospels, after the gods and christs of Christendom. But now he is going to plead your cause as written,

> "I have wounded thee with the wound of an enemy, with the chastisement of a cruel one, for the multitude of thine iniquity; because thy sins were increased. Why criest thou for thine affliction? thy sorrow is incurable for the multitude of thine iniquity: because thy sins were increased, I have done these things unto thee. Therefore all they that devour thee shall be devoured; and all thine adversaries, every one of them, shall go into captivity; and they that spoil thee shall be a spoil, and all that prey upon thee will I give for a prey. For I will restore health unto thee, and I will heal thee of thy wounds, saith the LORD; because they called thee an Outcast, saying, This is Zion, whom no man seeketh after." [46]

Until now you, his servants, his Zion, were scattered among all the denominations and sects of the Christendom the Earth bearing the indignation of your God. You were among them like accursed and forsaken by God. Your God gave you all these many years to the hand of your enemies because of the Spiritual iniquity of your fathers and you. You have fallen by their spiritual swords and gone into captivity among the heathen of the Christendom the Earth. But now your God is going to take away your reproach from among these heathen. For now, he is going to contend for the cause of his people and shall deliver them from all the hands of their enemies. He will deliver you from all the heathen denominations and sects of the Christendom the Earth. He will be sanctified in you before all these denominations and sects.[47] Now you are bearing his indignation and God did hide his face from you, but now your God is going to plead your cause, for he has come with vengeance. He has looked down from heaven and has seen the Earth, to hear the groaning of his prisoners and those appointed to death, and he has sent me to show these things unto you. He is executing Judgment for them, he is delivering Judgment on their behalf, as written, "I beheld, and the same horn made war with the saints and prevailed against them; Until the Ancient of days came, and judgment was given to the saints of the most High."[48] For the mighty one of Jesus Christ, even that Great God who will make Lord Jesus' enemies his footstool, he has come with vengeance to plead the cause of his servants, to execute judgment. He also said through Moses, "Is not this laid up in store with me, and sealed up among my treasures? To me, belongeth vengeance, and recompense; their foot shall slide in due time: for the day of their calamity is at hand, and the things that shall come upon them make haste. For the LORD shall judge his people, and repent himself for his servants."

For at the time when God pleads the cause of his servants and executes judgment for them, the calamity shall come on his enemies and all the heathen denominations and sects of the Christendom the Earth. Even at this time, he gave them to a strong delusion that they might be damned. But he will bring you back from their captivity first, and then he will punish the Beast, false prophet, whore, Satan and all these denominations and sects that were in the Christendom called the Earth. He will first turn away the captivity of those who had understanding among you and instructed people, yet had fallen by sword and gone into captivity, those who had the oil of understanding, yet were overcome by the enemy and spiritually killed. He will raise all these who were fallen; they shall stand on their feet and go back to Zion above,[49] for he will first turn away the captivity of Zion. He will punish the heathen and our enemies, and after that he will gather all the remnant of the seed of Jesus Christ the Israel whom he has chosen; he will gather them from the ends of world. But now he will turn away the captivity of the Zion, as also spoken by the prophets: "the salvation of Israel were come out of Zion! when the LORD bringeth back the captivity of his people, Jacob shall rejoice, and Israel shall be glad."[50] *And* "upon mount Zion shall be deliverance, and there shall be holiness, and the house of Jacob shall possess their possessions."[51]

Now Apostle John prophesied that a spirit of antichrist will come. This spirit of the enemy had come indeed long time ago (it was also in the time of John), but now this spirit is spread over all the denominations and sects of the Christendom the Earth, for this spirit denies subtly the true Lord Jesus unto whom we were called at the time of our conversion. For the Lord Jesus whom we received and believed in, at the time of our conversion when God has called us unto his fellowship, was like us in all things, except that he was sinless. I mean he was in our old spiritual estate like us before we were converted, like any human child that is in the world. He was made under beggarly elements of the world even law like all of us at that time. He become like us in all things, he was in our previous estate, which we had before our conversion, in the estate of any human child that is in that world, for he came to that world to save us, where we among the children of this world, being subjected unto beggarly elements of the world. For the Son of Man died in that estate and rose again making us free of the beggarly elements of the world. But this spirit of antichrist denies he came in that estate, it denies subtly that he came in flesh, although outwardly they accept that statement Jesus came in flesh. For very certainly the Christ unto whom we were called at that time was in our form, in perfect human child resemblance. Verily at that time we have confessed that he came in flesh, when we had the testimony of Jesus in us, but now that word is departed from our hearts. They made war with saints who had the testimony of Jesus (*for whosoever transgresses, and abides not in the doctrine of Christ, hath not God*) and took them captive to their false gospels. Whenever such people of understanding, the remnant who keep the testimony appeared, they killed them spiritually; now the Christendom is filled with those that were not from God and speak by the spirit of antichrist. Jesus of the spirit of antichrist is a Strange God of the whore and Barbarian the eighth king as spoken by Daniel.

But our Son of Man became no longer son of man for us, with their false gospels, with their strange God, which is the Christ of the Western nations of Barbarian. This strange god is without flesh and bones, an extractor, angry Judge: This is the Christ of the Spirit of antichrist, and this Spirit is upon all denominations and sects of the Christendom. You his saints who had understanding and had known your God, you have been overcome by the enemy and were spiritually killed, for they made you to move away from the true Gospel and true Christ with their craftiness. You lost his fellowship, by receiving another gospel, other christ and another spirit, which you haven't received at the time of your conversion, when God called you from that world unto the fellowship of his Son Jesus. But now you are fallen and spiritually dead by transgressing the holy commandment, which is the word of faith, which you heard at the time of your calling, even the Gospel of your salvation, the testimony of Jesus. For if it stays in you, only then we will remain in Father and Son, as written, "If what you have heard from the beginning should abide in you, you also will abide in the Son and in the Father. Whosoever transgresses, and abides not in the doctrine of Christ, hath not God."[52] Be not amazed at this for all this is truth, and your enemies have wonderfully destroyed you and your spiritual fathers as written, "his power shall be mighty, but not by his own power: and he shall destroy wonderfully, and shall prosper, and practise, and shall destroy the mighty and the holy people."[53] Now this Spirit is spread over all denominations and sects of the Christendom, their christs are not our Son of Man, they are strange gods without humanness. Nowhere in the world true Christ is being preached, for the Enemy has spiritually killed those who had the testimony of Jesus, and also killing them whenever such come into the world to give testimony. But now you who had understanding and gave testimony, but have been overcome and spiritually killed and received this spirit through another gospels and christs which you hadn't received at the time when God called you into his marvelous light to the fellowship of his Son Jesus at the time of your conversion, now your God will raise you back to life in this generation in few years on an appointed time. For among you, his servants, he will destroy this spirit of antichrist and its false christs, as spoken by the prophet that he will destroy it in you: "he will destroy in this mountain the faces of the covering cast over all people and the covering that is spread over all nations."[54] And as written, "therefore hast thou visited and destroyed them, and made all their memory to perish."[55] God is coming to destroy all false gods and christs of Christendom.

Now God is going to turn away the captivity of Jerusalem and will bring you back to Jerusalem above as spoken by the prophets. Now as the set time to favor has come, God has mercy on his servants; he going to raise you back to life. He is going to turn away the captivity of Jerusalem above in few years and will plead with denominations and sects of the heathen of the Christendom that tread upon it all these years; he shall be merciful unto his land. As noted in the book of prophecy, you shall be raised again back to life and shall go back to Jerusalem above. After these things, God will punish those that dwell in Christendom, all these denominations and sects of the Christendom called the Earth.[56] As also spoken by the prophets, "For, behold, in those days, and in that time, when I shall bring again the captivity of Judah and Jerusalem, I will also gather all nations, and will bring them down into the valley of Jehoshaphat, and will plead with them there for my people and for my heritage Israel, whom they have scattered among the nations, and parted my land."[57] For the time of harvest is near, but before that he will turn away your captivity, by bringing you, his witness, back to life, you who have been overcome and spiritually killed by the Beast. For now, God is coming with vengeance to deliver judgment on your behalf, to plead your cause. He will save you; all you that seek him, your hearts shall live forever. You, his witnesses, who had oil of understanding and yet fallen, the anointed ones, candlesticks, and olive trees, you shall arise and go back to Heaven to Jerusalem above, from whence the enemy cast down you, his messengers. As said by Daniel, "it cast down of the host and of the stars to the ground, and stamped upon them. Yea, he magnified even to the prince of the host."[58] I write, you once had the testimony of Jesus in you and kept the commandment of Faith, when that great God even Father called you to the fellowship of Lord Jesus when you were enlightened at the time of your conversion. You had his word, the fire, in your mouths, and had spoken against their preachers, teachings, and their books, which these christians who dwell in the Christendom the Earth read and have tormented the consciences of christians around you. But pretty soon you were overcome by the Enemy that fought against you subtly with another christ and perverted gospel; the beast overcame you and spiritually killed you, for you became like Samson whose hair was cut while he was sleeping.

But here is the patience and faith of saints who keep commandments of God, even the faith of Jesus, for they remember their God and Lord Jesus, and won't let go. For these denominations and sects won't treat you as spiritually dead and lost God, but as alive unto their strange god; they want a song and gladness from you, they want you to be glad and rejoice with them in their strange god. These saints will weep remembering the days in which they walked in the fellowship of God their Father and Jesus Christ their Lord, when God called them through gospel about his Son. They shall desire to see one of the days of the Son of Man, and they shall not see. When you suffer from lack of assurance, these heathen will say you are not keeping law of commandments perfectly, therefore he hid his face. Or they speak as if nothing happened and say it's a common thing, for first few days of your conversion are sweetest and such feelings have no importance, as if the fellowship of our God in his marvelous light that we had lost is just a feeling. They show themselves as godly and of understanding and walking in God's light, and they will take advantage of your helplessness to spoil you, to take you into the captivity into their denomination or sect and make you serve them and their strange gods under the light of their pseudo-religion. You lay dead spiritually, being carried unto bondage of the beggarly elements of the world again and being trampled underfoot of wicked, arrogant, and spiritual fornicators. There Son of Man will become crucified unto you and become unprofitable unto you, for by falling away you crucified him unto yourselves. Those who had understanding among God's people and had instructed others have fallen,[59] the mighty and holy people were been destroyed by the enemy, as written, "And his power shall be mighty, but not by his own power: and he shall destroy wonderfully, and shall prosper, and practice, and shall destroy the mighty and the holy people."[60] This barbarian the eighth king, even the Beast whose power is by Satan the prince of this world, has destroyed you with the craftiness, for as written in book of Revelation Satan gave his strength to them, for in the hand of the Beast, the craftiness of Satan has prospered all these centuries. As spoken by the Daniel the prophet, "And through his policy also he shall cause craft to prosper in his hand; and he shall magnify himself in his heart, and by peace shall destroy many."[61] But now that Great God even our Father will raise his servants back to life; they will go back to Zion above, as written, "*The deliverers will ascend Mount Zion.*"[62] He shall make all his servants spiritually strong and mighty; none of you shall be weak, the weakest among you shall be strong as David. You will be sent to reap, for the time of harvest of tares is very near. So fear not brethren greatly beloved of Lord Jesus and of the Father: Look, your Father is coming with vengeance, even that Great God is coming with great strength with recompense on your enemies; he will come and save you. His indignation is upon all denominations and sects of the Christendom the Earth, upon all their spiritual host of preachers, pastors, bishops, evangelists, theologians, etc. He will deliver you, his host which was cast down and trodden by the enemy; he will destroy from among you the spirit of antichrist and all false christs. He will raise you back to life, and you will go back to Father unto Zion above to heaven, from where the enemy cast you down, as spoken by the prophet, "it waxed great, even to the host of heaven; and it cast down of the host and of the stars to the ground."[63] He will come and save you pretty soon, for in a few days the years of the sixth trumpet are going to come to an end, and before that, he shall come, now also he came, for he visited us and he will execute judgment on your behalf, so that beast shall not prevail against you.[64] You shall pretty soon overcome the beast, for as prophets said, our God shall come with vengeance and recompense upon all our enemies who hated our God and destroyed us, his servants, among whom he dwells, the place of his sanctuary that was cast down. When he comes, he will first raise you back to life, your captivity shall be turned away and you shall return to Jerusalem above. With this event, the days of the of the voice of the sixth angel of trumpet shall finish. I call upon God to witness against my soul, if I am not telling you truth before that Great God, even your Father, who has sent me to show you these things that shall soon come to pass, to declare his works unto you: Pretty soon he will raise you back to life, bring you back to Jerusalem, which is above from the place where our Lord was crucified unto you,

For we and our fathers have sinned against our God grievously, against his holy and jealous love by forsaking our God for other gospels, another christs, other gods, righteousness of law, etc. We have dealt treacherously against our God by going after other gods and provoked him to jealousy with our vanities, as he said, "Surely as a wife treacherously departeth from her husband, so have ye dealt treacherously with me, O house of Israel, saith the Lord."[65] Because of our iniquities and unfaithfulness, our God hid his face from us, poured his anger on us, his jealousy burnt against us like fire for many centuries. For he has loved us with great and holy love, and we pierced him by our turning away from our God toward strangers and vanities. He loved us and created us new, begotten us by the death and resurrection of his Son, but we dealt treacherously against our God by going after strange gods of vanities and became defiled, therefore he consumed us in his jealousy. We despised the grace of Lord Jesus and God's grace, which he has shown toward us through his Son. We have destroyed ourselves, all the good things which our God and our Lord brought in us, for things of naught, as spoken by our God, "Behold, for your iniquities have ye sold yourselves."[66] But now our God says he will save us for his great name's sake, "Not for your sakes do I this, saith the Lord GOD, be it known unto you: be ashamed and confounded for your own ways, O house of Israel."[67] For he is still angry with us, the jealousy of his holy love burns against us greatly, for we have done like an unfaithful woman who defiles herself by going after strangers and destroys herself. Yet now he says concerning your captivity, "What have I here that my people are taken away for nothing?" You have sold yourselves for naught, and you shall be redeemed without money.[68] For he is going to turn away the captivity of Jerusalem above; therefore return and seek our great God and Lord Jesus with all your heart and soul. For now at this time, her time of captivity is coming to an end; if you seek him with all your heart, you will find him, as scripture says, "For I know the thoughts that I think toward you, saith the LORD, thoughts of peace, and not of evil, to give you an expected end."[69]

REFERENCES:

1. Isaiah 26:9;
2. 1 Peter 1:3; Romans 7:4;
3. Hebrews 10:20;
4. Ephesians 2:5; Colossians 1:22; Romans 6:3;
5. Ephesians 1:3; 2:5; Colossians 2:10. Romans 7:1;
6. Romans 7:6;
7. Colossians 1:13;
8. Acts 26:17-18;
9. Galatians 4:3-5; Romans 7:5;
10. Hebrews 12:22;
11. Isaiah 66:20;
12. Acts 22:21;
13. Romans 15:16;
14. Isaiah 63:19;
15. Daniel 8:12;
16. Isaiah 50:1;
17. 1 Corinthians 10:11;
18. Revelation 5:9-10; I Peter 2:9;
19. Isaiah 48:3; 53:10; I Peter 1:3;
20. Psalms 45:16;
21. Revelation 22:5;
22. Isaiah 43:10;
23. Ezekiel 39:23;
24. Revelation 11:2; Isaiah 51:23:
25. Daniel 11:33-35;
26. Ezekiel 39:23;
27. Joel 2:3; Obadiah 1:15; Isaiah 34:2;
28. Revelation 19:1; 16:6;
29. Matthew 24:29; Revelation 11:14;
30. Daniel 7:21-22;
31. Zechariah 14:9; Psalms 82:8; 2:8;
32. Isaiah 51:4;
33. Psalms 76:9; Isaiah 41:17;
34. Zephaniah 2:3;
35. Isaiah 66:4-5;
36. Isaiah 54:8-10;
37. Isaiah 50:1;
38. Isaiah 51:22-23;
39. Hebrews 6:7-8;
40. Isaiah 59:3-8;
41. Isaiah 60:10; 54:7-8;
42. Isaiah 49:14&21;
43. Isaiah 51:17;

44. Daniel 11:33-35;
45. Psalms 102:13;
46. Jeremiah 30:14-17;
47. Ezekiel 36:23; 39:21;
48. Daniel 7:21;
49. Revelation 11:11-13; Zephaniah 3:14-17;
50. Psalm 14:7; 53:6;
51. Obadiah 1:17;
52. 1 John 2:24; 2 John 1:9;
53. Daniel 8:24;
54. Isaiah 25:7;
55. Isaiah 26:14;
56. Revelation 11:18;
57. Joel 3:1-2;
58. Daniel 8:10-11;
59. Daniel 11:35;
60. Revelation 13: 2; Daniel 8:24;
61. Daniel 8:25;
62. Obadiah 1:21;
63. Daniel 8:10;
64. Daniel 7:22; 11:36;
65. Jeremiah 3:20;
66. Isaiah 52:3; 50:1;
67. Ezekiel 36:22;
68. Isaiah 52:3;
69. Jeremiah 29:11;

CHAPTER FIVE

Avenging of God for his servants

Now that Great and everlasting God, even Father of Lord Jesus is coming with vengeance and with recompense for enemies. He will come and save you. He shall subdue all things with his great strength, and first, he will turn away captivity of Jerusalem above and you shall go to Jerusalem above. You shall ascend to Zion to execute the spiritual judgments of our God upon on our enemies, as written, "saviors shall come up on mount Zion to judge the mount of Esau; and the kingdom shall be the Lord's,"[1] and,

> "The children also of Judah and the children of Jerusalem have ye sold unto the Grecians, that ye might remove them far from their border. Behold, I will raise them out of the place whither ye have sold them, and will return your recompense upon your own head: Proclaim ye this among the heathen; Prepare war, wake up the mighty men, let all the men of war draw near; let them come up: Beat your plowshares into swords, and your pruning hooks into spears: let the weak say, I am strong. Assemble yourselves, and come, all ye heathen, and gather yourselves

together round about: thither cause thy mighty ones to come down, O LORD."²

For truly very soon Father will turn away your captivity and in this generation. He fulfills his promise to Lord Jesus the making of his enemies his footstool. Daniel said the beast will prevail against you until Father comes and passes judgment on your favor.³

For your Father even that Great God now will plead your cause, and shall save you from all that your enemies have done unto you with their craftiness, and he shall bring an end to the shattering of your power,⁴ which was shattered in the place where your Lord was crucified and was made unprofitable unto you.⁵ He will bring you back to Jerusalem above, you will stop crucifying Lord Jesus unto yourselves, and Lord Jesus who loved us will no longer be as crucified unto us. Now, when the shattering of your power comes to an end as spoken by Daniel the prophet, when you will be raised back to life in place where your Lord was crucified and you will be brought to heaven to Jerusalem above to the place where you went at the time of your conversion, the days of the sixth trumpet will come to end, and in the days of the voice of the angel of the seventh trumpet, even the last trumpet, and that Great and dreadful God, even the God and the father of our Lord will take his Great might and shall begin to rule and he will execute judgments on Christendom the Earth upon these denominations and sects. Now after he turns the captivity of those who had understanding among his people, even the two olives and lampstands the candle sticks, they shall instruct and publish this good news unto people as written, "O Zion, that bringest good tidings, get thee up into the high mountain; O Jerusalem, that bringest good tidings, lift up thy voice with strength; lift it up, be not afraid; say unto the cities of Judah, Behold your God! Behold, the Lord GOD will come with strong hand, and his arm shall rule for him: behold, his reward is with him, and his work before him."[6] For the teachers of the people will be no longer removed into a corner,[7] they will gain victory over the beast and over his image, and over his mark, and over the number of his name. After these things in the beginning of days of seventh trumpet God shall cleanse from among you all spiritual iniquities, lies, and falsehoods and from the filthiness of all false gods and christs all the pollution. As spoken by Daniel Sanctuary shall be cleansed,[8] which the enemy has polluted and cast down, God also spoke through his prophet concerning these days saying, "I raise up the tabernacle of David that is fallen, and close up the breaches thereof; and I will raise up his ruins, and I will build it as in the days of old."[9] For God calls his beloved servant Jesus as David in the books of prophets,[10] Lord Jesus who dwells in the midst of lampstands the candlesticks is the prince of the host of heaven the Jerusalem, as written Ecclesiastical host the spiritual armies of the Beast cast down the place of his sanctuary.[11] God will cleanse you and put his word in you again. The testimony of Lord Jesus, the Gospel, and the word of the covenant, will be established in you again. After these things God will make Jerusalem a cup of trembling to all denominations and sects; you will become a burdensome stone to all heathen nations of the Earth, which were the sects and denominations of Christendom the Earth.[12]

All the foundations of Earth are out, of course. These mountains of the Earth are the foundations of the Earth, and even all these great denominations are the foundations of the Christendom the Earth, all these denominations are out of course, but God shall arise to judge the Christendom the Earth, for he shall inherit all the nations. For pretty soon, our God is coming with recompense and vengeance on his adversaries. Behold, the Lord GOD is coming with might, his arm, even Lord Jesus shall rule for him. Behold, his reward is with him. Behold, pretty soon our God is coming out of his place to punish to those who dwell in the Christendom the Earth. For their iniquity, he will utterly abolish idols, even the gods and christs of their imaginations. And Father shall be king over all the Christendom the earth. In that day shall there be one God, and his name one, and leftover of denominations and sects of Christendom the Earth shall come to you and multitude of the sea will be turned unto you.

Now he will take his great strength and will start to reign, after that, first thing he will do is, he will turn away the captivity of you who were two witnesses the olive trees the lampstands the candlesticks the churches,[13] which had the understanding among his people,[14] who, had the testimony of Jesus[15] and commandments of God, but became overcome by the enemy.[16] God will bring you back to Jerusalem above,[17] and you shall declare the good tidings of our God's kingdom and will instruct the people who were harassed and helpless, like sheep without a shepherd, the harvest of the earth will be ripe.[18] He shall enrich you spiritually, and strengthen you as spoken by prophets, "he that is feeble among them at that day shall be as David; and the house of David shall be as God, as the angel of the LORD before them,"[19] *and* "they shall be as mighty men, which tread down their enemies in the mire of the streets in the battle: and they shall fight, because the LORD is with them,"[20] *and* "O daughter of Zion, I will make your horn iron, and I will make your hoofs bronze;"[21] *and*, "I will make thee a new sharp threshing instrument having teeth:"[22]

Brethren, although father was angry with us, hid his face from us, and had given us unto the hand of our enemies because of the iniquities of us and our fathers, he reserved his anger on our enemies for all they had done unto us and our fathers as he declared, "Is not this laid up in store with me, and sealed up among my treasures? To me belongs vengeance, and recompense."[23] But now, after he raises you and brings you back to Jerusalem above, you shall publish this good news of the kingdom for a testimony to all.[24] After that you shall execute spiritual judgments of God on Christendom by pouring those vials, and then Jerusalem above shall become the cup of trembling to all denominations and sects. You will become a burdensome stone to all heathen nations of the Earth, which were all these sects and denominations of Christendom the Earth. And all these denominations and sects will be enraged against you,[25] but they know not the thoughts of the God, neither understand they his counsel; for he shall gather them as the sheaves into the floor.

For our God's anger is upon all nations of the Earth, which were the sects and denominations of Christendom the Earth. For all they have done unto us and our fathers, for all these Christians who dwell in Christendom of all denominations and sects have spiritually killed His saints and taken them captive and oppressed them, and parted His land,[26] but our God has reserved his anger upon them from a very long time. Therefore, a few centuries ago, souls of saints that were spiritually slain who were before you cried, "How long, O Lord, holy and true, dost thou not judge and avenge our blood on them that dwell on the earth?"[27] But our God's anger is upon denominations and sects of the Christendom the Earth, and upon all their spiritual host of preachers, theologians, bishops, pastors, etc. He has appointed them to utter destruction and to a spiritual slaughter, they now are shining as host in the heaven through their false religion, as a source of spiritual light, and ruling upon those that dwell in Christendom the Earth, but they shall fall to the ground and be cast out from above. And these denominations and sects will melt with their destruction, as spoken by the prophet,

> "Come near, ye nations, to hear; and hearken, ye people: let the earth hear, and all that is therein; the world, and all things that come forth of it. For the indignation of the LORD is upon all nations, and his fury upon all their armies: he hath utterly destroyed them, he hath delivered them to the slaughter. Their slain also shall be cast out, and their stink shall come up out of their carcasses, and the mountains shall be melted with their blood."[28]

Now after, you shall publish this good news of the kingdom after he raises you and brings you back to Jerusalem above, the captivity of Jerusalem and Judah will be turned away,²⁹ and God will judge heathen for you, and for all they have done to all his saints until now. He will enter into judgment with them,³⁰ even with all these denominations and sects of the Christendom the Earth, and he will make you his mighty messengers. Even you his messengers shall execute his spiritual judgments upon the Christendom, and upon those that dwell in Christendom the Earth upon all these denominations and sects, for our God will strengthen you and give you the things which you need to speak;³¹ for he shall send his messengers the mighty angels from among you to reap, then they shall speak and torment them that dwell in the Christendom all these denominations and sects. By speaking all those things, which God will give them, they shall torment the consciences of those who received the mark of the beast and worshiped his image, and shall make people from other religions no more converted unto they that dwell in Christendom the Earth. His messengers shall make them nauseating, even their material, written and spoken by their preachers of past and present, even every stream of the teaching and the theological fountains that were in these diverse sects and denominations, from which these Christians of all denominations and sects extinguish their thirst. And other spiritual judgments of our God, they shall execute upon the Christendom; thus they shall gather all tares and weeds together. According to the word of God, they shall gather all spiritual host of all denominations and sects of the Christendom the Earth to a battle of that Great day of God Almighty against the Jerusalem above, in a little time after when he turns away her captivity. According to which he declared to his prophets, "I will gather all the nations against

Jerusalem to battle".[32] They will be gathered as spoken by Prophet Zechariah in the last chapter of his book, therefore blessed he that watches and keeps his garments, then our God will come to fight against them, for it is his great day of battle, then Christendom will quake terribly as never before.

For our God will execute his Judgment upon Christendom, upon the heathen nations of the Earth, which were all the sects and denominations of Christendom the Earth, and he will gather them to judge them for all things they have done unto his saints as he declared to his prophet, "I will also gather all nations, and will bring them down into the valley of Jehoshaphat, and will plead with them there for my people and for my heritage Israel, whom they have scattered among the nations, and parted my land,"[33] and "Jehoshaphat" means God has judged. For our God will gather all these denominations and sects against you for a spiritual battle. His mighty messengers, even his angels among you, will gather all these heathen together by speaking the things which God will give them to speak, thus executing spiritual judgments of God upon the Christendom the Earth. They will gather all these to battle against Jerusalem above, even against you by pouring those seven vials on Christendom. As in parable, tares and weeds are gathered together and were bound in bundles to be burnt, for he shall gather them as the sheaves into the floor.[34] Our God will execute his judgment upon all denominations and sects of the Christendom, as he declared through his prophets. He has given all their spiritual host of preachers, pastors, evangelists, bishops, theologians, etc. to a spiritual slaughter. Darkness shall cover the Christendom; complete darkness to all the people of these denominations and sects, but you will have light.³⁵ As our Lord said the waves of the sea of other religions will be roaring against the Christendom the earth, and all these denominations and sects will be in distress with perplexity. And men in Christendom the Earth will be fainting from fear and expectation of things which are coming upon the Christendom. Because the powers of their religious heavens will be shaken, and all the starry host of their religion's preachers, pastors, bishops, theologians, etc., shall fall to the ground being slain by the sword of God, which is his word. As our God declared, "my sword shall be bathed in heaven, all the host of heaven shall be dissolved, and the heavens shall be rolled together as a scroll: and all their host shall fall down, as the leaf falls off from the vine, and as a falling fig from the fig tree."³⁶ After this, as spoken by prophets, Jerusalem above shall be holy and no more unclean men, uncircumcised in heart and in Christ shall enter her anymore, forever.³⁷

Now, the coming of Lord Jesus is like a thief in the night. It started from the time when the abomination that makes desolation, even the image of beast was set up,³⁸ and to the time when sign of the son of man appears in heaven,³⁹ and all the tribes of the Earth the Christendom shall wail because of him. For all these years, until sign of the son of man appears in heaven, the darkness of deception shall be upon the Christendom like a flood, and many people will be carried unto destruction. It came like a snare upon all the Christendom, and many were caught into it. Therefore the Lord said to always pray to escape these things that will come at his coming, saying, "Watch ye therefore, and pray always, that ye may be accounted worthy to escape all these things that shall come to pass, and to stand before the Son of man."[40] For when sign of the son of man appears in heaven, it shall be like the sunrise of the morning, and Christendom shall wake up to see the destruction that came upon them in unawares in the night like a thief, then all these heathen sects and denominations shall awake to see our God's judgment as he said, "I will set my glory among the heathen, and all the heathen shall see my judgment that I have executed, and my hand that I have laid upon them."[41] The coming of Son of man is throughout all this time, when the abomination that makes desolate was set up few years ago, and to the time when the sign of the son of man appears in heaven. Therefore, I exhort you to stay awake even after he brings you back from captivity, lest you might be deceived by the host of sects and denominations, and they might lead you again into spiritual captivity. For very certainly I say unto you, they will come against you and take many of you into captivity again. For all the coming years, the coming of the son of man is like a thief until their host shall fall to the ground and sign of the son of man appears in heaven. So, I exhort you to awake remembering Father and Lord Jesus from the time when you were called into his marvelous light in the beginning, to remember how you heard and received in the beginning, seeking our only God and Lord Jesus with all your hearts and souls by trying to remember, and praying and keeping yourselves away from all these sects and denominations, away from all the evil in Christendom and from anxieties of this life, love of riches, and other evils in the world, guarding your hearts from dullness, and keeping them always in right state. Importantly, always walking by faith in the Lord Jesus who loved you, and gave himself for your sins, and being dead unto the law. See, if you keep your conscience under the law and seek to be approved by it in your conscience, then you will find yourselves, sinners, with guilty consciences and naked, and you shall become weak and vulnerable before your enemies that deceive you and take you into captivity to their teachings (*So watch and keep your garment to cover your nakedness.*).

Now the deception in Christendom is like a flood that came in the days of Noah. People were being taken into it, yet they saw these days are of peace and safety. The false prophet, the spiritual host of the barbarian, these preachers are everywhere teaching Christians that dwell in Christendom that God is on their behalf, and is working for them in their lives, so that they all might receive this mark of beast, that no one can receive things that were preached in the Christendom nor he, his teaching will be received in the Christendom without the mark of the beast. Moreover, they were teaching to those in Christendom to aspire for the image of the Beast, which is a worldly prosperity like of the Beast that got healing. They are giving life to their aspirations of these Christians by their miracles these miracles and lying wonders of Satan, this speaking image of the beast, the lying wonder is testifying to lies, which is destroying many others by deceiving them who have not yet believed their teachings and not believed that these Satan's miracles done by God, as our Lord said if possible they shall deceive very elect. But God will shorten these days for the sake of the elect, whom he has chosen, even the spiritual seed of Jesus Christ the Israel whom he has chosen. Except these days should be shortened, no flesh will be saved, and all these Christians that were deceived never truly repented and loved the glorious gospel of our Lord they live as enemies of cross of Christ and hate self-denial; their god is their worldly craving, and their glory is in their shame, which loved and set their mind on earthly things of this life. Now they are rejoicing in the lies and falsehoods, making them their refuge and a cover over their love of this world, but when God turns away our captivity and brings back the light of glorious gospel as a clear sun without clouds, their folly will be discovered and you shall declare their iniquity and people will rise against them. They shall be detestable to all people forever, every one of them shall be tormented day and night in the burning lake with word of God the truth which he has despised. And such a man will be tormented in the presence of messengers; their cries of torment will ascend up as irritating odors forever. Their confidence will be rooted out, and their desire will perish; the fierce wrath of God without any drop of mercy rests upon them forever and ever. They shall be driven into darkness forever; sorrows shall be their portion and the terror on every side and will not have any rest. These Christians worshiped the beast, saying, "Which nation is like unto Beast, who is able to make war with these nations of Barbarian, even with these western nations?" And they worship the Satan, the ruler of this world, who gave these nations his seat, his strength, and great authority, saying God gave them such things. They changed the glory of God, which is on the face of Lord Jesus, the mighty signs by which God gave testimony about his Son into an abomination and work of Devils. They placed works of Satan, the image of the Beast whose deadly wound was healed and prospered in that

Holy place of Testimony Father given to his Son Jesus. They worshiped the health, life, wealth and worldly prosperity, the image they made for themselves in the fashion of beast, and they worshiped Satan as their God, who will realize their aspirations and give life to the image. They believed strongly that this God of the west is on the rise and is helping them to grow into prosperity in various things of this life and of the world. These wicked Christians boast themselves against the saints who remember their God who in the beginning called them through gospel of his Son as they seek their God and his fellowship. These wicked Christians boast themselves against the Saints, in their prosperity they have in the things of this life and of world, and they show themselves they are under God's favor and goodwill as opposed to saints that struggle in the things of this life and of world, and who all the day long get plagued, and chastened every day. But saints must endure their ridicule and boasting knowing their God, and love wherewith he loved them. Saints must understand these wicked Christians are set for destruction as Psalmist wrote, "Surely thou didst set them in slippery places: thou castedst them down into destruction. How are they brought into desolation, as in a moment! they are utterly consumed with terrors. As a dream when one awaketh; so, O Lord, when thou awakest, thou shalt despise their image."[42]

Lord Jesus also spoke about coming destruction upon the denominations and sects, which were nations of the earth the Christendom. For he said he will first tell his angels the messengers, who were reapers, first to gather the tares the weeds and bind them in bundles to burn them.[43] He said in those times, the waves of the sea will be roaring and the nations, even these denominations and sects of Christendom will be in bewilderment. When you, his messengers execute the spiritual judgments of our God on Christendom by speaking the things which will be given to you by God, and gather the tares and wicked together for the battle of the great day of God Almighty, the Beast and false prophet will be punished, and the sun be darkened, and the moon shall not give her light, and the stars shall fall from heaven, and the powers of the heavens shall be shaken; for all the spiritual host of these denominations and sects of the Christendom: the preachers, pastors, bishops, theologians, etc., will be spiritually slaughtered by word of God. Darkness shall cover the Christendom, complete darkness over all the people of these denominations and sects. Their religion shall be rolled like scroll, and all the starry host of their religion's preachers, pastors, evangelists, bishops, theologians, etc., shall fall to ground, being slain by the sword of God, which is his word. People will be fainting from fear and expectation of that which is coming on the Christendom.[44]

At that time after you gather the tares and weeds together in bundles when they were gathered to a spiritual battle in the Great day of God Almighty, God will remember the iniquity of the Church of Rome.[45] All that she has done against his servants, and how she corrupted the Christendom with her fornication, and how she exalted herself and lived in luxury he will avenge the blood of his servants on her. And our people should come out from there; for all her plagues will come on her suddenly she will be burned with fire, even by the word of Almighty God. He will pour fierceness of his wrath on her, all these denominations and sects upon whom she rules, for she sits on many waters. Even in our days, she sits on more than one billion and three hundred million people. All these kingdoms of the earth, these denominations and sects of Christendom the earth, who committed spiritual fornication of worshiping false gods and christs with her, shall weep and wail over her. Preachers and teachers of the Christendom will weep for her; for no man will receive their teachings any longer. In one hour her rich record of royalty and reputation of being virtuous adorned with saints, righteous and holy men will come to end. The missionaries that work in missions in sea of other faiths also will mourn for her when they see her tormented from being burned by the word of our God. And church at Rome the Babylon will be cast down with great violence and will no more appear, as Prophet Jeremiah wrote and also as written in the book of Revelation of Jesus Christ, our God will pronounce his judgment against her. The church at Rome will become great horror for all the denominations and sects of Christendom the Earth. For the sea of other religions will come upon it, its roaring waves will cover the Rome, the people of other religion that hate her will cover her. Thus church at Rome the Babylon will be cast down in violence and sink in the sea of other religion. It will never be seen again, neither its false religion ever appear again. Listen, he is saying to you who were in this generation, concerning your enemies, the day of their calamity is at hand, and the things that shall come upon them make haste.

After the Great day of God Almighty in which the Beast and false prophet will be thrown alive in lake of fire which burns with the breath of God, and leftover of the ecclesiastical host the spiritual armies of these denominations and sects will be killed by the word of God that comes out from the mouth of Lord Jesus,[46] then noise of strangers will go away. At that time the plunder and the wealth of these denominations will be gathered and will be given to those that dwell in Jerusalem above, against whom these denominations and sects came for battle. All their wealth will be gathered as spoken by the prophets "Judah also shall fight at Jerusalem; and the wealth of all the heathen round about shall be gathered together, gold, and silver, and apparel, in great abundance,"[47] *and* "Thy tacklings are loosed; they could not well strengthen their mast, they could not spread the sail: then is the prey of a great spoil divided; the lame take the prey. And the inhabitant shall not say, I am sick: the people that dwell therein shall be forgiven their iniquity."[48] As also written in the book of Revelation of Jesus Christ, that those who fly in the middle of heaven will eat the flesh of kings, captains, mighty men, horses, and riders of horses and all men both small and great. For the flesh of kings is nothing but the people that were in that kingdom, even in that denomination, therefore it was said that protestant denominations eat the flesh of Babylon, for they swallowed up her people upon whom she sat, into their denominations. Now at that time that Great and dreadful God, even the father of our Lord will give a great supper to those that dwell in Jerusalem, for he will do a great spiritual slaughter and give flesh of the kings of earth which were denominations sects of Christendom the earth; the flesh of captains, and the flesh of mighty men, even the followers of all these men, the flesh of horses, even the adherents of various doctrines, the flesh of riders of horses, the followers of these preachers, theologians that adhere to those doctrines, the flesh of all the host both small and great, and the inhabitants of Jerusalem shall be filled with their flesh. Jerusalem will spread abroad to the right and to the left, and her seed will possess gentiles. I "Jonathan Bijja Charles Spurgeon" the writer of this book, call upon that Great God to witness against me, if not all these things will soon take place before this generation passes away. All the heathen, the people of the nations, even denominations and sects of Christendom, they will come to you his people, to Jerusalem to worship before our God. If any denomination or sect that will be left in the Christendom will not come and refuse to serve you, our God will punish that denomination or sect.[49] And our Lord will rule nations with the iron scepter, even utmost parts of the Christendom he will shatter them like pottery.[50]

REFERENCES:

1. Obadiah 1:21;
2. Joel 3:6-11;
3. Daniel 7:21-22;
4. Daniel 12:7;
5. Revelation 11:8; Isaiah 51:20;
6. Isaiah 40:9-10;
7. Isaiah 30:20;
8. Daniel 8:14;
9. Amos 9:11;
10. Isaiah 55:4; Jeremiah 30:9; Ezekiel 37:25; Hosea 3:5;
11. Daniel 11:31; Daniel 8:11 & 24;
12. Zechariah 12:2;
13. Revelation 1:20; 11:3-4;
14. Daniel 11:33-35; 8:24;
15. Revelation 12:17;
16. Revelation 13:7&10;

17. Revelation 11:12; 15:2;

18. Mark 4:29;

19. Zechariah 12:8;

20. Zechariah 10:5;

21. Micah 4:13;

22. Isaiah 41:15;

23. Deuteronomy 32:34-35;

24. Matthew 24:15; Revelation 14:14;

25. Zechariah 12:3; Revelation 11:18;

26. Zephaniah 3:8; Joel 3:2; Matthew 24:9;

27. Revelation 6:10;

28. Isaiah 34:1-3;

29. Joel 1:3; Obadiah 1:21&22; Psalms 53:6;Revelation11:17;

30. Joel 3:12; Isaiah 59:17-19;

31. Revelation 15:7;

32. Zechariah 14:2; Revelation 16:16;

33. Joel 3:2;

34. Micah 4:12; Matthew 13:30;

35. Isaiah 60:2; 34:5; 24:21; Revelation 6:13; 16:21;

36. Isaiah 34:4-5;

37. Isaiah 52:1; Joel 3:17; Col 2:21; Ezekiel 44:9;

38. Daniel 12:12; Matthew 24:23-28; Luke 17:33-37; Revelation 13:14-18;

39. Matthew 24:29-30; Isaiah 11:10; 60:3;

40. Luke 21:36;

41. Ezekiel 39:21;

42. Psalms 73:18-20;

43. Matthew 13:30;

44. Luke 21:26;

45. Revelation 18:5; 16:19;

46. Revelation 19:21; Isaiah 34:5; Psalms 110:5;

47. Zechariah 14:14;

48. Isaiah 33:23-24;

49. Zephaniah 3:9; Isaiah 2:2-4; 60:12; Zechariah 14:17;

50. Psalms 2:18; Isaiah 11:1-10; Revelation 19:15;

CHAPTER SIX

Gathering the remnant of his people from the ends of Earth

Shall the plunder be taken from the mighty, or the lawful captive delivered? But that Great God, the mighty One of Lord Jesus, says that even the captives of the mighty shall be taken away, and the plunder of the terrible shall be delivered: For He will fight with him that fights with Zion, and He will save her children. And He will feed them that oppress her with their own flesh; and they shall be drunken with their own blood, as with sweet wine. When you, his messengers the angels, will gather the tares and weeds together and bind in bundles by speaking the things that God will give you to speak and thus tormenting those that dwell in Christendom. For you shall gather the Ecclesiastical host the spiritual armies of preachers, pastors, evangelists, bishops, theologians, etc, of denominations and the sects of the whole Christendom, along with Beast and false prophet to a spiritual battle in the Great day of God Almighty, by pouring those seven vials of wrath. At that time after seventh viol poured, God will remember the iniquity of the Church of Rome, all that she has done against his city, his temple and his servants and how she corrupted the Christendom with her teaching to do fornication with strange gods and how she exalted herself and lived in luxury and brethren that were there should escape. He will avenge the blood of his servants on her, all her plagues will come on her suddenly, and she will be burned with fire, even by the word of Almighty God. He will pour the fierceness of his wrath on her, and the denominations and sects upon whom she rules, all these kingdoms of Earth these denominations and sects of Christendom the Earth who committed spiritual fornication of worshiping false gods and christs with her and lived in luxury, shall be removed far from her and will weep and wail over her. Preachers and teachers of the Christendom will weep for her, for no man will receive their teachings any more.[1] Church at Rome the Babylon of the Christendom, the Earth shall be covered by sea of other religion and people that rage against her will cover her, as prophet Jeremiah said "The sea will come upon Babylon,; she is covered with multitude of waves thereof." As also written in the book of Revelation of Jesus Christ "A mighty angel took up a great stone like a millstone and cast it into the sea, saying, thus with violence shall that great city Babylon be thrown down, and shall be found no more at all".

When the seventh viol is poured the gross darkness will cover over the Christendom, over all denominations and sects in the Christendom, for their spiritual host will be slain by the word of God, even by the double-edged sharp sword that comes out of mouth of King of all kingdoms of the Earth. Their heaven of light, the religion under which they dwelt, will be rolled like a scroll, their refuge of lies and falsehoods will disappear, and they will open their eyes to the reality, even to the fierce wrath of our God and Lord Jesus that has come over them.² It is dreadful to fall into the hand of the living God who came to take vengeance on them. And to Jerusalem above, the kingdom and dominion will be given, as spoken by the prophets, "And thou, O tower of the flock the stronghold of the daughter of Zion, unto thee shall it come, even the first dominion; the kingdom shall come to the daughter of Jerusalem."³ Our God shall set his hand again, the second time to gather the Remnant of his people that were left in denominations and sects of the Christendom the Earth.⁴ And our God will start to thresh all the denominations and sects that were in Christendom. He will beat these nations of the earth, even denominations of the Christendom, like wheat bundles are beaten to remove the grain out of them. He will gather all spiritual seed of Israel the Jesus Christ, all remnant that were left among them, ⁴ as spoken by prophets, "In that day the LORD will start His threshing from the flowing stream of the Euphrates to the brook of Egypt, and you will be gathered up one by one, O sons of Israel." ⁵ I Jonathan Bijja Charles Spurgeon call upon that Great God to witness upon my soul, if not all these things will soon take place before this generation passes away.

Therefore, fear not brethren, you who were his mighty messengers that will do his harvest work. He will make Jerusalem above, you his kingdom strong as Iron and brass; you will thresh all these denominations and sects, and you will bring your brethren the seed of Jesus Christ the Israel that were left among these denominations and sects. For in Mount Zion and in Jerusalem there will be deliverance to the remnant of his elect whom God calls, and God will reign over the seed of Jesus Christ in his holy kingdom from henceforth, even forever, and they shall shine forth like the sun in their Father's kingdom. Now Jerusalem above is desolate, for God has smote her, because of the iniquity of her Children, which were us and our spiritual fathers before us. So God did hide his face from her and gave us to the hand of our enemies, but in these days when he punishes our enemies and saves us, God will make a unilateral Covenant of peace with her. He will make a covenant of peace[6] with the spiritual seed of Jesus Christ the Israel whom he has chosen, which shall be an everlasting covenant, according to that unilateral covenant that his word he puts in your mouth, even the Gospel, the testimony of Jesus, the word of God, from which we departed in the past, being overcome and spiritually killed by the enemy. Now it will never depart from your mouth and your children's children mouths forever, so that we, all his children, might abide in Father and Son forever, and your spiritual seed shall continue and be established before him and your fruit will remain, according to which he declared: "As for me, this is my covenant with them, saith the LORD; My spirit that is upon thee, and my words which I have put in thy mouth, shall not depart out of thy mouth, nor out of the mouth of thy seed, nor out of the mouth of thy seed's seed, saith the LORD, from henceforth and forever."[7] And according to this everlasting covenant of peace, Father will not hide his face from you anymore, as he spoken through his prophets, "Neither will I hide my face any more from them: for I have poured out my spirit upon the house of Israel, saith the Lord GOD."[8] According to this covenant he will make, Father will not be angry with you anymore, nor he will rebuke you, as spoken through his prophets: "For this is as the waters of Noah unto me: for as I have sworn that the waters of Noah should no more go over the earth; so have I sworn that I would not be wroth with thee, nor rebuke thee. For the mountains shall depart, and the hills be removed; but my kindness shall not depart from thee, neither shall the covenant of my peace be removed, saith the LORD that hath mercy on thee."[9] And he will not turn away from doing well to his people. In the coming ages he will show the exceeding riches of his grace in his kindness toward us through Christ Jesus.

Immediately after you gain victory over the Beast and his mark and over his image, harvest will begin. At the end of harvest of wicked, at the battle of the great day of God Almighty, the Beast and the false prophet, even the ecclesiastical host the spiritual army of the Beast which are doing miracles and deceived them that had received the mark of the Beast, and them that worshipped his image will be cast into what is spiritually called a lake of fire. All the remaining ecclesiastical host the spiritual armies of preachers, evangelists, pastors, bishops, theologians, etc, of all these denominations and sects of the Christendom the Earth will be dissolved and fall to the ground. Their religion, the heaven of their spiritual light, will be rolled together and Christendom the Earth shall be shaken terribly. Every denomination and sect will be moved from their place,[10] and all their cities that they fortified with their dogmas, articles of faith, catechisms and confessions, all their cities shall fall,[11] where they dwell spiritually and imprison your brethren. But we belong to his holy mountain his kingdom as prophets spoke, "The LORD also shall roar out of Zion, and utter his voice from Jerusalem; and the heavens and the earth shall shake."[12] *And* "all the host of heaven shall be dissolved, and the heavens shall be rolled together as a scroll: and all their host shall fall down, as the leaf falleth off from the vine, and as a falling fig from the fig tree."[13] Christendom will be covered with gross darkness and darkness will cover all the denominations and sects of the Christendom the Earth. Their heaven, the religion of lies and false assurances of safety, the illusion of standing on good graces of God will suddenly disappear. They will face the fierceness of the wrath of our God and Lord Jesus and they shall not be able to bear the wrath of our God. They will say to the mountains and rocks, "Fall on us, and hide us from the cruel wrath of God, and from the wrath of the Jesus Christ."[14] At the great day of God's wrath, sudden destruction will come upon them, as travail upon a woman with child, and they shall not escape.[15] And it is time of trouble for the elect also, even the seed of Jesus Christ the Israel and Jacob, for they are living among the strangers and they sincerely believed the denominations and sects in which they dwell were brethren and belong to Christ, and these brethren who were serving the heathen, think they are serving God, and his people, their spiritual rulers have continually fed them with blasphemies against their Father, but God will burst their bonds and will break their yoke. And God our Father will thresh the nations of earth, even these denominations and sects of the Christendom.

At that time, He shall stretch his hand for second time,[16] and shall again start to gather the Remnant of our brethren the seed of Lord Jesus, the Israel whom God has chosen, all that were left in denominations and sects, even if they are scattered in ends of Christendom among weird sects like Jehovah's Witnesses or Mormons, and even those that were left in sea. You, his messengers the angels, shall gather the spiritual seed of Lord Jesus from tribes of former Israel and from all tribes, nations and tongues. They shall be gathered unto Jerusalem above where we, his messengers were, after he called us and before the enemy cast us down. In that day, an ensign shall be lifted up on Jerusalem above for all the denominations and sects of Christendom,[17] and the glory of God shall be seen on her[18] and all the people that were leftover in the denominations and sects of the Christendom the Earth shall no more prevent his people as they are doing now by keeping them as captives with their teachings. For in that day, they shall be in great fear of you and they shall lay their hands on their mouths. As written, "They shall lick the dust like a serpent, they shall move out of their holes like worms of the earth: they shall be afraid of the LORD our God, and shall fear because of thee."[19] So fear them not, for in that day they will serve you and lick the dust of your feet. And Father shall lift his hand to gather his people as spoken by the prophet: "it shall come to pass in that day, that the Lord shall set his hand again the second time to recover the remnant of his people, which shall be left, from Assyria, and from Egypt, and from Pathros, and from Cush, and from Elam, and from Shinar, and from Hamath, and from the islands of the sea."[20] All of them shall come to Jerusalem above to worship before their God as spoken by the prophets, "the redeemed of the LORD shall return, and come with singing unto Zion; and everlasting joy shall be upon their head: they shall obtain gladness and joy"[21] *and* "it shall come to pass in that day, that the great trumpet shall be blown, and they shall come which were ready to perish in the land of Assyria, and the outcasts in the land of Egypt, and shall worship the LORD in the holy mount at Jerusalem."[22] For you, his messengers the angels, will go forth to gather all the remnant of his elect to Jesus Christ our Lord. In that time, great and terrible wrath of God will be on all the Christendom; it will be covered with darkness, and gross darkness will cover all these denominations and sects that were in Christendom, for he said he will pour wrath upon them such as they never heard. But upon Jerusalem his glory will be seen, and you messengers will go and bring his elect the seed of Jesus Christ the Israel to Jerusalem to their God. As also written in the Revelation of Jesus Christ, many from all tribes of the former Israel were sealed by receiving the Gospel, after that, threshing of wheat will begin and innumerable people from all nations and tribes will be gathered before the throne of God, which will worship him in his temple, as our Lord said he will send his messengers and they shall gather the elect the wheat to his barn. As our God also said "Behold, I will send for many fishers, saith the LORD, and they shall fish them; and after will I send for many hunters, and they shall hunt them from every mountain, and from every hill, and out of the holes of the rocks. For mine eyes are upon all their ways: they are not hid from my face, neither is their iniquity hid from mine eyes."[23]

Our Lord also said after sun and moon will be darkened and stars will fall to the ground, his sign will appear in heaven, and then all denominations and sects will wail because of him. For in that day all false christs and false gospels will perish and our Lord will be preached. The Son of Man will be like lighting in heaven that shines from one end of heaven to another end, from east to west, and his messengers will gather all his elect to Jerusalem above where we his witnesses were after he called us and before the enemy overcame us and cast us down. They will gather all of them to Jerusalem unto Jesus Christ, and the Lord Jesus himself shall feed them on the way, as spoken by the prophets, "Then the remnant of his brethren shall return unto the children of Israel. And he shall stand and feed in the strength of the LORD, in the majesty of the name of the LORD his God."[24] Lord Jesus will lead them to the living fountains of waters, even to God, and God shall wipe away all tears from their eyes, for at that time in those days God will swallow up death as spoken by the prophet: "He will swallow up death in victory; and the Lord GOD will wipe away tears from off all faces; and the rebuke of his people shall he take away from off all the earth: for the LORD hath spoken it."[25] The dead in Christ shall rise incorruptible, all the prophets, saints from the beginning of the world, saints both small and great will rise incorruptible. All his people that will be raised at that time will be clothed with immortal bodies, and all they that are alive will be caught up together with them in the clouds, to meet the Lord in the air. But exact year and the month God only knows. Thus they will enter into wedding banquet with him to the marriage and the door will be shut, for it is the hour of the marriage supper of Lamb. As spoken by the prophets, "awake and sing, ye that dwell in dust: for thy dew is as the dew of herbs, and the earth shall cast out the dead. Come, my people, enter thou into thy chambers, and shut thy doors about thee: hide thyself as it were for a little moment, until the indignation be overpast."[26] I testify to you before the living God, these sayings are faithful and true, and he sent me to show you his servants these things that shall soon take place.

Now Jerusalem is alone, desolate, having lost her children as captives moving to and fro, for she lost her children as they went into captivity among the heathen of the denominations and sects of the Christendom the Earth. She went on and became wilderness, and remnant of her children who keep the commandments of God, who kept the testimony of Jesus, who were of the understanding, were overcome by the Beast and spiritually slain and carried into captivity. Now our God will turn away her captivity. They that have understanding among his people, who were the two witnesses, the olive trees, the candlesticks whom the Beast overcame and spiritually killed, shall live and go there to the place where they were after God called them to the fellowship of his Son at the time of their conversion. But the Beast overcame them through its Ecclesiastical host the spiritual armies and cast them down as Daniel mentioned, "it waxed great, even to the host of heaven; and it cast down of the host and of the stars to the ground, and stamped upon them."[27] And they who knew their God and had an understanding among his people, who were two olives and candlesticks which witnessed after their conversion, but were overcome by the beast and were cast down from there, they shall ascend again to Jerusalem above, as also mentioned by the prophet, "saviours shall come up on mount Zion to judge the mount of Esau, and the kingdom shall be the Lord's."[28] And they shall be sent to reap, and they will first reap the tares and gather them in bundles to burn. After that, they will gather the remnant of his elect to Jerusalem. In that day, after Lord Jesus fights with all the spiritual armies of denominations and sects with the double-edged sword that comes out of his mouth, and the word of God slays them all,[29] his sign shall appear in Jerusalem and they will go and gather the wheat to his barn. And innumerable people shall be gathered, and Jerusalem above that was desolate and had lost her children from many centuries shall suddenly[30] have many children, as said by the prophet: "your waste and desolate places and your destroyed land Surely now you will be too cramped for the inhabitants, the children of whom you were bereaved will yet say in your ears, 'The place is too cramped for me; Make room for me that I may live here.'"[31]

For as the prophets said, God will have mercy on his afflicted people, he will be merciful unto his land, even unto Jerusalem above; his messengers will gather his elect, the wheat the children of the kingdom who were innumerable people from all the earth and sea, from all nations and tribes, and at that time many from all the tribes of former Israel shall receive Gospel, as mentioned in book of Revelation of Jesus Christ. Innumerable people that were now scattered in the Christendom shall come from great tribulation. For they are spiritually afflicted with hunger, thirst, and are painfully annoyed and dispirited like sheep without a shepherd, living under subjection to beggarly elements of the world. They lived in these times of great tribulation, and the providence of God saved them from being deceived by the false prophet, the spiritual host of the Beast, who were making all those dwell in the Christendom to worship the Beast, to worship his image and receive his mark. Even for these people's sake, God will reduce these days so that they might not be carried away in the flood of deception that is on Christendom the Earth. As prophets foretold these are the spiritual seed of Jesus Christ that were perishing in Christendom the Earth, being scattered among spiritual heathen of various denominations and sects as exiles and captives, shall come back to Zion, as written, "it shall come to pass in that day, that the LORD shall beat off from the channel of the river unto the stream of Egypt, and ye shall be gathered one by one, O ye children of Israel. And it shall come to pass in that day, that the great trumpet shall be blown, and they shall come which were ready to perish in the land of Assyria, and the outcasts in the land of Egypt, and shall worship the LORD in the holy mount at Jerusalem,"[32] *and* "the redeemed of the LORD shall return, and come with singing unto Zion; and everlasting joy shall be upon their head: they shall obtain gladness and joy, and sorrow and mourning shall flee away."[33] *Also*: "from heaven did the LORD behold the earth; To hear the groaning of the prisoner; to loose those that are appointed to death; To declare the name of the LORD in Zion, and his praise in Jerusalem."[34]

This Jerusalem above is our Spiritual place where our fathers in Christ dwelt. When our forefathers were in the world like us in the past, God sent apostles and evangelists and rescued them from the kingdom of darkness where they walked fulfilling the desires of flesh and mind according to the course of this world, according to the ruler of the authority of the air, the spirit that rules the world by means of fear of death. But merciful God, even our Father sent apostles and evangelists, and they proclaimed his glory and brought them to Jerusalem above to his holy hill to his kingdom in light, upon which he set his Son as king, as he said: "I set my king upon my holy hill."[35] Apostle Paul was also one such that was sent; he was chosen for that, according to which was foretold by God: "I will send those that escape of them unto the nations, to Tarshish, Pul, and Lud, that draw the bow, to Tubal, and Javan, to the isles afar off, that have not heard my fame, neither have seen my glory; and they shall declare my glory among the Gentiles. And they shall bring all your brethren for an offering unto the LORD out of all nations upon horses, and in chariots, and in litters, and upon mules, and upon swift beasts, to my holy mountain Jerusalem, saith the LORD, as the children of Israel bring an offering in a clean vessel into the house of the LORD. And I will also take of them for priests and for Levites, saith the LORD."[36] Therefore Paul wrote, "the grace that is given to me of God, That I should be the minister of Jesus Christ to the Gentiles, ministering the gospel of God, that the offering up of the Gentiles might be acceptable, being sanctified by the Holy Ghost."[37] For Paul was sent to gentiles that were far, that never heard Gospel of the glory of God.[38] In certain city called Corinth, the Lord said to him he has many people, as they went to preach glory of God, all those who were appointed to eternal life in the next age believed in God who raised Lord Jesus from death. They were all brought to Jerusalem above as offerings in clean vessels into the temple of God being sanctified by the Holy Ghost. These are called as dwellers of heaven, and their citizenship is in heaven, from whence also they look for the Savior, the Lord Jesus Christ. For God translated us to the kingdom of his Son, even to the kingdom of Heaven; we are children of Jerusalem above. And this Holy hill is not the physical mountain that can be seen by natural eye or touched with hands. For the Gospel didn't come unto us in word only but in strength, and in the Holy Ghost, and in much assurance; for we through Eternal Spirit, who transcends the time and space, have seen the days of the Son of Man as if we were with the twelve disciples of our Lord Jesus, as if our hands handled the Son of Man. And God has called us through hearing of the Gospel, and we went to Mount Zion and unto the city of the living God, the heavenly Jerusalem to his fellowship and presence, into his marvelous light and rejoiced with an inexpressible and glorious joy. But our enemies cast us down from our dwelling place. Now being fallen from grace and spiritually dead where our Lord is crucified unto us, we long to see one of the days of the Son of Man again, in which we were in the fellowship and in presence of our Father, when we remained with him in his marvelous light in Jerusalem above.

But now God will set the kingdom of Heaven forever, for from past 1,300 years the enemy was casting down the host of heaven to the ground and exalted himself against their prince the Anointed of God, as complained by Psalmist: "Thou hast broken down all his hedges; thou hast brought his strongholds to ruin. All that pass by the way spoil him: Thou hast set up the right hand of his adversaries; thou hast made all his enemies to rejoice. where are thy former lovingkindnesses, which thou swarest unto David in thy truth?"[39] For Lord Jesus is the prince of all saints that dwelt in Heaven in Jerusalem above, for he is the shepherd and prince of all Israel of God from all nations and tribes, and he was called as David figuratively in scriptures. God said to Lord Jesus he must rule his people in the midst of his enemies: "Sit at my right hand, rule in the midst of your enemies, until I make your enemies your footstool."[40] Therefore the Apostle wrote, "he must reign until he has put all his enemies under his feet. And last enemy to be destroyed is death."[41] But God's anger fell on the kingdom of Heaven because of the iniquity of us and our fathers who have forsaken the truth of the Gospel and gone after other gospels and other gods, and they didn't remain in the Father and Son. Therefore their God delivered them to the hand of their enemies. But now God will set the kingdom of Heaven forever, as spoken by Daniel the prophet, "And in the days of these kings shall the God of heaven set up a kingdom, which shall never be destroyed: and the kingdom shall not be left to other people, but it shall break in pieces and consume all these kingdoms, and it shall stand forever. Forasmuch as thou sawest that the stone was cut out of the mountain without hands, and that it brake in pieces the iron, the brass, the clay, the silver, and the gold."[42] Now that Great God says to Jesus Christ the Israel whom he upholds, and to you, his seed, "Fear not, thou worm Jacob, and ye men of Israel; I will help thee, saith the LORD, and thy redeemer, the Holy One of Israel. Behold, I will make thee a new sharp threshing instrument having teeth: thou shalt thresh the mountains, and beat them small, and shalt make the hills as chaff. Thou shalt fan them, and the wind shall carry them away, and the whirlwind shall scatter them: and thou shalt rejoice in the LORD, and shalt glory in the Holy One of Israel."[43]

Now in these days, in this generation, God will set the kingdom of heaven forever, for it is time to be gracious to her, for the appointed time has come. He will arise and have compassion on her. He will avenge the blood of his servants, render vengeance to his adversaries, and be merciful unto his land and to his people. As Daniel has said, stone smote the image upon his feet that were of iron and clay, and it will break them to pieces. In this generation, God will turn away spiritual captivity of those who were two olives and candlesticks, they of the understanding among his people. He brings you back to his holy hill, to Jerusalem above, and will set the kingdom of Heaven forever. This spiritual kingdom of God will smite feet and ten toes; these ten toes are Protestant denominations that grew out of these Western nations who gave their strength and authority to the Barbarian. Therefore, fear not brethren, you men of Israel, Father will help you. Before she was in labor, she gave birth; before her pain came upon her, she delivered a son. Who has heard such a thing? Who has seen such things? Shall an Earth be made to bring forth in one day? Shall a nation be brought forth in one moment? For as soon as Zion was in labor, she brought forth her children. The kingdom that God is going to set up will never be destroyed and shall not be left for other people. It shall break in pieces and consume all those kingdoms, and it shall stand forever. After the stone smote the image, it has become a Great and High Mountain and filled whole earth. As God foretold through his prophets,

"Enlarge the place of thy tent, and let them stretch forth the curtains of thine habitations: spare not, lengthen thy cords, and strengthen thy stakes; For thou shalt break forth on the right hand and on the left, and thy seed shall inherit the Gentiles, and make the desolate cities to be inhabited."[44] And as written, "Thou hast increased the nation, O Lord, thou hast increased the nation: thou art glorified: thou hadst removed it far unto all the ends of the earth."[45] For pretty soon God will punish our Lord's enemies, and Christendom will be covered with Darkness and the Jerusalem above will have light. Kingdoms of Earth will come to her light, and multitude of sea will be converted unto her, and her seed will be brought back to her, as spoken by prophets: "Lift up thine eyes round about, and see: all they gather themselves together, they come to thee: thy sons shall come from far, and thy daughters shall be nursed at thy side. Then thou shalt see, and flow together, and thine heart shall fear, and be enlarged; because the abundance of the sea shall be converted unto thee, the forces of the Gentiles shall come unto thee."[46]

When our God takes vengeance on his enemies and punishes the inhabitants of Christendom, when he destroys the Beast and the false prophet, our God will also punish the Satan, that old dragon that deceives the whole world, the ruler of the authority of the air the spirit that rules the humans by means of fear of death, through desires and lusts of mind and body. He will punish the Satan who was angry with his people and persecuted them, the Satan that made war with his witnesses and saints, the Satan used the Beast (also the whore) and spiritually killed these who had the testimony of Jesus and kept the commandments of God, the two olive trees and lampstands. He will punish the old serpent as said by prophet, "In that day the LORD with his sore and great and strong sword shall punish leviathan the piercing serpent, even leviathan that crooked serpent; and he shall slay the dragon that is in the sea."[47] For Satan initiates violence against those who seek to open the eyes of people to turn them from darkness to light of eternal life through testimony of Jesus and from the authority of Satan unto God. Satan initiated violence against apostles who were sent to declare our God's glory among those that never heard about him, to bring people from the kingdom of Satan. But now our God will punish Satan and shall take away his authority, and the multitude of the sea shall be converted to Jerusalem above[48] and the kingdom of the world will become our God's and our Lord's. Moreover, Satan and his messengers deceive all these nations of the earth, even these denominations, and sects; they oppose the truth and fill the Christendom with lies, devils, falsehoods, false gospels, gods and christs. Satan initiates the rebellion against God and Christ and a spiritual violence against the saints by these denominations and sects of Christendom. He takes people captive to false teaching and lies to do his will as spoken by the apostle.[49] But after the battle of the great day of God Almighty, Satan will be caught and will be chained, so that he may no longer deceive those who will be left in these denominations and sects. As written in the book of Revelation, Satan was caught and a seal set on Satan so that he will no longer deceive these denominations and sects; when Satan comes to deceive them, he will be identified. Satan will be in the bottomless pit, in migration, wandering from one place to other in all the Christendom, without a place for a foothold among the nations of Earth, even the denominations and sects of the Christendom, to deceive and establish himself there.

After you, his messengers, speak all things God gives to you, thus executing God's judgments on Christendom the Earth, then Beast and false prophet and denominations and sects of Christendom and their host of preachers, pastors, bishops, theologians, etc, will be gathered together to make war against the true Jesus Christ and them that were with him. At that time, their false religion, their heaven, will be rolled out like scroll; all the host of preachers, pastors, bishops, theologians, etc, will fall to the ground being slain by the double edged sword that comes out of mouth of our Lord. And God's wrath will be revealed to them from Heaven, even from Jerusalem above. Lord Jesus will send his messengers to gather his elect, and they will all be gathered unto him, and Lord Jesus will teach them and will lead them to Father. The Father will wipe all their tears and swallow up death, and the dead in Christ shall rise incorruptible. Those who from the past 1,300 years were killed for the word of God and testimony of Jesus, all those who were of understanding, two olive trees and candlesticks, who had testimony of Jesus and kept commandments of God, but overcame and spiritually got killed and taken into captivity, their souls will live; they will also partake in this first resurrection. And all his people who will be alive at that time will be clothed with immortal bodies, and will be caught up together with them in the clouds, to meet the Lord in the air. He will take them to his Father's house in Heaven, and they shall be with the Lord forever, as he said, "In my Father's house are many mansions:

if it were not so, I would have told you. I go to prepare a place for you. And if I go and prepare a place for you, I will come again, and receive you unto myself; that where I am, there ye may be also." [50] Thus you will enter into Marriage Ceremony with him to the marriage and the door will be shut, for it is the marriage supper of the Lamb.

REFERENCES:

1. Revelation 18:11;
2. Isaiah 24:16-21; Revelation 6:15-17;
3. Micah 4:8;
4. Isaiah 11:11; 49:22; 60:4; 27:12; Matthew 13:30; 24:31; Revelation 7:3-12;
5. Ezekiel 30:28;
6. Isaiah 27:12;
7. Ezekiel 37:26; Isaiah 54:10;
8. Ezekiel 39:29;
9. Isaiah 54:9-10;
10. Isaiah 13:13-14; 24:20-21: 2:21-22; Revelation 6:14; 11:19; 16:20;
11. Revelation 16:19; Isaiah 30:25; Michah7:12;
12. Joel 3:16;
13. Isaiah 30:4;
14. Revelation 6:16; Isaiah 2:21; 13:9;
15. 1 Thessalonians 5:3;
16. Isaiah 11:11; Hosea 11:11;
17. Isaiah 11:12 &10; 49:22; Matthew 24:30; Luke 17:24;
18. Isaiah 60:2;
19. Micah 7:17;
20. Isaiah 11:11;
21. Isaiah 51:11;
22. Isaiah 27:13;
23. Micah 5:15; Jeremiah 16:16-17; Revelation 7:9-11;
24. Micah 5:3-4;
25. Isaiah 25:8;
26. Isaiah 26:19-20;
27. Daniel 8:10;
28. Obadiah 1:21;

29. Isaiah 24:21; 34:5; Matthew 24:29; Revelation 19:21;
30. Isaiah 66:8;
31. Isaiah 49:19-20;
32. Isaiah 27:12-13;
33. Isaiah 51:11;
34. Psalms 102:19-21;
35. Psalms 2:6;
36. Isaiah 66:19-21;
37. Romans 15:16;
38. Acts 22:21; 18:10;
39. Psalms 89:40-41;
40. Psalms 110:1;
41. 1 Corinthians 15:25-26;
42. Daniel 2:44-45;
43. Isaiah 41:14-16;
44. Isaiah 54:2-3; Zephaniah 3:19-20;
45. Isaiah 26:15;
46. Isaiah 60:4-5;
47. Isaiah 27:1; Revelation 20:1-3;
48. Isaiah 60:5;
49. 2 Timothy 2:26;
50. John 14:2-3;

SECTION FOUR:
BOOK OF PROPHECY

CHAPTER SEVEN

The Revelation of Jesus Christ

The Book of Revelation is about the revelation God gave to Lord Jesus to show his servants at the time of end about the things that must soon take place. He sends his messenger the angel just before the last trumpet and signified it by him unto his servant John. Nevertheless, Lord Jesus showed John all the things that were at the time of John and the things that shall come after that period along with the time until the end. John was in Spirit who transcends time and space and he was carried into future and went back and forth in future. We know from the book of Daniel that Daniel was asked to seal the prophecy which was revealed to him in the last vision he got, which, was noted in last three chapters of his book, and this is that background of that vision. Daniel in those days set his heart to understand the vision he saw about the He-goat and Ram. In those days Daniel mourned three full weeks. He ate no pleasant bread, neither came flesh nor wine in his mouth, neither did he anoint himself at all, till three whole weeks were fulfilled. And a messenger was sent to him to make him understand the vision. After revealing those things Daniel was instructed to seal it until the time of End.[1]

Now the things written in Book of Revelation are not about just a revelation about things that will happen in the unknown distant future, as many wicked dogs that teach futurism and dispensationalism affirm. These are the most insane heretics and ingrafters of heretical perversity. These scoundrels don't know anything but deceive many and seek to rob the scripture of truth from servants of Lord Jesus, there are so many workers of iniquity in the Christendom and it is filled with such people who seek to destroy the truth of the prophecy and rob it from servants of God, as written, "The wicked walk on every side, when the vilest men are exalted."[2] No denomination and sect are exempt. There are liars of historicism, surely each one of these lying sects passover the Barbarian, and speak that the church of Rome, or papacy, or some other is the Beast. Also, there are scandalous preterist pigs, these mad senseless fools and mockers teach prophecy of the book were fulfilled in 70 AD, and there are blind guides which say it is not a book of prophecy at all. And there are so many evil theories, which Satan planted from the beginning, even from the second century to deceive people. All these insane liars, deceivers and wicked workers of iniquity will soon get the punishment due for their teachings, which were the works of iniquity.

But the things written in the book of Revelation are about things that were present at the time John was, in the first century, and all things that shall come to pass, one after another, along the way until the end of this present age. Also, the things that shall come to pass in the coming age, and things that will be in that age that shall come after the coming age, in which New heavens and earth were created, as Lord said unto John, "Write the things which thou hast seen, and the things which are, and the things which shall be hereafter;"[3] It was also said to John at the beginning of the book, *"I will show you things which must be hereafter."*[4] As written, Lord Jesus himself directly showed these things to John. The things that are from John's time to almost end of this age, and at the time when the end is near, John was asked to receive the little scroll opened from a messenger who came at that time. The things that were written in the book of Revelation are about things that happened from that time of John in the first century, and all the things happened along the way until the end of this present age, and also things that shall come to pass after the end of this age and the things that will happen in the coming age, and things will be in that eternal age in which new heaven and earth were created and the extinction of the sea. But at the end of the Sixth trumpet, and before last trumpet, Lord Jesus will send his angel as written in Chapter ten and that angel will show John *(for John was in Spirit carried unto our time)* the things that must shortly come to pass at that time, as also written at the beginning of the book, "The Revelation of Jesus Christ, which God gave unto him, to shew unto his servants things which must shortly come to pass; and he sent and signified it by his angel unto his servant John:"[5]

Now John saw in God's hand a scroll sealed with seven seals written within and on the back side, and there was found no man worthy to open the scroll and read it. No man, saint, prophet, or apostle was found able to unseal to seals of the scroll, surely none not even among the dead. But Lord Jesus was only found worthy and prevailed to open the seals, and all of these mysteries are revealed to the Lord Jesus, by God his Father. Now when Lord opens the six seals of the scroll, a brief summary of things that will come to pass from the time of John to time of the end of this age are revealed. It was a brief summary of things that shall come to pass until the time of harvest, which shall take place at the time of the end of this age. When he opened the first seal, it was about the saints who went ahead preaching gospel, conquering new dry land out of the sea, and establishing new churches and adding people to it. All these pockets of land which shall later become Christendom and was called as Earth, after this time period of spiritual prosperity and growth, the peace was taken out of the earth; people in Christendom started hating one another. After this time period there came spiritual famine, and after this time period there came a spiritual death through fighting with one another, through famine, through false teachers the beasts of Earth, and through the spread of evil teachings. After this period the spiritual death of saints started, a long time of sorrows, and they were killed for a long time and it was said them it shall continue for some more time. This is a very long period therefore they cried, *"how long?"* After this, when he opens the sixth seal, the harvest of earth will take place, for it is the Great day of wrath of God upon all the kingdoms of Earth the denominations and sects of Christendom the Earth, their light of religion the heaven will be rolled, he will avenge his saints on dwellers of Christendom the earth, this is the first phase of harvest. His messengers shall gather tares the weed and throw them in what is spiritually called fire as spoken by Lord in a parable. After this they will gather his elect from the four winds from the ends of the earth, and from one end of the heaven to the other end, as noted in the seventh chapter of the book.

After this, when Lord Jesus opens the final seal, Seven trumpets are blown, and again, the sequence of God's Judgment the woes, one after another, throughout these centuries shall come upon Christendom the earth from the sixth century until time of end of this age. These were revealed to John, and John notes down and prophesied all those things that shall come to pass from the sixth century. But, just before the end of the sixth trumpet and before the beginning of the seventh trumpet, John saw an angel came down from heaven, and this messenger had a little Book opened in his hand, and the face of the messenger was as if it were sun.[6] Mind the feet of the angel were like the pillars of fire, the feet on which he stood appeared to John like pillars of scripture the word of God. And these things show way to those that dwell in the Christendom the Earth and also to those that were in sea of other religions. For God said he will make his Judgment for a light unto people and inhabitants of world will learn righteousness, and God is known by the judgment, which he executes. John saw this messenger at the end of the sixth trumpet and just before the beginning of the seventh trumpet, and before harvest at the end of this age. John was asked to take the little scroll from his hand, John did receive it and was told to John he must prophesy again, and then John prophesied the things which he received from the messenger in the subsequent chapters of the book of Revelation. This angel is also the third angel mentioned in Chapter fourteen of the book and Martin Luther being the second angel, for until this messenger comes, the mystery of iniquity and other mysteries are hidden from men. Moreover, the angel said to Daniel about the last two chapters of his book, seal and shut up the words until the end. But these things were made known unto this messenger by Lord Jesus. This is the messenger that signified the things that must shortly come to pass to John just before the end as stated at the beginning of book of Revelation and also as stated at the end of the book of Revelation," the Lord God of the holy prophets sent his angel to shew unto his servants the things which must shortly be done."[7] and after this messenger speaks those mysteries just before the beginning of the seventh trumpet at end of this age before harvest, those mysteries will no longer be sealed to the servants of God, as written in end of the book of Revelation, "Seal not the sayings of the prophecy of this book: for the time is at hand." For they must be sealed until the end,[8] and in the time of harvest, Lord Jesus will send his mighty messengers the reapers,[9] and they shall gather together all the tares the weeds[10] by pouring the vials of wrath on Christendom the Earth. I "Jonathan Bijja Charles Spurgeon" who wrote this book testify you before the living God that I am this messenger and scriptures testify about me,[11] He sent me to show unto you his servants the things which must shortly be done. I am that angel sent by Lord Jesus that signified to John about the things which must shortly come to pass. I am writing these things that you might know about the things happened in the past, things that are now and importantly the things that soon shall be done. After I utter my voice and speak these things, even these things that were written in this book, which I need to speak in these days, the days of the last trumpet, even the seventh trumpet will begin. At that time Lord Jesus will send his angels to reap, they will first gather together wicked and cast them in lake of fire, and then the sign of the Son of Man will appear in heaven, and then all the tribes of the earth will mourn. And they will see the Son of Man coming on the clouds of heaven, with power and great glory. It shall be well with those that seek their God who hid his face from them, he shall be merciful unto you, and your hearts shall live.[12] I didn't come to speak these things on my own, but they whom you say our God and our Lord, Even God, and Lord Jesus has sent me to speak these things to the servants of Lord Jesus. The very things that I wrote in this book itself testify that God and Lord Jesus have sent me. Therefore he who refuses to obey my voice and speak against the things written in this book will receive his punishment from God.

Now John was in Spirit who is transcendent of time, he came into the future and went forward and backward in the future along with one of the messengers who were reapers.[13] After the pouring of the seven vials of wrath at the end of age to gather the tares, one of the Angels carries John, who was in Spirit, backwards into the times of Dark ages, and has shown him things from the time of dark ages and shows John, a woman riding the Beast, and after that John was shown Martin Luther who was also a messenger that came with great authority, whose glory has lightened the Christendom the Earth.[14] After that he was shown the judgment that will come upon the whore, when God remembers her sin at the time of the seventh vial, after that John saw the hour of Marriage supper of Jesus. And again, John wrote that the things happen after the sixth vial is poured and the end of this age. And then first resurrection and the coming age and its end, and second, resurrection and new heaven and the new earth which stay forever and the new Jerusalem that is going to come out of heaven from God.

Now in the Book of Revelation, the things that shall happen along with the time until Harvest at the end of this age were shown and prophesied four times. The first time the quick summary and brief overview of the sequence of things that shall happen, one after another all this time period, even from the first century until the harvest at the end of this present age was shown by opening six seals of the scroll. And after opening of the sixth seal, the punishment to tares, the wicked was shown, how God's anger will come on these Kingdoms of Earth, even these denominations and sects of the Christendom, over both small and great that dwell in Christendom the earth, on the great day of his anger and how the lights of their religion were taken away, and how all their spiritual starry host of preachers, pastors, evangelists, bishops, theologians etc shall fall to the ground was revealed. After the end of the harvest of tares, at the time of angels ready to hurt Christendom and Sea, it was revealed that many from tribes of Israel were sealed by receiving the faith of the Gospel, and an innumerable number of his people, the elect the spiritual seed of Jesus Christ the Israel from all tongues, kindred and nations were gathered from four winds of heaven. From the ends of the Earth and heaven, they came from great tribulation, for whose sake God reduces these days.

For the second time, again it was shown the overview of the sequence of things that shall happen one after another all this time period, even from the sixth century until the harvest at the end of this present age was shown by opening the seventh seal of the scroll in which seven trumpets were blown. When the fifth trumpet was blown it was shown the end of migration period the bottomless pit for many Germanic tribes in Europe, the barbarians come upon Christendom the earth, and John wrote their kingdom's name is the Destroyer, for he shall destroy the mighty and holy people. And the things that shall happen during the days of the voice of the sixth angel were explained and it is shown that it is very long period in those times that the saints are defeated and spiritually killed by the Beast, and 1260 years the holy city will be trodden under foot by the heathen, It was also made known the devastation in Christendom caused by the Pentecostal and charismatic, and the rest of Christians repent not and continue in their wickedness.[15] But, in the days of the voice of the angel of the seventh trumpet, the end of this age will come and God's anger shall come upon the nations of the earth, even over the denominations and sects of the Christendom, in the days of the voice of the seventh angel the temple of the ark of his testament, the temple in heaven will be opened and the many mighty messengers of the Lord Jesus, even those seven angels with vials of wrath shall do the harvest and gather all wicked tares together to be punished on the great day of the Wrath of God Almighty.

For the third time, again it was shown the overview of the sequence of things that shall happen all this time period, from the first century until the time of Abomination that makes desolation, which happened in our times. This was shown in the twelfth and thirteenth chapters of the book of Revelation. John saw the kingdom of heaven coming with power, how saints overcame Satan and his messengers; he saw how the dragon persecuted the woman and how Satan had instigated the pagans in Roman empire against them, like a flood against the woman, but how Christendom opened her mouth and swallowed up all the flood of ungodly pagan people into itself which Satan send against the woman. He saw woman fleeing into the wilderness away from the wrath of the serpent. He saw how the Dragon, the old serpent, the Satan, was angry with woman and went to fight against the remaining seed of the woman who have testimony of Jesus. And John saw the beast coming out of the sea, and said it continues in power for 1260 years and he saw the dominion and great authority of beast among the nations of world, he saw its ten horns the Protestant denominations were in authority like kingdoms; he saw how those that dwell in the Christendom worshipped the Beast, saying, "Who is like Beast, who is able to make war with these western nations?" and how Christians worshipped Satan, by saying God gave the Beast that authority and strength. He spoke about the defeat of saints in the hands of Beast, John saw the second beast coming out of Christendom, even false prophets doing signs and miracles and deceiving those that dwell in Christendom, He saw the image of the Beast even the abomination that makes desolate, which was set up in our times.

For the Fourth time, again it was shown the quick summary and brief overview of the sequence of things that shall happen one after another all this time period, even from the beginning to the harvest at the end of this present age was revealed in chapter fourteen of the book of Revelation, John saw those men who were not defiled their clothes standing upon mount Zion and they have not defiled themselves with spiritual fornication with churches nor they spoke falsehoods. After that he saw three messengers followed by another, the first one warns those dwell in the Christendom about the judgment that is coming on the Christendom. The second messenger cries against Babylon, that it was spiritually fallen and an apostate, which made denominations and sects of the Christendom to be drunken with her teaching of superstitions, extra merit works, this teaching the wine was the product of wrath produced in their conscience by law because of their spiritual fornication. And the third messenger shall follow them and he shall cry against the Beast that carried the whore throughout the dark ages, and against his image and mark. He is that messenger mentioned in chapter ten of the book of Revelation. After that, many in Christendom shall be reaped; for the instructors of the people will come. And the harvest of the wicked of Christendom shall take place and they shall be gathered together by his messengers for the great day of the wrath of God Almighty.

John also saw quickly the sequence of things that shall happen in all that time period, from the time of dark ages, and it was revealed in chapters seventeen, eighteen, and nineteen of the book of Revelation. One of the messengers who poured seven vials of wrath on Christendom and gathered the tares together has carried John back in time to times of dark ages, and has shown the beast even the nations of the

Barbarian carrying a woman, even the Church of Rome the papacy. He showed John the mystery of the Beast and its horns which have not become Kingdoms (denominations) yet, at that point of time, and showed him the mystery of the woman, that ruled over the denominations and sects of the Christendom which were spiritually called as kings of Earth. After these, John saw a messenger even Luther who cried against the whore, calling, "It is spiritually fallen and is become the habitation of devils, and the hold of every foul spirit, and a cage of every unclean and hateful bird."[16] He spoke against her wine which is her teaching, her teachings of appeasement, extra merit works, relics, superstitions, indulgence, vigils, celibacy, ascetic, monkery, etc. are the result of the wrath produced in them by the law, because they fornicate themselves with another gospel and another christ. After this, John goes forward into the future, into the end of this age to the time of the harvest of tares and weeds. At that time of the seventh vial, when God remembers the iniquity of the whore, even the Church of Rome and saw the Judgment of God on the whore, and saw how God avenged the blood of his servants at her hand, and after that he saw the hour of marriage, the supper of lamb come, and after that again John goes backward to the time of the sixth vial and saw the punishment on the wicked the tares which were gathered together by pouring vials of wrath for the great day of God Almighty. After that, in the twentieth chapter, he saw the binding of Satan by one of the messengers, and the first resurrection.

In the book of Revelation, it was shown how the Harvest will take place and how the tares are gathered together by the reapers, even by the messengers whom Lord Jesus will send to reap. The first phase of the harvest, which is gathering of tares and weeds, was written clearly in chapter sixteen of the book. It will be how the messengers of Lord Jesus pour those vials upon Christendom the earth and gather the wicked together. And the second phase of Harvest, the gathering of wheat, was mentioned in the seventh chapter of the book of Revelation, that many people from the tribes of former Israel will be sealed by receiving of Gospel and all the remnant of the elect from all nations, kindreds, and tongues were gathered by his messengers.

And in the book of Revelation, it is written of four Spiritual battles in various chapters. These four battles between Satan and his associates against the saints were shown and prophesied in the Book of Revelation. The first battle happened in the first century, and saints overcame Satan and his messengers, and the second battle happened after beast came and the saints were defeated by him for 1260 years. The third battle takes place at the end of this age, at the time of the harvest of tares and weeds on the Great day of wrath of God Almighty, and enemies of saints will be destroyed. Again, a fourth battle takes place at the end of coming age after Satan will be loosed from prison, after that battle Satan will be thrown in lake of Fire forever.

And a very quick summary and brief overview of the sequence of things that shall happen one after another in the coming age, from the beginning of that age to the end of that age as was shown in the twentieth chapter of the book of Revelation, the things that shall be after the harvest of wicked and the end of this age were shown and prophesied. John saw one messenger who came with a great chain and bound Satan such a long time a thousand years and set a seal upon him, that he no longer deceive those that dwell in Christendom. The first resurrection in which dead in Christ will rise and reign of saints with Christ for thousand years, which is 360,000 days. Remember the beast only rules for 1260 days, starting from 800 AD to 2040's. Jesus Christ our Lord, and those who partake in the first resurrection, will reign over all nations of Earth, even all denominations and sects that will be in Christendom the Earth. For that Great God even Father of our Lord must inherit nations of Earth, he will give heathen to Lord Jesus as possession and he will rule them with a rod of iron, and Saints will receive authority from Lord Jesus. The stone that smote the image shall become Great and High Mountain and will be established on the top of the sects of Christendom, and will be exalted above all mountains of Earth and all nations shall flow unto it. Lord Jesus shall judge the poor with righteousness, and reprove with equity for the meek of the Christendom, and he shall smite the Christendom with the rod of his mouth, and with the breath of his lips shall he slay the wicked. And after thousand years finishes, the Satan will be loosed from his prison for a little season. He will go to deceive the sects that will be in the Christendom, and to deceive the nations of Earth that are at the four corners of the earth. They will come with all weaponry needed for spiritual battle with a great number of spiritual hosts. Like the spiritual host of beast in the past, this host will go there to cast them down, these evil people come to take prey and plunder to lead saints into spiritual captivity, to destroy the spiritual seed of Jesus Christ the Israel whom God has Chosen, to destroy saints who are living in God their Father's fellowship without any fear, in safety, in their Father's kingdom, without battle horses of doctrines, without chariots of theologies, without catechisms, confessions, etc. But God saves the saints and fire from God, the word of God out of Jerusalem above will devour them and Satan will be cast into the lake of fire. In the past their God hid his face from them because of their evil doings and delivered them to the hand of their enemies, but from a little time now he will never hide his face from them. The last and fourth battle the final attempt of Satan against the Saints at the end of the coming age will end in failure as prophesied by prophets, Satan will be cast into the lake of fire. The judgment of all the dead will take place; they will be judged according to their works, all those whose names were not written in book of life will be cast in lake of fire, death and hell will be cast in Lake of fire. This is the second death, as the Lord said in the parable of sheep and goats; nations who were kind toward children of God and done good to them as spoken in parable, being received blessing of forgiveness shall enter into eternal life.

In the Last two chapters of the book of Revelation, were written about the age that is going to come after the next age, and this age remains forever. As God said, "the new heavens and the new earth, which I will make, shall remain before me, saith the LORD,"[17] There shall be no more sea, and there shall be no more death. God creates new Heaven and Earth, so there will be three places for men, one in Heaven, another is Earth, and another is Lake of fire. One of the Angels that had seven vials has shown John Jerusalem the bride coming down from heaven, John wrote that throne of God and Jesus Christ is in it, and saw no temple in it, for God and Jesus Christ is the temple of the city, for those who were part of city, even Apostles, prophets, saints both small and great, are living stones and walls of the city they don't need to go anywhere like the temple to see God and Christ, for they were of those who were always inside the temple before throne and always seeing the face of God. The city was built upon the foundations of Apostles as it was in the old time as was written, saints are citizens and "are household of God; and are built upon the foundation of the apostles and prophets, Jesus Christ himself being the chief corner stone; In whom all the building fitly framed together grows unto an holy temple in the Lord build together for an habitation of God through the Spirit."[18] But God has promised to Jerusalem above whom he has forsook for a while and hid his face from her, that will built her as written "O afflicted one, storm-tossed, and not comforted, Behold, I will set your stones in antimony, And your foundations I will lay in sapphires, moreover, I will make your battlements of rubies, And your gates of crystal, And your entire wall of precious stones."[19] For God will built Jerusalem above after the Harvest that takes place in the end of this present age, for the set time of his favor on her has come, he will send his messengers soon, to gather his children, his elect, the outcasts of seed of Jesus Christ the Israel from the ends of world, and he will heal their broken hearts and binds up their wounds. John wrote his servants shall serve him, and they shall see his face, and his name shall be in their foreheads. And there shall be no night there; and they need no candle, neither light of the sun; for the Lord God gives them light: and they shall reign forever and ever. They are priests of God and Christ and will reign on earth forever. All the seed of Jesus Christ the beloved, of that Great God, will be as priests and gates to all those saved nations, and there will be angels at the gates of City, no idolater, liar, or anything that defiles will ever enter in them. The kingdoms of that new Earth, even the nations of the Earth, are saved and their names will be in book of life, not as some foolish people who teach only the bride the saints the elect will be saved and rest of all others will perish. These nations who were not seed of Jesus Christ the Israel will walk in the light of bride, and they will bring glory and honor of nations into the city. They all will come and worship before our God, they shall be people of our God and he will wipe away all their tears,[20] but dogs, and sorcerers, and whoremongers, and murderers, and idolaters, and whosoever loves and makes a lie, and all those whose names were not written in book of life will be outside City and cannot enter into it, and they will be in lake of fire the second death. They and their idols shall be an abhorring to all flesh, they shall be disgusting to all, forever; their fire will not be quenched, forever.

Now you his servants, whom he called into fellowship of his Son through Gospel at the time your new birth, now tell me you foolish people who forsook him and went to serve the gods and christs of the Christendom, the idols of heathen made after the imaginations of men, does any of these gods and christs of the denominations and sects whom you serve has shown any of you these things in all these past centuries, for you say you are alive, seeing and walking in light and in fellowship with God, does those gods and christs in whose fellowship you are, did they shown your fathers or you these things in all these centuries? Hear all you denominations and sects of Christendom, let all denominations and sects be gathered, let all Christians in the world be gathered. For thus says, the one who is the God, Father, King, Mighty one, Savior, Holy One and Redeemer of Jesus Christ and his saints, who among them can declare this, and show us former things? Let them bring forth their witnesses, that they may be justified: so, therefore, bring your evidence that who among you has been able to show us these former things, that you may be justified: or hear these things, and say, it is the truth.[21] Or else stand up and produce your case for your gods and christs, bring your evidence, says King of Jesus Christ. Who among you has shown these former things in all these centuries, who among you that his god or christ has shown these former things, that we may consider your gods and christs are capable of showing the things to come and can show things hereafter, that we may know that they are gods: and can do good, or do evil, that we may be dismayed,[22] look they are nothing, and their work is less than nothing, you choose your abominations, idols of your imaginations? Oh you who dwell in the Sea of other religions, this is that Great and everlasting God who created all things and all of us, whose works I have declared. Come and see the judgments of God upon the Earth the Christendom, who changes times and seasons. Who says and does all things.

Who among in all the denominations and sects of Christendom has shown these things? To whom his god or christ has shown these things, or any god of other religions has ever shown all these things to any one of those that were in other religions? Is not my God in whose name I am speaking these things, has shown all things from those ancient times? He says, "who hath declared this from ancient time? who hath told it from that time? have not I the LORD? and there is no God else beside me; a just God and a Saviour; there is none beside me. Look unto me, and be ye saved, all the ends of the earth: for I am God, and there is none else."[23] Therefore all you spiritual seed of Jesus Christ the Israel, whom that great God has chosen, fear not these gods and christs of heathen called by his name. You shall possess the remnant of these denominations and sects that will be left in Christendom the Earth. Fear our only true God all you seed of Lord Jesus Christ, all you descendants of Jesus whom he has begotten through his death and resurrection, glorify the one who is our Lord's God and our God, his Father and our Father, and stand in awe of Him, sanctify his name, and sanctify the Holy One of Jesus Christ, and fear his God, all you, his seed. Fear not the gods and christs of denominations and sects of Christendom the Earth. Fear not says our God, to gods and christs of these nations of Earth the Christendom. Thus says the LORD the King of Israel, and his redeemer the LORD of hosts; I am the first, and I am the last, and beside me, there is no God. And who, as I, shall call, and shall declare it, and set it in order for me, since I appointed the ancient people? And the things that are coming, and shall come, let them show unto them. Fear you not, neither be afraid: have not I told you from that time, and have declared it? You are even my witnesses. Is there a God beside me? Yes, there is no God; I know not any.

Therefore brethren come out from them, every one of you, turn away from the gods and christs of those that were in Christendom, let us seek our God who has hid his face from us. For this is iniquity of our fathers and us, that we forsake our God who called us to his fellowship in his son through Gospel at the time of our calling, and has gone after the idols of gods and christs made after imaginations of the men who dwell in Christendom, we forsook our only true God and Lord Jesus for another gospels, and gone after other gods and christs and provoked our God to jealousy, therefore our God's anger burnt against our fathers and us and he fought against them and delivered them to the hand of their enemies. For he is a jealous God, and we sinned against him as a woman does treacherously toward her husband, therefore he consumed us in his jealousy and torn us into pieces in his anger. For he loved us with great and jealous love and saved us through the death and resurrection of his Son the Israel whom he has chosen, but we despised his grace and his love and dealt treacherously against our God, all this great wrath of our God that came upon us throughout all these centuries testify us, how sore he was broken by our unfaithfulness and treachery. Therefore, stop your fornications with the gods and christs of denominations and sects of Christendom. Let us return to seek our God and Christ with all our heart and soul, by trying to remember our God and Christ from the time of our new birth, and press on to know our God. Let us wait for our God who hid his face from us, without going after gods and christs the work of imaginations of men, let us live in this world like as those who lost their everything knowing we lost God our Father, for in him such will find mercy, let us live like fatherless and stop calling other god an idol of an imagination, you are my father, you have made me. Let us entreat our God with prayer and supplication, say "take away all our iniquity, heal our apostasy, hide not your face from us, forsake us not forever, receive us back into your fellowship so that we might praise and thank you from the heart". Let us acknowledge our sin and of our fathers. Let us acknowledge no denomination and sect, and their gods can save us, and say we won't ride upon the doctrines and theologies of Christendom, for in returning and rest you shall be saved; in quietness and in trust shall be your strength. So take you, the words and turn to your God as spoken by the prophet, "O Israel, return unto the LORD thy God; for thou hast fallen by thine iniquity. Take with you words, and turn to the LORD: say unto him, Take away all iniquity, and receive us graciously: so will we render the calves of our lips. Asshur shall not save us; we will not ride upon horses: neither will we say any more to the work of our hands, Ye are our gods: for in thee the fatherless findeth mercy."[24] Therefore return in your hearts away from the things for whose sake you have forsaken God your father and gone astray from him, you can't have both God and those things at the same time, for you can't set your hearts on both. Therefore turn away your whoring hearts from all things for which you have forsaken your God, whether they be your theologies and doctrines, these denominations, sects, their teachings, their gods and christs, or your righteousness, justification, eternal life, or whatever they may be for which you have forsaken your God.

Therefore, turn away every one of you from the idols of gods and christs made after the imaginations of men, idols of the denominations and sects, which were nations of earth. For this is high time to return to our God and seek him. I write you, brethren, who had the understanding among his people. You, who gave witness against these Christians of various denominations and sects after your new birth, but pretty soon were overcome by enemies and got spiritually killed, come out from them, and do not enter into any sect, neither believe anyone who says here or there is true Christ preached; don't go after them. Let us seek our God with all your hearts and souls. You who still remember your Father and Lord Jesus and long to see one the days of son of man while you are still in his fellowship at the time of your calling, return and seek our God, for he has torn us, and he will also heal us; he has smitten, and he will bind us up. He will raise us back to life and we will live before him, for we robbed from him his little children whom he has begotten again through suffering, death, and resurrection of his Son Jesus Christ. We robbed from him his little children whom he loved, by forsaking him for idols of gods and christs of the heathen, therefore the anger of the jealousy of his great love for us has burned against us, he fought against us like a bear that lost her cubs. Lord Jesus and we all belong to Father and to him alone, and the God of Israel is a jealous God. Therefore take with you words, and turn to your God. So stop riding upon your foolish and vain theologies and doctrines that were in Christendom, and stop thinking foolishly any particular denomination or sect is good. For I testify you before the living God, they are all heathen nations of Earth the Christendom. I beg you brethren the servants of God and Lord Jesus, come back from among heathen and seek our God and Lord Jesus, for the time of the indignation of our God on us his saints is coming to End.

All you seed of Lord Jesus, who was begotten by his bodily death and resurrection, return and seek our God, all you seed of Lord Jesus the Israel whom that great God has chosen, your God is calling you to return, and your God will heal your backsliding. For you perverted your ways and have forgotten your God. All these denominations and sects of Christendom will lead you further astray from your Father, for you and your fathers indeed bore the shame of serving the idols of heathen day and night as spoken by Moses,[25] so turn away from them and their gods and christs, and return and seek our God. For you and your fathers bore your shame among the heathen, even you all, among all these denominations and sects, the nations of the earth the Christendom, among whom you were scattered. But now that Great God even our Father is going to rule the Christendom, he will visit and destroy all other gods and christs and will make their memory to perish,[26] therefore fear not them. As the seed of the beloved of that Great God, sanctify the one who is his God and his Father.

The woman whom the dragon persecuted went into the wilderness for a period of 1260 years, away from the sight of angry Satan, who sought to kill them all physically. She went according to the providence of God to spend time of her rebuke and chastisement among heathen, where they who have understanding among his people nourished her in captivity. Even those were two olive trees and lampstands the candlesticks, even the remnant of her sons who keep commandments of God, and have the testimony of Jesus, but these mighty and holy people were defeated, destroyed and spiritually killed by their enemies throughout this period of wilderness. For they will prevail over saints and wear out them all these 1260 years. As the prophet said, they are fainted and lie helpless in streets filled with rebuke of her God, and Jerusalem above will be trodden by heathen. But now her God Who contends for His people, says "Behold, I have taken out of your hand the cup of reeling, The chalice of My anger; You will never drink it again."[27] Now our God says to her, that he will gather her, as he spoke by the prophet, "For the LORD has called you as a woman forsaken and grieved in spirit, and a wife of youth, when thou was refused, says your God. For a small moment have I forsaken you; but with great mercies will I gather you."[28] So therefore, be courageous you children of Jerusalem above, you will be gathered unto your mother, then the wilderness and the solitary place shall be glad for you; you shall see the glory of our God. Therefore brethren, strengthen those who were of weak conscience and weak hearts. Fear not, behold your God will come with vengeance, even your Father with a recompense; he will come and save you. Therefore awake and shake yourselves from the dust; and loose yourselves from the chains of your denominations and sects, even from the their statements of faith, doctrines, theologies and the teachings of heathen from your neck. For now God shall comfort Zion. He will comfort all her waste places, and he will make her wilderness like Eden, and her desert like the garden of the God; Fear not the reproach of men and don't be afraid of their insults, neither be afraid of their idols when they curse you by the names of their gods and christs, they shall wither away like grass and their glory and pomp will perish in the grave and their idols will perish from the Christendom. But that Great God is very near, even the mighty one of Jesus who is going to make his enemies his footstool, look our God will come and save you; he will swallow up death for you and will wipe away all your tears and take away your rebuke from the face of earth. And you brethren from these western nations, this you surely know, that your identity is in Jesus Christ our Lord, not in your tribe, or nation, or language, you are purchased with his blood, children whom he has begotten again through his death and resurrection, together with all your brethren from all other nations and tribes, you are household of God and fellow citizens. Pray that these things reach your brethren all over the world without trouble.

Now brethren, the set time has come, as written "Thou shalt arise, and have mercy upon Zion: for the time to favor her, yea, the set time, is come. For thy servants take pleasure in her stones, and favor the dust thereof. So the heathen shall fear the name of the LORD, and all the kings of the earth thy glory. When the LORD shall build up Zion, he shall appear in his glory."[29] Therefore, pray to God without ceasing until he establishes Jerusalem above, as praise of all the Earth, as our Lord also said give him no rest until he makes Jerusalem a praise in Earth. For now, the set time has come. All these heathen, even the kingdoms of Earth, even all these denominations and sects of Christendom the Earth will fear the glory of our God. Let this be recorded for the generation to come, and the people yet to be created shall praise our God. For He hath looked down from the height of his sanctuary; from heaven did the Father behold the earth; to hear the groaning of the prisoner, to loose those that are appointed to death. Indeed, he looked upon the Christendom; he heard the groaning of his prisoners and those that were appointed to death, even for their sake he will shorten these days. After the Harvest of the wicked, our Lord will send his messengers the angels who were among you, you his messengers will gather them, and then all remnant will come from the great tribulation in which they are now. Then those who were perishing in prison, and those who were appointed to death, will come to Zion to declare his name and his praise in Jerusalem above, as spoken by prophet, "It will come about also in that day that a great trumpet will be blown, and those who were perishing in the land of Assyria and who were scattered in the land of Egypt will come and worship the LORD in the holy mountain at Jerusalem."[30] Brethren, I "Jonathan Bijja Charles Spurgeon" the writer of this book, call upon that Great God to witness against my soul, if not all these things shall soon take place before this generation passes away. I testify to you before God that this generation shall not pass away until all these things take place. It is easier for heaven and earth to pass away than these things fail to take place before this generation passes away. Therefore, brethren, know for certain that our God is very soon going to save the seed of Lord Jesus Christ his beloved; all his seed will be saved in that Great God with an everlasting salvation and you will not be put to shame or humiliated, to ages everlasting. In our Great God, all you the seed of his beloved will be justified and shall glory. These are the true and faithful sayings of that Great God, he has sent me to show you his servants what must soon take place. Return O brethren for the time of your rebuke has come to an end, and the restoration of all things is at hand, as our God declared through his servants the prophets.

But he will first turn away your captivity, you who were of understanding among his people, the two olive trees and lampstands the candlesticks, you who had the testimony of Jesus, but overcome by enemies and spiritually killed for the sake of word of God, you shall live and go back to Jerusalem above unto your God and you shall teach the people that were now distressed and dispirited like sheep without a shepherd. And you will be sent to do the harvest work, the harvest of wicked must be finished quickly and God will give you the all things you need to speak and the needed wisdom, you will do the first stage of harvest work by pouring those seven vials of wrath on Christendom, by speaking the things that will be given to you to speak. So fear not brethren, Lord Jesus will strengthen you in God your Father, he will give you wisdom, understanding, strength, and utterance, and you shall be mighty angels of that Great God and Lord Jesus. He will give you mouth and wisdom which none of your opponents will be able to resist or refute. Look ahead and see the Eternity which is laid before you, years without end. You will inherit the ages to come and you will partake in the first resurrection, which will take place after harvest. We will live forever with Father and Lord Jesus. So, be courageous with hope by belief and understanding of these things, be of sound judgment and sober spirit for the purpose of prayer and love brethren, see, in a few more years enemies of our Lord will be destroyed and our God will make them his footstool. Happy and Joyful things are very near, even in this generation, the salvation of our God is very near and all nations shall see it, for who is like our God that changes times and seasons? Blessing, and glory, and wisdom, and thanksgiving, and honor, and power, and might, be unto our God forever and ever. Amen.

> "You has rebuked the heathen, you has destroyed the wicked, you has put out their name forever and ever. O you enemy, destructions are come to a perpetual end: and you has destroyed cities; their memorial is perished with them. But the GOD shall endure for ever: he had prepared his throne for judgment. And he shall judge the world in righteousness; he shall minister judgment to the people in uprightness. The GOD also will be a refuge for the oppressed, a refuge in times of trouble. And they that know your name will put their trust in thee: for you, GOD, has not forsaken them that seek thee. Sing praises to the GOD, which dwells in Zion: declare among the people his doings. When he makes inquisition for blood, he remembers them: he forgets not the cry of the humble."

Let him be accursed that argue and speak against the things written in this book. Blessed is he that reads, and they that hear the words of this prophecy, and keep the things which are written in the book: for the time is at hand.

The grace of our Lord Jesus Christ be with your spirit, brethren. Amen.

REFERENCES:

1. Daniel 12:4&9;
2. Psalms 12:8;
3. Revelation 1:19;
4. Revelation 4:1;
5. Revelation 1:1; 4:16;
6. Revelation 10:1; Psalms 19;6-9; Ecclesiastes 8:1;
7. Revelation 22:6;
8. Revelation 22:10; Daniel 12:4&9;
9. Revelation 16:1 &16; Matthew 13:30 & 40-41;
10. Revelation 16:1-16;
11. Psalms 102; Isaiah 52: 7; 41:27; Matthew 25:6; 1 Revelation 1:1; Chapter 10; 14: 9-12; 22:6 & 16;
12. Lamentations 3:25; Psalms 22:26;
13. Revelation 17:3; 1:10;
14. Revelation 18:1;
15. Revelation 9:20-21;
16. Revelation 18:2;
17. Isaiah 66:22;
18. Ephesians 2:20-21;
19. Isaiah 54:11-12;
20. Revelation 21:2-4;
21. Isaiah 43:9;
22. Isaiah 41:22-23;
23. Isaiah 45:21-22;
24. Hosea 14:1-3;
25. Deuteronomy 4:26-28;
26. Isaiah 26:14;
27. Isaiah 51:22;
28. Isaiah 54:6-7;
29. Psalms 102:13-16;
30. Isaiah 27:13;

SECTION FIVE:
HELP TO UNDERSTAND

CHAPTER EIGHT

Little help for the saints

When God created Man and placed them in a Garden, He commanded him saying, of every tree of the garden you may freely eat. But of the tree of the knowledge of good and evil, you shall not eat of it; for in the day that you eat thereof, you shall surely die. Now this commandment of God was intended for the good of man, for that commandment is life to man so that he won't die by eating from the tree of knowledge of good and evil. So, therefore, the commandment is holy, just, and righteous.

But the Serpent, who has the power of death, which is Sin, beguiled the woman and brought all manners of strong desire in her mind to eat the fruit of the tree. When the woman saw that the tree was good for food, that it was pleasant to the eyes, and that it was a tree to be desired to make one wise, she took of the fruit thereof and did eat. This same effect occurs among many who hear the Law that gives knowledge of good and evil; it will be good for spiritual food, pleasant to the heart, and desired to make wise. For the Law is righteous, pure, just, holy, and perfect; it gives knowledge of good and evil, as Moses said when he gave the Law. "I have set before you today life and good, death and evil."[1]

When Adam and Eve ate the fruit of the tree of knowledge of good and evil, their eyes were opened and they understood that they were naked, and they came to the sense of shame.

So also Law causes the sense of shame in our conscience, and reveals our own nakedness, for it gives sufficient knowledge of good and evil, right and wrong. For the Law is righteous, just, holy, and perfect. It shows our unrighteousness, unjustness, and imperfectness in our conscience, for it gives the knowledge of good and evil, right and wrong, like a mirror it shows how we look like, for the Law is pure and perfect like God.

The Law of God is like a ruler and instructor to all humans that were born in the world and until the time of their death. Although God gave the written Law to the children of Israel of old time through Moses, it existed and started working before Moses, even from the time when Adam and Eve received from the tree of good and evil. The work of the Law, this knowledge of good and evil, and the authority of the Law was upon all the children of Adam. For whenever a human comes into this world, he will be naked and will not be ashamed until he reaches a certain age; then he will know good and evil because the Law gives knowledge of good and evil in his conscience. Some humans may obey and do what seems to be right according to their conscience, and some may harden themselves and do things which they know are Evil and wrong. When that great God, the ruler and judge of all things, judges humans, he will bring all these things into judgment; even the thoughts of humans in their conscience, the deeds, words, and imaginations performed by humans which were approved as good, just, perfect, and right in their conscience. And the deeds, words and imaginations by humans which were not approved by all their thoughts wholly as good, just, perfect and right in their conscience.

Now Moses wrote in some places to show us that the work of the Law in human conscience was there before it was given as Ten Commandments as a covenant to the children of Israel. He wrote, "his master's wife cast her eyes upon Joseph; and she said, Lie with me. But he refused, and said unto his master's wife, Behold, my master wotteth not what is with me in the house, and he hath committed all that he hath to my hand; There is none greater in this house than I; neither hath he kept back anything from me but thee, because thou art his wife: how then can I do this great wickedness, and sin against God?"[2] *and* "Jacob said unto his household, and to all that were with him, Put away the strange gods that are among you,"[3] *and* "Abimelech said to Isaac, What is this thou hast done unto us? one of the people might lightly have lien with thy wife, and thou shouldest have brought guiltiness upon us."[4]

When Adam and Eve ate the fruit of the tree of knowledge of good and evil, their eyes of understanding were opened and they came to the sense of shame and knew they were naked. So also the Law causes a sense of shame in our conscience, and reveals our own nakedness, for when the Law is expounded clearly, it will show our nakedness and will bring in us a sense of guilt and shame, and like a mirror it shows what we look like; for the Law is pure and perfect. For by the Law we come to the knowledge of our shamefulness, guilt, and sin. As Adam and Eve sewed fig leaves together, and made themselves aprons to cover up shame and nakedness, so also we do some kind of appeasement works and good works to cover up our shame. These aprons will not last before the Perfect Law of God, and we will find ourselves naked, for before the perfect Law of God no living flesh is justified in their conscience. They will find themselves guilty, and all their efforts will amount to nothing but the aprons of fig leaves that will not last .

Like Adam hid himself from God, they will be terrified to go into the presence of God, because of a guilty conscience that condemns them in their heart. For the Law opens their mind to know their wickedness; as the body that is naked shows the shamefulness of our own self, so also the Law opens our eyes to our own self, which is the personification of wickedness and Sin without any good. The Law of God is very perfect, and all human beings are the very personification of wickedness and Sin without any good before it. Oh man, it is the Law of God in whose sight the very heavens are unclean; how will the Law of God show the human race, whose imagination and intention of heart is evil from childhood?

The Law of God is holy and perfect; its standard is as high as heaven. If you see a woman with lustful eyes for a fraction of second, in that very moment you have committed adultery with her by that blink of thought. Whosoever divorces his wife and marries other woman, his relationship with his former wife amounts to adultery, and his relationship with his wife was never was as it should be between husband

and wife. A woman who leaves her husband and marries another man is committing adultery with her new man, for her husband is still alive and she was unfaithful toward her husband and not done virtuously, and she will be called an adulterous woman. The man who marries a divorced woman is committing adultery with the other man's wife. The Law of God is perfect and holy; the commandment is in-lined with the nature of God. For our God is a jealous God, and he loves his people with holy and jealous love, as in manner of Man's love toward his wife. Therefore he can't bear his people going after any other gods, for love is as strong as death; jealousy is as cruel as the grave; the coals thereof are coals of fire, which hath a most vehement flame. Many waters cannot quench love; neither can the floods drown it. Therefore the Psalmist complains about God's anger on us. "How long, God? wilt thou be angry forever? Shall thy jealousy burn like fire?"[5]

The Law of God is perfect and good; the commandment is in-lined with the nature of God. It is knowledge of good and evil where we can find good, for there is none good, but God alone is good. Our Father is a merciful God, and he is kind unto the unthankful and to the evil. He makes his sun to rise on the evil and on the good, and sends rain on the just and on the unjust. Therefore Love your enemies; bless those that curse you, do good to those that hate you, and pray for those who despitefully use you and persecute you. The commandment of the Law of God is perfect, and loving *neighbor as thyself* is not a vague phrase. If you have riches with you, then you are not keeping the commandment as long as your neighbors are poor; therefore you ought to distribute your riches among the poor. One having two coats, let him impart to the one having none; and the one having food, let him do likewise. When a rich young man approached Lord Jesus, the young man thought that he was keeping all the commandments from childhood.[6] The Lord said to young man that he lacks one thing, for that young man failed to keep this commandment. For the commandment of the Law of our God is perfect; it has no loopholes, and just giving some alms to the poor doesn't make a substitute for the commandment.

Neither loving *God withal heart, soul, wisdom and strength* is a vague phrase; it's not mere loving him more than other things and people we love. It's madly and deeply loving God, just as the Lord Jesus loved him, and he loved him as no one has ever loved him. It is to love him unto death, as if we can't live without him, with a killing love as strong as death. Lord Jesus expounded many commandments, but this he showed us in himself, for he is the personification of such love towards God his father; we can see it in his life, in his love towards us and in his prayers and supplications[7]. If we love God for eternal life, salvation, righteousness, or some other thing, that can't be a true love; verily people pretend to love God, but they neither know him nor love him. But God is well pleased in his Son, and his love alone is sufficient, which always makes God's soul to delight.

The Law of God is holy and perfect, and its standard is high as heaven. But hypocrites sought to nullify the commandments of God, just as in old times. They said "that if anyone says to his father or mother, 'The help you would have received from me has been given to God,' he need not honor his father or mother with it."⁸ The Law is like a light that shows what is in us, but it will show the evil in us, for that is only thing we have abundant in us. Like a mirror, it shows us what we look like. The Law is like the tree of knowledge of good and evil, and we are sinful and evil like our parents were naked before they ate fruit, and the Law shows only what we are. If we sit under it and eat its fruit, it should give humans knowledge of good and evil. The Law appears as good for food, and that it was pleasant to the heart, and it is to be desired to make one wise. It will make one's eyes of understanding open, as it made Adam and Eve to know that they were naked without clothes. Wherever a little fainting light of knowledge of the Law falls in the consciences of humans, people know that they are naked without clothes. Therefore people in all places and among all religions seek to sew the aprons with fig leaves, like their first parents of all human beings did. They seek to help with some supposed good works and superstitions of religions or dietary laws, etc. Hypocrites and deceivers are everywhere to deceive them that those efforts of leaves are sufficient to hide their nakedness of their evil. And because of the lack of sufficient knowledge of good and evil, which the Law of God gives, they will be easily deceived by them. The Law gives the knowledge of Evil, for I had not known lust, except the law had said, "You shall not covet. anything that belongs to your neighbor."⁹ Remember, Adam and Eve were naked even before they ate the fruit of tree of knowledge of good and evil. It is not the knowledge of good and evil that made them naked; it only opened their understanding to know that they were naked..

So also all their children are naked. Evil dwells in all humans; evil desires and motions of Sin in members of human bodies.[10] For whenever a human comes into this world, he will be naked and will not be ashamed until he reaches certain age; then he will know good and evil. The Law gives knowledge of good and evil in his conscience; then from that time of puberty, evil desires and motions of Sin in members of human bodies will become active. For until that time of understanding of good and evil, they were there but were unknown to them, as Adam and Eve knew not the nakedness until they ate fruit. When the time to know good and evil in the life of a human child comes, the evil that dwells in them becomes active, and the Law of God is perfect and it supplies all that is lacking in knowledge of good and evil which naturally occurs in humans from that time. When they come to the knowledge of the evil in their conscience, the sin in them will get revived; when they know that evil which is not right to do, the Sin that is in their flesh will bring all kinds of strong desires toward it. For knowledge of good and evil gives sufficient knowledge of evil, and they will know what lust is by eating the fruit of the Law which says "you shall not covet anything that belong to neighbor." For sin that is in them will work and bring all manner of concupiscence in them, and they will know what lust is from within them.[11]

The knowledge of good and evil will give them understanding in their conscience that adultery is wrong, but the Sin in their members of body will bring all manner of concupiscence in their mind toward it. For knowledge of good and evil throws light on them and reveals that such and such thing is in them, and that light falls on the Sin that is in them. The Sin will appear to them and become revived, and will start working in them actively. The Law and commandment is not Sin, but gives knowledge of good and evil, it opens their eyes of understanding toward the evil. The Sin already exists in them; just as it opened their eyes to know they are naked, and they were naked even before their eyes were opened. Therefore, the knowledge of good and evil is good and just; it is the Sin that dwells in human flesh that uses the commandment of knowledge of good and evil, and brings all manner of concupiscence in their mind. Sin deceives them, and will kill them by that which was ordained for life. For Sin by the commandment will become exceedingly sinful, and brings the terror of God in their conscience. Just as Adam and Eve were afraid of God, because they knew they were naked and hid themselves behind the tree.

The Law of God that gives the knowledge of good and evil is Holy, just, and good. The commandments are good, but if humans fail to do what is good, which they desired, and do the shameful and sinful things which they hated to do, they will consent that the commandments of God are good and desire to do what is good. They might delight in the Law of God in their mind, knowing it is just and good, and desire do that which is good, but this desire in the human mind will meet the opposition from the Sin in the flesh. It will bring all manners of concupiscence into the mind and bring them back into the captivity of the Law of Sin in their flesh. And they will do not which they want to do, but they will do which they hate to do. Sin works death in humans using the commandment of Law of knowledge of good and evil. Sin will appear as Sin, and that Sin by the commandment will become exceedingly sinful. Thus the knowledge of good and evil bring condemnation, wrath, and the displeasure of God into the human conscience. For it shows our Sin to us, and our Sin will become exceedingly sinful, and conscience withers and dies. Like the first parents of humans, they will be afraid, and they will flee and hide from God.

For the Law of Knowledge of good and evil is given for condemnation; not that the Law is bad or unjust, but the Law is Just and holy. It shows the evil that is in humans, and it opens the understanding to that which is in humans. Just as it opened the minds of our first parents to know that they are naked, and brought the terror of God in them so they went to hide from him, the Law requires perfect obedience to God, and it requires perfect obedience to the commandments of God. Christ said to the rich young ruler to sell what he had and give it to the poor, for that man thought he was keeping the commandment. To love thy neighbor as thyself, it requires perfect obedience. Even committing adultery in the heart is counted as adultery. Everyone who knows what is good and doesn't abide by it will be condemned.

Just like the fruit of the tree of knowledge of good and evil, the words of the Law of commandments appear as good for food, is pleasant to the heart, and is to be desired to make one wise. It will makes one's eyes of understanding open;

so they like to sit under it and eat its fruit. But it should open their mind to understand their shame; when the Law is preached correctly without reducing its standard, it should bring out the all wickedness, rebellion, and evil that is inside the humans to light, to show them how they are. Humans think that they can keep the Law and become perfect according to the works of the Law by their efforts in keeping it, just as their first parents tried to make aprons of fig leaves to cover their shame. Hypocrites and deceivers in all places and all religions try to reduce the standard of the Law, and will try to nullify the commandments of God. These wicked people think God as altogether like them and try to reduce the standards of the Law by their teachings and deceiving people, so that they can obtain righteousness by doing certain works and by abstaining from certain things. But the Law of God is perfect, and its standards are high and it will never justify a naked sinner. For the first parents of humans were naked, and so it opened their eyes to understand to their shame. The Law only shows what is inside a man; it will never justify anyone who will not love God with all his heart, soul, wisdom, and strength.

The Law is in-line with the nature of God. Its standard is as high as heaven, and all humans will get condemnation as worthless sinners by it and the whole world should keep its mouth shut before the Law of God. I speak to those who know Lord Jesus; if you know him, you should know that he is the personification of all righteousness. He is the standard for the Law of God, and the Law teaches us to love God as he loved him. The Law of God will condemn you unless your righteousness is close to the righteousness of Lord Jesus; if anyone thinks himself righteous enough to be justified before the Law of God, he is a fool that doesn't know the standard of the Law. There are so many fools in this world who think their good works are up to the standard of God's holy Law; it is evident that they don't know the standard of the Law of our God. The Law is given for condemnation because no human is justified before it, for we are all like our first parents naked, as they were naked before they ate the fruit of the knowledge of good and evil. So we are all sinners from birth and conceived in Sin; Sin and wickedness are natural things to us. Sin dwells in us, even before we ever come to the little knowledge of good and evil.

The Law was not given with the intention to justify humans, doing charity, piety, mercy, humility, doing good, abstaining from sins, abstaining from doing forbidden things, and keeping the Christ's commandments of doing good works which Christ spoke expounding the Law, which was written in the Gospels. Keeping the Ten Commandments will never justify any man, for there is no such Law given to humans that will justify humans. They are only given for condemnation to show our Sin and not for justification. The same Christ who said "if you want to enter into life, keep the commandments" also said "It is impossible for men,"[12] for salvation, righteousness, and life was promised to those who can be justified according to the Law. On the other hand, it is impossible for humans to be justified by keeping the commandments of God and Christ that were of the Law, for by good deeds no flesh will be justified in God's sight; the knowledge of good and evil was never given with the intention to justify the humans, for they were already naked and sinners. The Law was only given for condemnation; yes it was given only for condemnation, to show their shame and Sin. For this reason, God said to our first parents who were naked, "The day in which you eat the fruit of the knowledge of good and evil, you shall die,"[13] for God knew it would open their understanding and would show them their shame. So they were afraid of the knowledge of their shame and hid from God. People not knowing the standard of the Law think they can do good works of the Law that will make them justified before God, but the Law was only given for condemnation, not for justification. No human being can be justified before God according to the standard of the Law, for they are already sinners and Sin dwells in them, just as their first parents were naked. Therefore, the Law given for the sinners, it is given for transgression.

As long as a man is not a murderer, adulterer, or thief, he would swear he is righteous. Just as the rich young ruler who said he was keeping all the commandments, but he was obliged to distribute his wealth to his poor neighbors according to the commandments. The Law shows transgressions to people. For perfect obedience is required to the Law, and it won't give any concessions as hypocrites think; thus transgressions might be recognized as such and thus increased. When Sin, death, and the wrath of God is revealed, people will grow impatient and complain against God and Christ, just as the slothful servant did; they will say you are an austere person, and to reap where you haven't sown. The joyful and thankful attitude towards master will change, and the Law brings enmity with God in their mind, because the Law reveals the wrath of God in their conscience against every thought, word, and action that is evil, and thus the Law inspires hatred towards God. For their conscience will be whipped continually by the condemnation of the Law; thus the Law is a burdensome yoke of bondage. Before, that man was a very happy and holy man, and can say I am not as other men are: extortioners, unjust, murders, idolaters, and adulterers.

The Law is useful, like a hammer to smash self righteousness, self wisdom, and self help. It will bring out the wickedness, rebellion, and evil that is deep inside a human to light, and will show them how evil and shameful they are. It will destroy the aprons of fig leaves of the self-help and self-righteousness, for the Law was given only for condemnation; it will pronounce the judgments on human conscience, thunder claps and lightings upon their conscience, and the people will quake with terror. The Law requires perfect obedience; it will not stay quiet. It will continuously slam the human conscience for every little evil in their actions, words, and thoughts. Its voice against them will increase further and further. As their first parents hide themselves because of fear of God, who earlier were never afraid to stand before him nakedly, so also their children will be terrified and flee from God. For the Law brings the wrath of God in to their conscience. It will make them destitute of all righteousness, it will bring out the all wickedness, rebellion, and evil that is inside a human to light, and it will show them how evil and shameful they are.

This is the knowledge of their great evil, transgressions, helplessness, despair, condemnation, and death, delivered by the Law of knowledge of good and evil to its students. For the Law only shows humans what is inside them and they are only wicked, rebellious, and evil; for this reason the Law never justifies any man. Even if he is a born again Christian, Saint, prophet, or an even an apostle of Christ, it is evil and wicked teaching of enemies of Christ, that the purpose of law will change and it won't condemn the saints in their conscience after their conversion, no law will ever justify any man. For inside every man is nothing but only wickedness, rebellion, and evil; therefore the Law of God shuts every mouth and condemns the whole world and makes them guilty before God. Therefore servant of God said "enter not into judgment with thy servant: for in thy sight shall no man living be justified."[14] the Law is the ministration of death, just as God told them the day in which they eat the fruit of knowledge of good and evil, they will die.

The Law destroys universal illusions of righteousness in a human. In the world, it appears as though some are righteous when compared to others; such illusions of righteousness will be destroyed when it opens the eyes of understanding to those who keep commandments and live holy lives. For the Law of God demands perfect obedience and will bring out the all wickedness, rebellion, and evil that is inside of them to light, and will make them as worthless sinners in their own sight before God. It will open their understanding to know their shame and nakedness. The Law is a spiritual prison; it arouses the conscience. Before the Law begins its work perfectly, a person will not have a sense of Sin and guilt, as their parents did when they walked nakedly before God with without feeling shame. When it starts its work, it will pronounce the judgments on human conscience, there will be thunder claps and lightings upon their conscience, and the people will quake with terror. The Law requires perfect obedience; it will not stay quiet, it will continually slam human's conscience for every little evil in their actions, words, and thoughts. Its voice against them will increase further and further. Those who were acquainted with perfect standards of the Law will quake as greatly as Mount Sinai; it whips the conscience with judgments and condemnations upon all the deeds, words, and thoughts.

The Law brings conscience to turmoil, the sore displeasure and wrath of God revealed against them in their conscience. It drives them to terror and despair; they will be terrified and the feeling of hatred will be in them against God, being alienated in their heart[15] from the God who is angry with them and wants to destroy them for their evil. Therefore, the Law is a ministration of death, for it will bring such terror and the wrath of God to conscience and continually slams the human conscience for every evil in their actions, words, and thoughts. It opens their eyes to all wickedness, all the evil in them, and thus makes them guilty before God. This is the good service the Law provides to humans. Hypocrites, the foolish and childish people who were not acquainted with standards of Holy Law of God think it will justify them. The Law of God is perfect, good, and just; it gives knowledge of good and evil to humans, the children of Adam and Eve. It has dominion over all the human beings who were born in the world, and it rules over every human until he dies and will be delivered to the domain of death. This Law was given to the children of Israel of the old time in written form on the tablets of stone. These Ten Commandments were written on stones and were handed over to Moses as a covenant to the children of Israel.

And so the whole human race is subjected to the dominion of Sin and Law, and they are under the bondage of Sin because they Sin. Moses wrote that God would raise a prophet like him from Israel, for that man was to deliver the people from the yoke of bondage as Moses delivered the people from bondage in Egypt. Prophets wrote he would be the savior of the human race; he would be the salvation of God unto the ends of Earth. God said he would give this man as a covenant. This man was to deliver the people from the yoke of bondage of Law and Sin; from the dominion of Law and Sin, and from the authority of Satan. That old serpent who had the Sin; by it Satan rules the human world through desires of the flesh and mind. For the whole world is in wickedness and serves the Sin in harmony with a spirit that works in them through desires of flesh and mind, accumulating the wrath of God against them. And so the Law becomes the strength to Sin, for it gives the knowledge of Sin. By it Sin is imputed, and Sin uses the Law to produce all manner of concupiscence in the minds and will carry humans to fulfill the desires of flesh and mind unto death. Thus Satan, through Sin, rules the world, and they serve the Sin as slaves. Sin is the strength of death, and death is the reward of Sin. But God promised a savior who would save the people from the bondage, as Moses saved the Israel of old time from the slavery unto Pharaoh in Egypt.

He is the God's Holy One, whom he has begotten from death. He has not abandoned his soul to Sheol, nor did he let his Holy One see decay. He made known to him the path of life; He promised his chosen servant that he would keep him and preserve him, and promised to give him as a covenant to the people as written. "I the LORD have called thee in righteousness, and will hold thine hand, and will keep thee, preserve thee, and give thee for a covenant of the people, for a light of the Gentiles; that thou mayest be my salvation unto the ends of the earth."[16] This man God has appointed as the Covenant, the light and Salvation of God to all humans, so that whosoever hear his word and believes in God that raised him from dead, shall have eternal life. He will not come into judgment, but has passed from death to life. For this man is the covenant, and the testimony about him is the word of faith of the covenant; that must be kept in faith. It is not of works like the Law of good and evil, but it is of Faith. For this man is the covenant, and in this man that great God has created the way and the salvation to all those that believe in him. Through this man, the very God, who in the old time made the way in the depths of sea, a path in the mighty waters, has made a way to Heaven in him through the depths of the Earth, through powers and principalities and through the domain of death, by raising him from the dead and making him to sit at his right hand. For the Law and Sin will have dominion over a humans as long as they live;[17] after they die they will enter into the domain of death. For this reason, the Law won't speak anything to the dead, and if any man is dead he is freed from the Law. So, according to the Law, a married woman is bound to her husband as long as he lives; when he dies, he will be away from the domain and reach of the Law, and it cannot bind the woman to him anymore.[18]

God calls man whom he gave covenant as Israel, and he made his servant Israel's mouth as a sharp sword. He formed him from the womb to be His Servant, to bring back the children of Jacob back to God. The children of former Israel had not obeyed the voice of this Israel, the Servant of God whom he has chosen, but they despised him and abhorred him; therefore this man complains, "God said unto me, Thou art my servant, O Israel, in whom I will be glorified. Then I said, I have laboured in vain, I have spent my strength for nought, and in vain: yet surely my judgment is with the LORD, and my work with my God."[19] But God said to him, "It is a light thing that you should be my servant to raise up the tribes of Jacob, and to restore the preserved of Israel. I will also give you for a light to the Gentiles, that you may be my salvation unto the end of the earth."[20] And this man God has appointed as his Salvation unto the ends of the earth. For there is only one God; to all the humans he alone is the savior, and besides him there is no savior. This man whom God has chosen is the salvation of that one true God unto the ends of Earth; He is the savior appointed by that great God to the world. In this man, that great God has made salvation for humans, even in the fleshly body of this man God made deliverance for humans. For in him God gave forgiveness of sins to people through faith, for God hath set forth him to be a propitiation through faith in his blood and to declare his righteousness for the remission of Sins that are past, through the forbearance of God. To declare, at this time his righteousness, that he might be just, and the justifier of him who believes in Jesus.[21]

God has set forth this righteous man as the propitiation for whole world. God will not impute their Sins to those who obey the faith in this man, whom he has begotten from death. Evil dwells in all humans, evil desires and motions of Sin in members of human bodies. For whenever a human comes into this world, he will be naked and will not be ashamed until he reaches a certain age; then he will know good and evil. The Law gives knowledge of good and evil in his conscience; then, from that time of puberty, evil desires and motions of Sin in members of the human body will become active. For until that time of understanding of good and evil, they were there but were unknown to them, as Adam and Eve knew no shame and nakedness until they ate fruit. When the time to know good and evil in the life of a human child comes, the evil that dwells in them becomes active, Sin that is in the members of the human body brings all manners of concupiscence against the good to Sin, and brings human into subjection to fulfill the lusts of flesh and mind produced in their minds by Sin. Even if the will is present in a man to do good, the Sin in the members of his body will fight against his will, and will bring him to its subjection to fulfill its lusts.[22]

For this cause, God has appointed punishment for the Sin that is in the flesh; the destruction of the body of Sin on the cross. The Cross is an instrument of torture, a means of execution. Crucifixion is an ancient method of painful execution in which the condemned person is nailed to a large wooden Cross and left to hang until death. A cruel prelude was scourging; the convict then usually had to carry the cross to the place of execution. Crucifixion was usually intended to provide a death that was particularly slow, painful (hence the term Excruciating, literally "out of crucifying"), gruesome, humiliating, and public. The whole body will suffer, as it is stretched and hung upon a cross, as written. "They pierced my hands and my feet. I am poured out like water, And all my bones are out of joint; I can count all my bones."[23] God has provided through faith the destruction of the body of Sin for humans in this man, even in the fleshly body of this man Jesus. God, sending his own Son in the likeness of sinful flesh, and for Sin, condemned Sin in the flesh, so that they should not serve Sin, so that they do not live out their remaining time on earth for human passions,[24] but for the will of God.

The Law is given for condemnation, to show humans their Sin and transgression; every one that doesn't fulfill it are condemned and cursed. The Law curses everyone as written, "Cursed is every one that continueth not in all things which are written in the book of the law to do them."[25] And for curse of the Law, God made his son a curse, as written: "Cursed is every one that hangeth on a tree,"[26] so that all who believe in him might be made free from its curse. The Law shows our transgressions and Sins; it speaks against us in our conscience before God, and shows us our shame and Sin. It won't justify any man, for all men are evil by nature, and it requires perfect obedience to its commandments. But God in Jesus Christ has nailed the Law to the cross and blotted out all the handwritings that was on it. Not as some false teachers speak the partition wall of ceremonial laws only, which were kept by Jews, but more importantly the moral law, which strongly speaks against both Jews and Gentiles. He blotted by the blood of his son, to reconcile both unto himself in his Son, by giving them redemption, even forgiveness of sins to the humans in him, and in his Son he took out of the way the Law and all its ordinances that were against them. And the Law has dominion over all humans; all humans will be under it until they die and go in the domain of death. That great God has given freedom from the dominion of the Law to humans in this man Jesus, even in the fleshly body of him through his death and resurrection, for God sent his son into the world in the likeness of sinful flesh. He took the form of a servant and was made under the law;[27] he was under the subjection of the Law like all humans, but by his death he was made free from its authority and domain. All those who believe in him will obtain the freedom from the dominion of Law by the deliverance that is in him.

God also gave humans freedom from the dominion of sin in this man, in the body of his flesh; for when he died, he died unto Sin as well. And this man Jesus, whom God appointed to be his salvation, has died unto the Law and Sin, and rose again from the dead. Upon this man death has no more dominion, and he was raised from the dead by God and is to never die anymore. God preserved him and gave him as covenant and light, and in him is the salvation of God unto the ends of Earth. For as many as believe in him will receive the eternal Spirit, who transcends time and space, and by the Spirit of God they will all be baptized into his body, into his death and resurrection, and they will all be legally made free from the dominion of the Law and Sin. As Jesus said to his disciples "Ye shall drink indeed of my cup, and be baptized with the baptism that I am baptized with:"[28] They will become children of God, for God begets them again through faith by the resurrection of Jesus Christ his Son.[29]

God has shown before they ate the fruit of tree of knowledge of good and evil, in the creation of Woman; even the Eve, for God created Woman by causing Man to fall into a deep sleep and removed a rib from him and made the rib as Woman. It is a foreshadowing of the One who was to come, and his church, for God has created them new. Those who were dead in Sin, He brought them to new life, through the death and resurrection of the man called Jesus Christ. Jesus, who knew no Sin, bore their Sins on his own body and suffered on the Cross and God chastised him for their Sins as written "the LORD hath laid on him the iniquity of us all. the chastisement of our peace was upon him."[30] He died having cleansed the members of his body from all Sin by his blood; when he died, he died unto Sin and the Law. God raised him from the dead, declaring him just and forgiving the members of his body of the all Sin laid upon his body. They that were baptized into his body by the Spirit are baptized into his death, dead with him by his body, for they were made his members of his body. They died with him unto the Law and Sin, and God has forgiven them and raised them with him and made them to sit with Christ in a heavenly places. Being dead with Christ to the Law and raised with him, they will not be under the Law.

Christ said to his disciples, "Ye shall drink indeed of my cup, and be baptized with the baptism that I am baptized with." Now, a dead man is dead; he can't hear, can't see, and can't do anything. But, if a man lives unto the Law in his conscience, he can't live unto God through faith in Christ, who loved us and gave himself for our sins. The Law was not given with the intention to justify humans, but to show Sin for condemnation, doing charity, piety, mercy, humility, doing good, abstaining from sins, abstaining from doing forbidden things, and keeping the Christ's commandments of doing good works. Christ spoke expounding the Law, which was written in the Gospels, and keeping the Ten Commandments will not justify any man before God. They are not given for justification, but show our Sin and bring condemnation; as long as man lives unto the Law, he can't live unto God. Yes when Lord Jesus was in the world, he did expound the Law of God, and preached it in accordance with its standard. We can find it in his teachings on the Sermon on the Mount, and in other places written in Gospel of Matthew, Mark, and Luke.

The children of Israel, unto whom he was sent, were going about to establish their own righteousness by the works of the Law; they sought be justified of their works by keeping the Law. On the other hand, publicans and harlots, who can't aspire for the righteousness of their own, submitted to the mercy of God by believing in Jesus Christ with the hope of righteousness. For all the spiritually poor sinners who were destitute of righteousness in their own eyes, he appeared as the propitiation and light of life. The Law was given, even the Ten Commandments, as covenant to children of Israel:

it ministered transgression, condemnation, and death. For it was given to show transgression, Sin, evil, and to bring condemnation and the wrath of God upon a conscience leading to death. But this covenant, even Jesus Christ ministered the free righteousness of God, free justification, and Life. For this covenant was not given like the Law to show our transgression, Sin, evil, and to impute the sin, but to show the goodness and righteousness of God in forgiving us and not imputing our Sin on us. It was not given to bring condemnation and wrath upon conscience, but to bring justification and tranquility upon conscience, leading to life. Not to bring terror in conscience and to make people to flee and hide themselves from God, but to bring peace and tranquility in the conscience and to come to the presence of God.[31] It was not given to show the sinfulness, wickedness, and evil that is in us, and to found ourselves as sinners,[32] but to die unto the Law and live by our faith in the son of God, who loved us and gave himself for our Sins.

The word of this covenant, even the Gospel about Lord Jesus Christ, is the word of faith; it has to be kept by faith, and it was called the Law of faith. The Law works alienation in the heart, for it will show transgression, condemnation, and work terror in the heart. They will be alienated in their heart from the God who is angry with them and wants to destroy them for their evil; they will be alienated and will become enemies in their own mind against God. But this covenant is a ministration of reconciliation, to witness that God was in Christ and reconciling the world unto himself, not imputing their trespasses unto them; as if God and Christ beseeched them, to be reconciled and saying don't be alienated in your heart, to come near, because for them God made his son who knew no sin to be Sin, to be them, that they might be made the righteousness of God in the body of his flesh. The Law is a burdensome yoke of bondage, and no living flesh can fulfill its demands; their conscience would be whipped continuously by the condemnation of the Law. Therefore, Christ called to those that were toiling under it, "Come unto me, all ye that labour and are heavy laden, and I will give you rest. Take my yoke upon you, and learn of me; for I am meek and lowly in heart: and ye shall find rest unto your souls, for my yoke is easy, and my burden is light."[33] For Christ is the end of the Law for righteousness to all that believe in him, for righteousness comes by Christ not by the Law; it was only given to show transgression. For the Law only gives knowledge of good and evil and shows us our Sin, as it opened the understanding of our parents to know they naked and made them ashamed.

Therefore, they made aprons with fig leaves, which was useless to cover themselves their shame; so also our own efforts of doing works of the Law, keeping the commandments, and doing good work is not useful like the aprons of fig tree to cover us from our shame. But that Great God, who made coats of skin and clothed Adam and Eve, also made clothes for us their children and clothed us with his own Son. As the scripture says, we are clothed with Christ through baptism into his body by Spirit;[34] therefore Christ is the end of the Law for righteousness to everyone that believes in him. Also in Christ we have the deliverance from the dominion of the Law by his body; through his death and resurrection,[35] he will give the people rest from that heavy yoke. He is not a taskmaster who puts the burdens of the Law on people as Satan depicts him using his own words against him, but he is a merciful savior. If we start to know him, he reveals the Father to us, both his love and Father's love toward us, and we can live by trusting in the Father's love and his love toward us. His yoke is not the good works according to the standard of the Law, but his yoke is faith in him, and we should learn from him to trust him. God will teach Lord Jesus his way and he is with him. God has given him the tongue of discipleship, to sustain the weary with a word. This man Jesus is meek and lowly to receive and teach us; his yoke is justification in conscience, his yoke is peace and serenity on conscience wrath and terror will be far. His yoke is liberty, and his yoke is life to conscience.

The whole human world is under the Law, but you who were called by God to the fellowship of his son, whom he has begotten again to new life by the resurrection of his son; you are not under the Law, for you are dead unto the Law by death and resurrection of his son, as written. "My brethren, ye become dead to the law by the body of Christ; that you might live unto God." If you are dead, then you are free from its dominion; it has no authority over you, for you don't come under its jurisdiction. A dead servant can't hear, see, or do anything for his master; likewise reckon yourselves dead unto law. If you live unto the Law in conscience and keep your conscience under its judgments and seek to be found just in your thoughts, deeds, and words, you will find yourselves sinners.[36] For the Law won't justify any; it will condemn you in your conscience. You can't live unto God. If an Apostle himself can't live unto God, without dying unto the Law, then surely you will not live, as spoken by Paul: "I through the law am dead to the law, that I might live unto God." For you are dead unto the Law by the body of Christ who is our Law; the Law of faith, that we might live by faith in him, who loved us and gave himself for our sins. If you seek to be justified in the conscience according to works of the Law by keeping the Christ's commandments of doing good works which were written in gospels and keeping ten Commandments and other similar commandments written in the old testament and new testament books and epistles, you will find yourselves sinners and guilty in your conscience. If any one of you seek to be justified by keeping these things, that person is separated from Christ and he is fallen from grace, as written. "You have been severed from Christ, you who are seeking to be justified by law; you have fallen from grace."[37] To him, the death and resurrection of Christ and his cross; all will become unprofitable. Christ's work won't avail anything to him, and he has fallen from grace. He needs to earn his own righteousness by keeping the whole Law, by loving God with all his heart, soul, wisdom, and strength, and by loving his neighbor as himself, and by keeping all those related commandments written in old and New Testament books, in the gospels and epistles.

If we sinners and wicked people can obtain forgiveness and justification by keeping the Law or by any other means, then for what purpose did Christ die? Why would God give his son, if righteousness can come to us by any other way? On one hand, we evil people do Sin and wickedness against God, and on the other we despise his free grace and mercy. To keep the commandments and do good works for the sake of justification is to despise God's grace and the sacrificial death of Christ. It is a Sin unto death,[38] against this Holy covenant, against the gospel. By denying grace of God and the sacrifice of Christ you do like this as written "he trampled on the Son of God, profaned the blood of the covenant that sanctified him, and insulted the Spirit of grace?"[39] I don't assume you do these things knowingly. Therefore, whosoever teaches to those who were dead and rose with Christ, that good works and keeping the commandments were necessary for salvation apart from faith, is the despiser of God's grace and the sacrificial death of Christ. He is an enemy of Christ, and he is a worker of iniquity; a dog and a wicked worker who seeks to destroy saints and wants to take them to bondage. There are so many such people in the world, and beginning from the Church of Rome, also the rest of the denominations and sects, and also many people from them. These evil people do so much harm, even to this day; these evil people show some small danger or evil of some people who don't belong to Christ turning grace into sensuality,[40] they use these things to make their wickedness against the truth be justified. As Apostle wrote, whosoever seeks to be justified according to the works of the Law, that is by keeping Christ's commandments of doing good works which were written in gospels and keeping the ten Commandments and other similar commandments written in the old testament and new testament books and epistles, such people are fallen from grace and to them the death and resurrection of Christ, his cross, all will become unprofitable. Christ's work won't avail anything to them.[41] They won't come under this covenant; they are separated from Christ, as written, "You have been severed from Christ, you who are seeking to be justified by law; you have fallen from grace." They need to earn their righteousness by their works; their wage is not credited as a grace, but as what is due.[42] But to us who do not work, but believe in Him who justifies the ungodly, our faith is credited as righteousness.[43]

For to us, justification is by grace, and we gain access to this grace is by Faith.[44] It is no longer on the basis of works; otherwise grace is no longer grace. For no man can be justified partly by his works and partly by grace; it can be either by grace or by work, for it can't be both. It can be either be a gift or a reward. Therefore, those who despise God's grace and seek to be justified also by their works are fallen from grace; they need to earn it by keeping the whole law, if they want to be justified before God. But all of you who were called by God to the fellowship of his son through Gospel, and were baptized by the Spirit into his body are dead unto the Law by his body as scripture says my brethren; you also are to become dead to the Law by the body of Christ. But if you keep your conscience under the Law and sought to be justified in your deeds, words, and thoughts, then you will be found yourselves sinners and guilty and you shall die unto God. For as long as you will be alive in your conscience unto the Law you shall not live unto God, for the Law was given to see what is in yourself, and there is no good in any humans; we are all sinners and sin dwells in us, and the Law will only show us as evil, wicked, and sinful. For we the humans are like children of Israel bitten by a poisonous serpent in the wilderness; there is nothing in us but Sin. It dwells in our bodies, and the Law of knowledge of good and evil shows us what is in us and what we look like, and we will find ourselves evil, wicked, and sinners. As long as you see into yourselves through the Law, you will not live unto God.

We need to look unto our brazen serpent that was lifted up for us, and we need look unto the one who it a made sin for us, unto the son of man who was lifted up for us. Therefore we need look unto the son of God, who loved us and gave himself for our sins, that he might save us from this present evil world. For unto us righteousness is not in us. In ourselves we found only Sin, as the scripture says that God has given his son to be our righteousness.[45] Therefore he is our justification, and in him we have righteousness and justification, and in us we have Sin and condemnation. We look at him, the one who is our righteousness, the one who is salvation given by God. It is Satan that depicts the son of man as a lawgiver and more stringent than Moses. Christ is not the minister of sin and condemnation to enforce the Law that was given for the purpose of showing Sin and condemnation.

He didn't come to lead the people under bondage, but to save them from bondage. Yes he expounded the Law to people as it is, but it was a secondary thing, and it was a minor thing with him. He didn't come into the world to preach the Law, he came to save sinners and he came to save people from the dominion of the Law, Sin and death. *Law is good, if one uses it rightly*. He instructed many things to do, to the people seeking after righteousness of Law, which were written in the Gospels. Yet when they hear Lord Jesus, who says "your Father which is in heaven," they get comfort, hope, and some courage to believe in God through him. The Holy Spirit will make them trust in Lord Jesus, and they obey the faith of Lord Jesus Christ through the Holy Spirit. Poor sinners who didn't dare to lift up their heads to look unto heaven now look at God in Christ, which gives them hope. He was before them as a personification of all righteousness, with full of grace and truth, and they found eternal life manifested from the father in the person of Jesus Christ in conscience. These newborn babies by new nature are eager to hear and do what Lord tells them. They will know intuitively the importance of walking in this marvelous light and to have this revelation about Jesus Christ which God has revealed to them newly and holding this faith in pure conscience, obeying to this faith through the Spirit which dwells with them unto keeping Lords sayings with pure and fervent heart.

Thus they do the works that meet for repentance, and they intuitively keep Lord's sayings through Spirit with joy and like a humble little child without any second thought. They do these things through the Spirit of God, who dwell with them to teach them. As God is light, they walk in light; these newborn walk in his presence. They will have the fellowship with the father, they will see how glorious it is to walk by the grace of God in this way than to have the glory of men, and they will take all the care to please the God who sees in secret and rejoice in his praise. In light of the glory of God, they will see the greatness and glory of God's commandments over the traditions of men, because they see the glory and greatness of God. In this new and marvelous light they experience people's rejection and disregard of the things which were of high esteem and precious to these newly born Christians before God. They see what a glorious thing it is to suffer for Lord Jesus' sake, and they rejoice in it through the Holy Spirit. These are the days in the beginning at the time of their conversion to Christ, and these are the days of the son of man in their life. These newly born babies were only able to drink milk, yet they did so wisely with intuitive conviction in laying their foundation upon Jesus Christ the eternal life manifested to them from the Father. They lay the foundation of their house upon rock. For God reveals knowledge, concealed in his son, to these newborn babies in their innermost part, in the hidden part. This is the hidden wisdom, which God ordained before the world unto our glory. As Lord Jesus said, "I praise You, O Father, Lord of heaven and earth, that You have hidden these things from the wise and intelligent and have revealed them to infants. Yes, Father, for this way was well-pleasing in Your sight."[46]

Therefore Peter, with intuitive conviction, confessed his faith in Jesus, and Jesus said the Father revealed that to him. They intuitively will seek to live in the way that pleases God, and do the works to meet repentance and keep the sayings of Lord Jesus through the Spirit with joy. "Then came Peter to him, and said, Lord, how oft shall my brother sin against me, and I forgive him? till seven times?"[47] For they, because of Joy, they found the hidden treasure in Christ their eternal life. They will do all these things spontaneously and joyfully lose the things they own. For God reveals report to these newborn babies in their innermost part, in the hidden part, and God desires truth in the innermost being of his worshipers. They heard the Father and learned from Him to go to Christ, to trust in whom he gave eternal life. But if they kept their conscience under his sayings and commandments and sought to be justified in conscience by their works before God according to them, then they would be going against the truth and his word would not have a place in them. They won't abide in Christ, and they will turn salvation upside down and fall from the fellowship of God. For the Law is not of faith, and it will show them their Sin and work wrath in their conscience.

We will do Sin that leads to spiritual death, when we seek to be justified in our conscience before God by keeping the commandments of God and Christ. For doing that means we are seeking to be justified by our works and thus rejecting grace and the work of Christ; rejecting the free righteousness of God by seeking to earn our own righteousness by our works, and going astray from grace and truth. For we were called to be justified by our faith in Christ, and to us justification and righteousness are made available freely in Christ through faith in him. If we seek to earn them by our works being obedient to the commandments, so that we desire to find them within ourselves, then we will be doing contrary to the grace of God and Jesus Christ the covenant. For by doing like that we are utterly rejecting the grace of God and Christ; it's like saying righteousness, justification (which God brought for us in his Son by his death and resurrection) is of no worth, and Christ died in vain.[48] We will be breaking the actual commandment of faith, which is Christ the Word, whom we heard from the beginning, which God gave us to keep under this covenant. We will be going against the faith that was delivered to us and will be making God a liar, for he testified to us that he gave eternal life to us in his Son.[49]

We heard and received his Son as our eternal life manifested from the Father, and we will be going against the faith of the covenant that was delivered unto us, when God called us into the grace of Lord Jesus. And all things will turn upside down to us; the Gospel will become another Gospel, a perverted Gospel and a law. Christ will become a tyrant and no more gracious, as in the beginning. Grace will be no more. Christ will become crucified unto us and will become no more useful to us, and we will die and wither away. A free gift becomes a reward beyond our reach; a marvelous light becomes darkness and confusion; faith becomes hard labor; justification and peace becomes guilty conscience and condemnation; life turns into death; the yoke of Christ, which was light, and the yoke of liberty will become a heavy burden and a yoke of bondage; love toward Christ turns into suspicion and hate; joy turns into despair, and we will fall from the presence and the fellowship of God in Christ and die spiritually, as spoken by lord. "If a man abide not in me, he is cast forth as a branch, and is withered; and men gather them, and cast them into the fire, and they are burned."[50] For these are the commandments given to us. The First and Holy commandment is the word we heard in the beginning, which needs to be kept by faith, even word of faith. Jesus Christ is the covenant whom we heard at the beginning, the good news of our salvation. The Second commandment is to love brethren as he loved us. Breaking this Holy commandment, even the Jesus Christ the covenant whom we heard at the beginning, is a Sin unto death.

From the beginning, Satan and his messengers who sought to take saints into captivity, back into bondage, tried to turn things upside down for the saints by perverting the Gospel of Christ. Therefore they thought to the saints, that they needed to keep the Law in order to be saved. But it will kill saints; they can't live unto God if they live unto the Law, no matter how great a saint a person might be. Even apostle said he couldn't live unto God. If he lives unto the Law for as I said earlier, the Law works wrath in conscience the Law requires perfect obedience. It will not stay quiet; it will continuously slam the human conscience for every little evil in their actions, words, and thoughts. It will not give them clean chit in anything they do; they do things out of fear and disbelief, and everything that is done without faith is Sin.[51] The Law's voice against them will increase further and further, and those who were acquainted with perfect standards of the Law will quake greatly like Mount Sinai. It whips the conscience with continual judgment and condemnations upon all the deeds, words and thoughts. The Law brings conscience to a turmoil; by it the sore displeasure and the wrath of God is revealed against them in their conscience. It drives them to terror and despair; they will be terrified and the feeling of hatred will be in them against God. They will be alienated in their heart from the God against whom they will sin, with guilty conscience they stay away from him. Therefore the Law is a ministration of death, for it will bring such terror and the wrath of God to conscience and will continuously slam the human conscience for every little evil in their actions, words, and thoughts. It opens their eyes to all wickedness and evil in them, thus making them more and more guilty before God. And all things will turn upside down to us; the Gospel will become another Gospel, a perverted Gospel and a Law; Christ will become a tyrant, as one who seeks their harm and no more gracious as in the beginning; justification and peace in the conscience will become a guilty conscience and condemnation; the yoke of Christ, which was light, and the yoke of liberty will become a heavy burden and a yoke of bondage.

Christ will become crucified unto us, and will become no more useful to us, and our hearts will die and wither away before God. All those who trouble the saints by teaching that they were in an obligation to keep the moral law also, apart from faith, in order be saved, they will get their due punishment for destroying the saints. It would be better for them for a millstone to be hung about their neck and be drowned in the sea, than to offend these little children who believe in the Son of God who loved them. The Law is not of faith; Christ is of faith, and he is an object of faith. Saints live by faith in the Son of God who loved them and gave himself for their Sins. They love Jesus because he loved them first and gave himself for them, and they love the Father because he is their Father. He loved them first and gave for them his only Son, whom he loved more than all things. Saints love the Father and Lord Jesus because they have known and believed in the love that God and Jesus has toward them, and because they were first loved by God and Christ. Knowledge of God's love that he has toward them in his own heart has been shed abroad in their hearts by his Spirit, as it was evidently demonstrated when he gave his son for their Sins to save them. They love the Father and Lord Jesus freely without any compulsion, and they love their brethren because they are brethren for whom Lord Jesus died, and they love their brethren because they love the Father and Lord Jesus.

Those saints who fall and entangle themselves under the Law, their situation will be like this; the Law will keep a knife on their throat and threatens them, saying "you shall love God with all your heart, and you shall love your neighbor as thyself; otherwise I will slit your throat." The Law will whip the conscience of those that are under its yoke; their obedience will be tainted by fear, doubt, and compulsion, and their hearts will be far from God. They are not cheerful doers, and they are not worshiping God in truth and spirit. The Law also condemns them, for it is spiritual; it will find out and condemn them, for there is no truth in their love for God, and it will terrorize them by showing their Sin and the wrath upon their Sin.

Very soon, these people will start to murmur against God. The Law is not of faith, for there is no grace in it. But you saints, who once walked in God's marvelous light and liberty, and who walked in Father's fellowship in joy and did good works and his sayings with joy, freely and spontaneously, but are now entangled under the yoke of bondage; you were bewitched like the Galatians by false brethren to believe that keeping the commandments and doing good works are necessary apart from faith in Jesus Christ, for the salvation. Brethren, we are called to be saved by grace and by faith in Jesus Christ alone. It's completely free and by faith alone, but if you believe you need to keep commandments also apart from faith in Christ in order to be saved, then you will turn the Gospel into a perverted Gospel, Christ into a perverted Christ, and everything will be turned upside down. We are called to serve in the newness of spirit, not in the oldness of the letter, because you are entangled under the law; you can't serve in the newness of the spirit and in truth, but you will be doing everything as if you are under obligation to do them. You will be doing it under compulsion, in fear and doubt, your hearts will be far from God, and there will remain no more true love in you as once you had toward him. Because the enemy has blinded your mind, so that you no longer look unto Jesus Christ and his love toward you, unto the one whom you were acquainted, at the time of your new birth; unto that Jesus Christ who loved us so much, such that he gave himself for our sins that he might save us from this present evil world.

He didn't give silver or gold, but gave himself; not for your obedience, righteous deeds and good works, but for your disobedience, Sins, wickedness, iniquity, and evil deeds. Therefore your disobedience, sin, wickedness, iniquity, and evil belongs to him; he gave himself for them. You are the flesh of his flesh, and the bone of his bone; you belong to him, and very certainly he belongs to you. For it is God, your Father, who gave him to you, and it was your Father's will that he should give himself for your Sins, disobedience, wickedness, iniquity, and evil deeds, that he might save you. Therefore brethren, your disobedience, Sin, wickedness, iniquity, and evil belongs to this man; all things that belong to him are yours and all things that belong to you are his.

Therefore, remember the man named Jesus Christ, whom you have tasted and known that he was gracious at the time of your new birth; he was not a tyrant, stringent, oppressor, or a cruel judge who would be provoked at the slightest provocation, as you see him now being bewitched by the enemy. For you were bewitched to believe that you are obligated to keep the Law and good works or some other thing, whatever it is, apart from faith in Jesus Christ in order to be saved. Therefore, remember how you heard and received all the things you've heard and seen at the time of conversion and at time of the new birth; what happened to the confidence of your faith, where is that joy unspeakable when you are in Father's marvelous light, where is that unrestrained love toward Father and Lord Jesus in the heart that was so free, without any pressure, delightful, cheerful, and truthful. If it were possible to die, you would have died to go to the Father and Lord Jesus. But now, why you are so far away from Father and Lord Jesus in your hearts? It's as if you never knew them. Who has distorted and changed them unto you that you refrain; they wonderfully destroyed you by perverting the Gospel unto you, and have turned everything upside down unto you. They made you alive unto law and to die unto God and Christ by teaching you are under the Law and in an obligation to keep the commandments, and has blinded your minds so that you no longer look unto Jesus Christ and his love toward you.

But you should know, as the scripture says, you are dead with the body of Jesus Christ and God has begotten you again by the resurrection of Christ. At that time and in that world you used to walk conformed to the ways of this world and of the ruler of the power of the air. When you are under the dominion of Sin and Law, God made you to die unto the Sin and Law through the fleshly body of Jesus Christ by baptizing you into his fleshly body by the eternal Spirit of God, who transcends time and space, making you to die with him in his body and through faith in the resurrection of Christ he raised you with Christ to a new life; his resurrection giving you a new birth in the body of his flesh. Therefore, you are not legally under the Law from the time of your new birth, and it is God who made you free from dominion of the Law. Therefore, as the scripture says, you are clothed with Jesus Christ, whom your Father has given to you. Your righteousness is neither in your works, words, or thoughts, nor in anything that is in you, so search not to find it within you. But by the work of God you are in Christ Jesus, whom God has given to you to be your righteousness; he became your wisdom, righteousness, sanctification, and redemption given to you by your Father.[52]

As the Father said by his prophet, "their righteousness is of me, saith the LORD."[53] Therefore, wake up and seek again what the Father has given to you; don't let your enemies deprive you of the claim of your faith forever, even Lord Jesus your righteousness whom God gave to you, that you might live again by faith. We are called to be saved by faith alone, not by faith and works, for salvation to us is by the grace of God and Lord Jesus alone, not by your works. If you think you need to add any work, even works of Law, that is keeping commandments, along with faith in order to be saved, then it will become no more grace and you will be separated from Jesus Christ. You need to keep the whole

Law and commandments, and you will be judged according to your works, and Jesus will become no more profitable to you. So strive hard to regain that most holy faith delivered to you at the time of your new birth, and seek the one who is the author of your faith, even Lord Jesus who loved you and gave himself for your Sins. Try to remember him from that time when you tasted his mercy at the time of your new birth, before your enemies distorted him unto you, and strive hard to not let Satan and his messengers frighten you by any means; for very certainly they will frighten you with scriptures and the very words of Lord Jesus.

Now faith is not an easy and simple thing; it is a precious thing. Faith is reflection of other people through our judgment, for if we judge that the other person is speaking truth, and then we believe. If we won't believe the other person is speaking the truth, then we judge him as a liar. If we believe in a person who promised to do some good to us, that means we judged if he is speaking truth, if he is capable of doing that, if he is trustworthy, etc. For without these things about that person in your heart, you will never truly put your faith in him. So our faith is based on the mental image formed in us about the other person. If Christ formed in you that he is gracious, loving, truthful, righteous, trustworthy, eternal life, and is precious, which means you have really precious faith; if he will be precious unto you, then you will not hesitate to lose anything of the life and of the world for him. You will be as joyful as one who found treasure hidden in the field. We are called to be transformed by the Spirit beholding as in a mirror the glory of the Lord, and are being transformed into the same image.

Since his image is distorted by enemies unto you, they tread upon you who were fallen on the ground, try slowly to come and trust in him like in the beginning; try to know him again like in the beginning, try to strengthen yourself in his love toward you. If the image of Christ formed in you becomes that he loved you so much and gave himself for your Sins, then you will slowly stop becoming fearful and stop fleeing from him. And slowly, you will come to him and trust in him and live by faith in his love. On the other hand, if you judge Christ like this and the image of Christ formed in you is that he is an angry judge, an impatient and a stringent person provoked with the slightest provocation and who will seek your destruction, then you will surely become fearful and flee from him and entangle yourselves with the Law. You will try to do things out of servitude, fear, and even in hatred over him, not out of true love for him. Therefore, strive to regain the most holy faith, which is truly a precious faith which you have been given at the time of new birth. Strive hard to not let Satan and his messengers frighten you by any means, for very certainly they will frighten you with scriptures and with very words of Lord Jesus. Love produced by true faith should be in the heart first, not the works from a servitude fear. "If ye love me, keep my commandments."

Before keeping them you should have love for him in your heart, but what commandments are they that were mentioned in Gospel of John? These are the two commandments of God and Christ, and they that are going to be justified by faith the need to keep. The First one is to continue in the Faith of the Gospel, the word of faith we heard in the beginning, and the Second one is to love our brethren. These are the two commandments given to those who seek to be justified by faith in him, as also confirmed by Apostle John, "Brethren, I write no new commandment unto you, but an old commandment which ye had from the beginning. The old commandment is the word which ye have heard from the beginning."[54] *And* "this commandment have we from him, That he who loveth God love his brother also."[55] *And* "this is his commandment, That we should believe on the name of his Son Jesus Christ, and love one another, as he gave us commandment. And he that keepeth his commandments dwelleth in him, and he in him."[56]

So don't let them put the yoke of burden upon you. Some might ask that, if we were made free from the dominion of the Law and were not in an obligation to keep it, shall we go and Sin then? Shall we continue in lasciviousness and fornication? Because we are not under the Law, but we are not under Sin either; how shall we who are dead to sin live any longer therein? Neither did we learn Christ in this way at the time of new birth, if indeed we have heard Him and have been taught in Him just as the truth is in Jesus. If it happens to appear that we also naturally do some of the things that were in the Law, it's not apart from the First commandment, which is the Gospel of the word of Faith; we won't live before God if we keep conscience under judgment of the commandments of the Law and try to walk before God, because there is no such Law given that gives life. The Law is not of faith, for it's not by grace; it always condemns and never justifies us in conscience before God, so if we live unto it, we shall die unto God.

If someone desires to do Sin, if he is made free from the obligation to keep the Law, then he is like wild beast that was chained; only the chains are preventing the wild beast from harming people. But a sheep needs no chains, for it's a different creature. Therefore let us forsake our old nature and walk in a new nature in liberty, given to us at our new birth by dying in conscience unto the Law and living by faith in Jesus who loved us. The Law doesn't help a man against the Sin as these false teachers assert; if you put your conscience under the commandments of law as an obligation to keep them, then the Sin is revived in you and will become even more powerful. For it gives strength to Sin; Sin will bring all manner of concupiscence in you, and sin will become exceedingly sinful. Therefore, it is the wrong notion of workers of iniquity that teaching saints are under the obligation to keep the moral law will make them fruitful in good works.

On the contrary, the scripture says that the constant teaching of justification and eternal life by the grace of God will make them careful in doing good works, as written. "Not by works of righteousness which we have done, but according to his mercy he saved us, by the washing of regeneration, and renewing of the Holy Ghost; Which he shed on us abundantly through Jesus Christ our Saviour; That being justified by his grace, we should be made heirs according to the hope of eternal life. This is a faithful saying, and these things I will that thou affirm constantly, that they which have believed in God might be careful to maintain good works. These things are good and profitable unto men,"[57] *and* "sin shall not have dominion over you: for ye are not under the law, but under grace."⁵⁸ These dogs who teach saints are under the Law, think that liberty makes a believer reckless and he will go and do Sin, because they think sheep are also wild beasts like them that need to be tied by some chains. They seek to turn everything upside down for you; they misquote scriptures, and say Christ didn't came to abolish the Law.

We are not saying the Law was abolished, we know the whole world is under it, including those workers of iniquity. Christ, who once was under the law, and those who were died with him are no longer under the dominion of the Law. If Christ is now under the Law, then they are under it, but he is not under its dominion; likewise, they that are raised with him and in him into new birth. These Law workers can't understand that we, who were of faith, can't live unto the Father in our conscience by faith in Lord Jesus who loved us without dying unto the Law in the conscience. It was the father of these false teachers who, day and night, accuse saints in their conscience before God; it's not that God didn't know about his saints and needed to learn from Satan, but Satan accuse saints in their conscience before God, that he might make them terrified and flee from Christ and God. They need to overcome him by faith in the Son of God who loved them and gave himself for their sins, by blood of Jesus the redemption God gave to them in Christ,⁵⁹ and by keeping the faith of the Gospel, the word we heard in the beginning.

The first time the false teachers, the messengers the angels of Satan, created this confusion among the believers by teaching that they need to keep the Law apart from faith in Lord Jesus, the Lord's holy Apostles and elders decided on this matter. Within the church, believers from the Pharisee sect said that it was needful to circumcise the gentiles, and to command them to keep the Law of Moses. But the Apostle Peter stood and said, "God put no difference between us and them, purifying their hearts by faith. Now therefore why tempt ye God, to put a yoke upon the neck of the disciples, which neither our fathers nor we were able to bear? But we believe that through the grace of the Lord Jesus Christ we shall be saved, even as they."[60] The Apostles and the Holy Ghost did not even allow small obligation of the Law, such as circumcision to add to faith. But for the sake of the Jewish believers, that they might not offended, they suggested them to do certain things. "For it seemed good to the Holy Ghost, and to us, to lay upon you no greater burden than these necessary things; That ye abstain from meats offered to idols, and from blood, and from things strangled, and from fornication: from which if ye keep yourselves, ye shall do well."[61]

The Apostles believed the gentiles would be saved by the grace of Lord Jesus, without keeping any works of the Law. If they had already thought them to keep moral law in addition to faith; there would be no necessity to write to abstain from idolatry and fornication in this letter. These things are the truth and were written for our admonition, but brethren you were cast down by the enemy to the ground, entangled with the burdensome yoke of bondage and are getting trampled under the feet of this spiritual armies the ecclesiastical host of the enemy, which were pastors, priests, evangelists, preachers, theologians, bishops, etc of the denominations and sects that were in Christendom. Brethren, get rid of the yoke that they laid around your neck, and try to die unto law in your conscience; die unto its preferences, judgments, condemnations, and threats like the dead who can't hear or see anything, so that you may slowly live in your conscience unto God by faith in Jesus Christ who loved you and gave himself for your Sins. Remember the man named Jesus Christ, whom you tasted and have known that he was gracious at the time of your new birth. He was not a tyrant, oppressor, or a cruel judge who will be provoked at the slightest provocation; a stringent person, as you see him now being bewitched by enemy. Therefore, remember how you heard and received all things you heard and saw at the time of conversion at time of new birth; what happened to the confidence of your faith, and what happened to that unspeakable joy when you were in the Father's marvelous light. Try to come back to Jesus Christ, your life and your righteousness, the Son of man who loved you and gave himself for your Sins; for you are his and he is yours.

So drive away the fears and delusions that his enemies produced in your heart against him by turning him unto you into another Christ, which he is not. No, he is not angry at you; there is nothing in him against you before God, for it is your father that has given forgiveness for your Sins by his blood in the body of his flesh, and you are in Christ. He has begotten you through the fleshly body of Jesus Christ by his death and resurrection, and so Lord Jesus Christ is your Father in our Father, even in that great God who raised him from the death. Brethren, look unto your Father and Lord Jesus; they are not against you, but for you. Therefore, be reconciled in your hearts with your Father and Lord Jesus, and let not your enemies drive you away in your hearts far from your Father and Lord Jesus. I wish that you could be bold like the Apostle John to lean on the bosom of one who loved us.

Now, brethren, I am writing these things not on my own, for I was sent by your Father and Lord Jesus to speak these things that were written in this book unto you. Why do you count me as your enemy of righteousness? For there are two ways to obtain righteousness, eternal life, and salvation, and these ways are mutually exclusive ways. The first way is to obtain those things by way of obedience to the Law and keeping all the commandments, and to do all the works needed for righteousness, eternal life, and salvation, and earn them as a reward. Lord Jesus also taught this way, when he expounded the Law. We know that when a rich young ruler asked him how to obtain eternal life in this way, he told him to keep the commandments and perfectly fulfill them. The second way to obtain these things is to obtain them as a gift by God's grace, through faith in Jesus without the works of the Law, whom God hath set forth to be a propitiation through faith in his blood and to declare his righteousness for the remission of sins. We see this when Lord Jesus forgives the sinners and says to them that their sins are forgiven, and he also taught this second way when he taught about faith in him, therefore let them that were thirsty for righteousness come and whosoever desires let him drink from him freely. He will not cast away anyone who desires to lay his faith in him to draw from him water of righteousness freely.

We can see it in his conversation with the Samaritan woman when he said to her, "If you knew the gift of God, and who it is that said to you, Give me to drink, you would have asked of him, and he would have given you living water."[62] To walk in the first way is to earn them as a reward; here, Jesus is not profitable to those that walk in this way. Except his teachings in expounding the Law, there won't be grace; you have to work and earn them by your works. To walk in the second way is to die unto the Law and walk by faith in Jesus. Here Jesus Christ, our sanctification[63] himself, becomes all those things to those who trust in him for the grace of God; here we, through the Spirit by faith, wait for the hope of righteousness, eternal life, salvation etc.

If we hope for righteousness, let us with perseverance wait eagerly for it, for who hopes for what he already has? Let them get all these things by their works as they speak; faith alone is insufficient, but we will seek our Father. We will seek our Father and our Lord, for nothing is more important to us than our Father and then Lord Jesus. Eternal life, righteousness, sanctification and justification are gifts of God to you. Oh poor people, what shall you do with these gifts? You have lost your Father and Lord Jesus. Yet we will be fulfilling the Lord's saying to seek his kingdom and righteousness first, for Father himself has become our righteousness, eternal life, justification, sanctification and our King; the God of the righteousness of our faith and the God of our Salvation we hope for. For as the scripture says, in the Father, all the seed of Jesus Christ will be justified and will have glory. He is our Lord's Holy one; he sanctified the Father in his heart above all and everything. Our Father has begotten us again unto new life in the body of his flesh through the death and resurrection of Jesus Christ, and we are the seed of Lord Jesus Christ by the work of that great God. As the prophet said, "he hath put him to grief: when thou shalt make his soul an offering for sin, he shall see his seed, he shall prolong his days."[64]

Therefore, let us return to our Father and our Lord, and seek them by trying to remember our Father and Lord Jesus, and by trying to die unto the Law in our conscience and living by our faith in Lord Jesus, who loved us and gave himself for our Sins. Don't look upon your fragile love for him, for it should be only a small reflection of what you see when you see his love for us; know it and trust in it, for we need to live by looking continuously on him, for he is the source of our faith. Don't let this enemy's spiritual army the ecclesiastical host of pastors, preachers, bishops, and theologians of past and present distort him unto you. For they will verily use his very person and his own words to frighten you and make you to flee from him in your conscience, but Lord Jesus is whom you've tasted and found gracious in the beginning at the time of your new birth, and is with whom you were acquainted in the past, as he is same today as he was yesterday. So beware of the dogs and workers of iniquity. If you live unto the Law in your conscience, you can't live unto God in your conscience by faith in Jesus; those who teach to you that you are under the Law and obliged to keep its commandments will bear their punishment. These fanatics teach you that you are under the Law and are obliged to keep it, but they themselves won't keep it; they appear outwardly as godly, but inside their hearts are filled with iniquity, filthiness, and sinful passions. Inside they are wild beasts who need to be restrained with chains.

You are called to walk in liberty in newness of life, for you were created as a new creature by God at the time of your new birth. He has cleansed your hearts by faith in Jesus; therefore, let us seek to regain that precious faith. Let us seek our Father and Lord Jesus, and die unto the law in our conscience and try to live by faith in our Lord who loved us and gave himself for us by the will of our Father. Let us seek to know and believe the love that God has toward us. For God is love; and he that dwells in love dwells in God. Love is of faith, there is no fear in love, but perfect love casts out fear. If you truly come to know and trust in the love that the Father and Lord Jesus has toward us and are able to comprehend its breadth, length, depth, and height, then it will cast away fear from you. You will come boldly to the Father and Lord Jesus, and you won't be fearful in your conscience and flee from them. Now you are not perfected in love, and your consciences are weak and have feeble knees. The Law is not of faith, and it works wrath in your conscience and torments you; you will become fearful and flee from Father and Lord Jesus. Brethren, let us die unto the law that we may live by faith in the love of our Father and of Lord Jesus, who loved us and gave himself for our Sins. To die unto the Law is to die unto it in your conscience, like the dead, won't see or hear anything; we die unto its demands and condemnations. Since you entangled yourselves with it and are trodden by your enemies, and the Law condemns your thoughts, words, and deeds, and works wrath and a guilty conscience in you, and cause you to become fearful and flee from God and

Christ in your conscience; become deaf and blind to it like the dead. Don't look at what it shows, and don't hear what it says to you in your conscience, for all the Law has to show us is what in you and what is in your deeds, thoughts, and words. We know there is nothing good in us or in them, nor we put our trust in them, but try to avoid looking at the things it wants to show you. Look unto our brazen serpent, the one who loved us and was made sin for us.

Tell the Law that I have nothing to do with your likes and dislikes, and I am dead to you and not under you; Mr. Law, you have no authority to speak to my conscience. When the Law starts its screaming with accusations and condemnations against you, don't be terrified and seek to be justified according to the Law in your conscience before God, for it is the denial of Christ and his work in the grace of God. Rather, rest your conscience in the love the Father and Lord Jesus has toward us, and in the work of Lord Jesus and the grace of God, even if the Law terrifies you in the words of Lord Jesus and of Father. For you are not under the Law like all the other human beings that are in this world and you are not in same status with other humans; you are heirs to God and Christ. The scripture says that the Father has seated you in heavenly places with Christ. You don't come under the dominion of the God's law to men living under heaven in this world; it has no dominion over you. I say that the heir, as long as he is a child, different nothing from a servant, though he be lord of all; but he will, under tutors and governors until the time appointed of the Father. Likewise, when you were among them in world you were under the Law, but the Father has called you with a heavenly calling unto his fellowship in Lord Jesus. He has begotten you again by the body of Jesus Christ, through his death and resurrection, and blessed you in a heavenly places in Jesus and made you sit together with Lord Jesus in heavenly places; above powers and principalities, for you are heirs to God and Lord Jesus and all things that belong to Father and Lord Jesus belongs to you. You have not received the spirit of bondage to fear again, but you have received the Spirit of adoption, whereby we cry, Abba, Father. Therefore, throw away your fear and disbelief of all this grace Father has given to you, and be confident. Fear not, for you won't come under the Law of God given to the men who dwell on earth. If you live unto the Law in your conscience, you will die unto God; but if you die unto the Law, you will live unto God by faith in Jesus.

If the Law accuses you in your conscience, tell it, "Mr. Law, go ahead and accuse me as much as you like. I know I have done many sins, and I sin daily, but that doesn't bother me. Talk as much as you want, but I am deaf to you, and I am dead unto you. Don't talk to my conscience. I have nothing to do with your likes and dislikes, for my conscience lives unto another Law, which is Christ. It's a better Law, and the Law of Grace needs to be kept by faith." You need to cry louder and stronger against the accuser, the devil who accuses you in your conscience before God day and night.

When Satan accuses you in your conscience showing scriptures and words of God and Christ, say, "I confess. I have sinned."

"Then you are condemned, and God will punish you."

"No I am not. He will not punish."

"Why not? Does not the God say so?"

"I have nothing to do with the Law of God."

"How so?"

"For in Christ in whom I am, God gave me forgiveness to all my transgressions by his blood. He also made me free from the dominion and the obligation to the Law by the body of Jesus through death. I have another Law, the Law of liberty, which is the love of my Father and Lord Jesus who I need to keep by faith. It teaches me to die unto the Law, and to not become fearful and flee from Christ with a guilty conscience for anything."

Thus fortify yourself against the accuser, the devil, with a strong faith in Lord Jesus and his work, his love, and our Father's love. Know the grace the Father and Lord Jesus has bestowed on us, and know who you are to the Father and Lord Jesus. The just shall live by faith,; as for the proud one, his soul is not right within him, because he is deceived by the teachings and doctrines he cling to.[65]

But verily, that crafty Serpent frightens you with the very person of Lord Jesus, creating darkness and confusion and leaving you nowhere to go but to the yoke of bondage. For Satan uses the very words of Lord Jesus, and the things he has spoken or done to frighten you with his very person. He describes Christ as an extractor, stringent, and cruel judge who condemns and punishes men. Tell him this definition of the son of man is wrong; the man whose name is Jesus Christ dwelt among us on earth, loved us, and gave himself for our Sins by the will of God to save us from this evil world. You need to believe this truth strongly, that he loved you and gave himself for your Sins; he doesn't tread upon the fallen but raises them. He is the propitiation for our Sins, and not only for ours but also for the Sins of the whole world. He is not a minister of Sin like Moses, to give the Law to condemn us for Sin. He is not an extractor or an oppressor to require the impossible from us, but he is the bringer of grace and truth, and from him we receive grace upon grace, as he is our high priest who intercedes for our Sins.

I would like you to know this truth, that all love of Christ toward all of us is one. It is not divided among the many of us; like a father sees his many children as one, he sees us as one. His love towards all of us is one and undivided among us, and his love towards each one of you is the same as towards all of us. He sees each one of you as all, even as the whole church, and he loves each of you equivalent to the love with which he loves the whole church, not as a part or member of church. Therefore you need to believe that Lord Jesus' love towards each of you is equivalent to his love towards Peter, Paul, John and toward whole church, for in his eyes you are all one. A man leaves ninety nine sheep in wilderness and will go after one sheep that was lost, until he finds it. Let your conscience dwell in these things, that you may dwell in God.

These Law workers boast about how first century saints were; how they were martyrs and how they loved God, and how they endured sufferings and happily lost their lives for him. But they ignore the root of the thing which worked all those things in them, as they boast on what it appears to be a human virtue and works. For they have not done these things by their moral virtue by following exemplary Christ, but by trusting in redeeming Christ. For this is the strength and root of their faith which works by love, even knowledge of the love that God and Christ has toward us, as Apostle John testifies, "We have known and believed the love that God hath toward us. We love him, because he first loved us." Likewise Apostle Paul wrote it is knowledge of God's love shed abroad in heart, and he says he lives by faith in Christ's love. If we dwell in love Father and Lord Jesus has toward us, by knowing it and trusting in it, then our love will be in a right way, for its just reflection of love we see in Father and Lord Jesus for us. Apostle John wrote "There is no fear in love; but perfect love casteth out fear: because fear hath torment. He that feareth is not made perfect in love."[66] If you become rooted and grounded in this love, and truly come to know and trust in the love our Father and Lord Jesus has towards us and become able to comprehend it's the breadth, and length, and depth, and height; then it will cast away fear from you. You will come boldly to Father and Lord Jesus, and you won't become fearful in your conscience and flee from the Father and Lord Jesus, for this love is of faith and works love in your conscience.

Therefore brethren, try hard to know and trust in the love the Father and Lord Jesus has towards us, and lay hold on it by faith. Then your faith works out all things by love towards God and Christ. Before you do any good work you need to have love in your heart first, so therefore first seek to take hold of the love the Father and Lord Jesus has toward you, and let your conscience richly dwell in it, that you may get rooted and grounded in this love. If you are becoming fearful and fleeing from Lord Jesus in your conscience, then you are not perfected in this love. So strive hard to get perfected in the love of the Father and Christ towards us through faith in it, trusting and understanding it; and then you will also love the Father, Lord Jesus, and your brethren, as your faith also works by love. Therefore die unto the Law that works wrath in your conscience and live by faith in the love of Lord Jesus, who gave himself for our Sins in love, toward us.[67]

When the Law raises its voice against you in your conscience, bidding you to do something or forbidding you something, accusing and condemning you in your conscience; tell it loudly, "I don't need your righteousness, as I have another righteousness, which is Christ himself given by God." Tell it loudly, "I don't have anything to do with your likes and dislikes. I am dead to you, and I don't have anything to do with you. I have the liberty to do anything." You should stop listening to it. You should become deaf to it, like the dead man who can't hear or see anything, when it accuses and curses you.

Tell it, "I have forgiveness in Jesus Christ by his blood for all my Sins. He loved me and gave himself for me." For Satan will accuse you continuously in your conscience before God using the Law against you, finding fault with your deeds, thoughts, and words, to frighten you by making you feel guilty and thereby making you become fearful and flee from Christ in your conscience. When you allow yourself to do something, later don't condemn yourselves for doing that.

But in actual conflict, when Satan frightens you of the very person of Christ and distorts him to you, it's not easy to regain the sight of our sweet savior quickly. So brethren, don't keep the works of the Law for justification in conscience, and always put your trust in the sacrifice of Christ as a source of our Justification and forgiveness.

Always strive hard to get perfected in the love of the Father and Christ towards us through faith in it: trusting it, understanding it, and dwelling in it constantly, so that you may be grounded and rooted firmly in the love Christ has towards you, for this is the root and strength of your faith. You are made as a new creation, so walk in liberty without the chains of the Law on your neck. Put out the old creation the old man that was needed to be restrained with chains, for the Law was not made for new creatures, but for old creatures. False teachers will say that the Law was made for you. Sin will not rule over you if you die unto the Law and become perfected in the love which God and Christ has toward us, so that you might live by faith in Christ without becoming fearful and going far in our hearts from him. But you will turn things upside down, if you live unto the Law of commandments in your conscience and seek to be approved by them in your conscience. Then you will die unto God and Christ in your conscience, and you won't be grounded in the love of Christ toward us, for the Law works wrath in your conscience.

You will also be walking against the truth and will be denying Christ and his work. You will be walking in the oldness of the letter, as old creatures and like beasts in restraining chains with all sinful passions aroused in you by the Law;

there will be no fruit, peace, joy, love, faith, etc. Satan has sowed tares among you, and they will cling to you. All these preachers of the past and present to whom you listen, who has reputation of being great and exemplary preachers; those wicked will get their punishment due to them for teaching you that you are under the Law and were obliged to keep moral law. They turned all things upside down to you,. The Gospel became another Gospel, a perverted Gospel; Christ became a tyrant, an extractor, and no more gracious as in the beginning; grace became no more grace,; and Christ became crucified unto you, and became no more useful to you and you died and withered away.

Remember the Father and Lord Jesus from the time when God has called you, from the time of your new birth; remember what you heard, received, and saw in the beginning. Try hard to regain the true picture of Christ that loved us; you can't do these things without dying unto the Law in your conscience. Our faith is based on the mental image formed in us about the other person; how can you truly love him without Christ formed in you as the one who is gracious, loving, truthful, longsuffering, righteous, trustworthy, eternal life, and is precious. Therefore, try to regain the picture of Christ who loved us and gave himself for our sins. Let your minds dwell in the love the Father and Lord Jesus has towards us, by knowing it and trusting in it, that you might live by faith in Christ. You need to fight against the reason, fear, doubt, Satan's accusations against you using the Law and his distortion of Lord Jesus unto you. You ought to be in faith like Father Abraham, whose body was, dead being a hundred years old, and Sarah's womb was dead; yet he didn't consider these things that were in him against the Gospel promised to him. He trusted in God with a strong faith and didn't waver through disbelief at the Gospel.

Therefore strengthen your faith in the love the Father and Lord Jesus have towards you, for you are children of God. He has begotten you again through by the body of Christ, through his death and resurrection. You are made free from the Law and Sin by the death of Jesus Christ our Lord. So don't put your conscience under the Law of commandments and seek to be approved by them in your thoughts and deeds; rest your conscience in the grace and love of the Father and Lord Jesus, in the sacrifice of Lord Jesus. You are called to walk in liberty, for it is your Father who justifies you and it is Lord Jesus who died for you. Be perfected in the love of the Father and Lord Jesus towards you; it will cast away your fear. You should come to the understanding of your Father's love towards you in Christ, for you are all in Christ and Christ is in the Father. You should be confident like the Apostle who said "I am persuaded, that neither death, nor life, nor angels, nor principalities, nor powers, nor things present, nor things to come, Nor height, nor depth, nor any other creature, shall be able to separate us from the love of God, which is in Christ Jesus our Lord."[68] Then your faith also will work by faith in that love. Apostles, or first century saints, didn't love the Father, Lord Jesus, and their brethren by closing their eyes towards the love the Father and Jesus has towards them. Rather, they saw it and understood it, and their love was a reflection of that love,. As Apostle wrote *"We love him, because he first loved us."* Brethren, I wrote these things so that you may seek the Father and Lord Jesus, and may seek to know, understand, and trust in the love the Father and Lord Jesus have towards you. You may die unto the Law in your conscience and live by faith in the love of Jesus Christ. I wrote so that you may not walk wickedly against the holy covenant; even Jesus Christ that was preached, the word of faith you heard in the beginning. I wrote so that you may become strong in the love the Father and Lord Jesus have towards us, and might be able to understand the word of prophecy written in this book. Nevertheless I want you to read Martin Luther's commentary on Galatians, to understand these things and to avail more help for your conscience. The grace of our Lord Jesus Christ be with you all. Amen.

REFERENCES:

1. Deuteronomy 30:15;
2. Genesis 39:7-9;
3. Genesis 35:2;
4. Genesis 26:10;
5. Psalms 79:5;
6. Matthew 19:20; Mark 10:20;
7. John 4:34; 14:31; 18:11; 15:9; 10:15; Philippians 2:7-8; Psalms 9:13-14; 22; 30; 17; 28; 35; 71; 77; 88; 142; 118:22-27; 69:14-17;
8. Matthew 15:5-6;
9. Exodus 20:17;
10. Romans 7:17-18;
11. Romans 7:8;
12. Matthew 19:26; Mark 10:27;
13. Genesis 2:17;
14. Psalms 143:2;
15. Colossians 1:21; Galatians 1:6;
16. Isaiah 42:6;
17. Romans 7:1; Romans 6:7;
18. Romans 7:2;
19. Isaiah 49:3-4;

20. Isaiah 42:6;
21. Romans 3:26;
22. Romans 7:8 &23;
23. Psalms 22:14;
24. 1 Peter 4:2; Romans 8:3;
25. Galatians 3:10; Deuteronomy 27:26;
26. Galatians 3:13; Deuteronomy 21:23;
27. Galatians 4:4; Philippians 2:7;
28. Matthew 20:23; Mark 10:39;
29. 1 Peter 1:3; Ephesians 2:5-6;
30. Isaiah 53:5;
31. Hebrews 10:20; Romans 5:1; 8:15-16; Galatians 4:7;
32. Galatians 2:17-21; Romans 1:17; 2 Corinthians 5;19; 3:6-9;
33. Matthew 11:28-29;
34. Galatians 3:27; 1 Corinthians 12:13; Romans 6:3;
35. Romans 7:1-4; Ephesians 2:6; Colossians 2:10-15;
36. Galatians 2:17; 3:19; Romans 4:15;
37. Galatians 5:4;
38. 1 John 5:16; Hebrew 6:4-8; 2 Peter 2:21;
39. Hebrews 10-26-29;
40. Jude 1:4 & 19;
41. Hebrews 6:6; Galatians 5:4;
42. Romans 4:4;
43. Romans 4:5;
44. Romans 5:1-2;
45. 1 Corinthians 1:30;
46. Matthew 11:25;
47. Matthew 18:21;
48. Galatians 2:21;Hebrews 10:29;
49. 1 John 5:10-11;
50. John 15:6;
51. Romans 14:23;
52. 1 Corinthians 1:30; 1 John 5:11;
53. Isaiah 54:17;
54. 1 John 2:7;
55. 1 John 4:21;
56. 1 John 3:23-24;
57. Titus 3:5-8;
58. Romans 6:14;

59. Ephesians 1:7; Colossians 1:14;

60. Acts 15:9-11;

61. Acts 15:28-29;

62. John 4:10;

63. 1 Corinthians 1:30;

64. Isaiah 53:10;

65. Habakkuk 2:5;

66. 1 John 4:18;

67. Galatians 1:4; 2:20; John 15:13;

68. Romans 8:38-39;

ABOUT THE AUTHOR

Jonathan, was born in India on September 14 1979, in a small town called Nandyal in state of Andhra Pradesh, he did masters in computer science from a university in California.

www.ingramcontent.com/pod-product-compliance
Lightning Source LLC
Chambersburg PA
CBHW020357080526
44584CB00014B/1052